MW01639579

# Pennsylvania

A Field Guide to State History

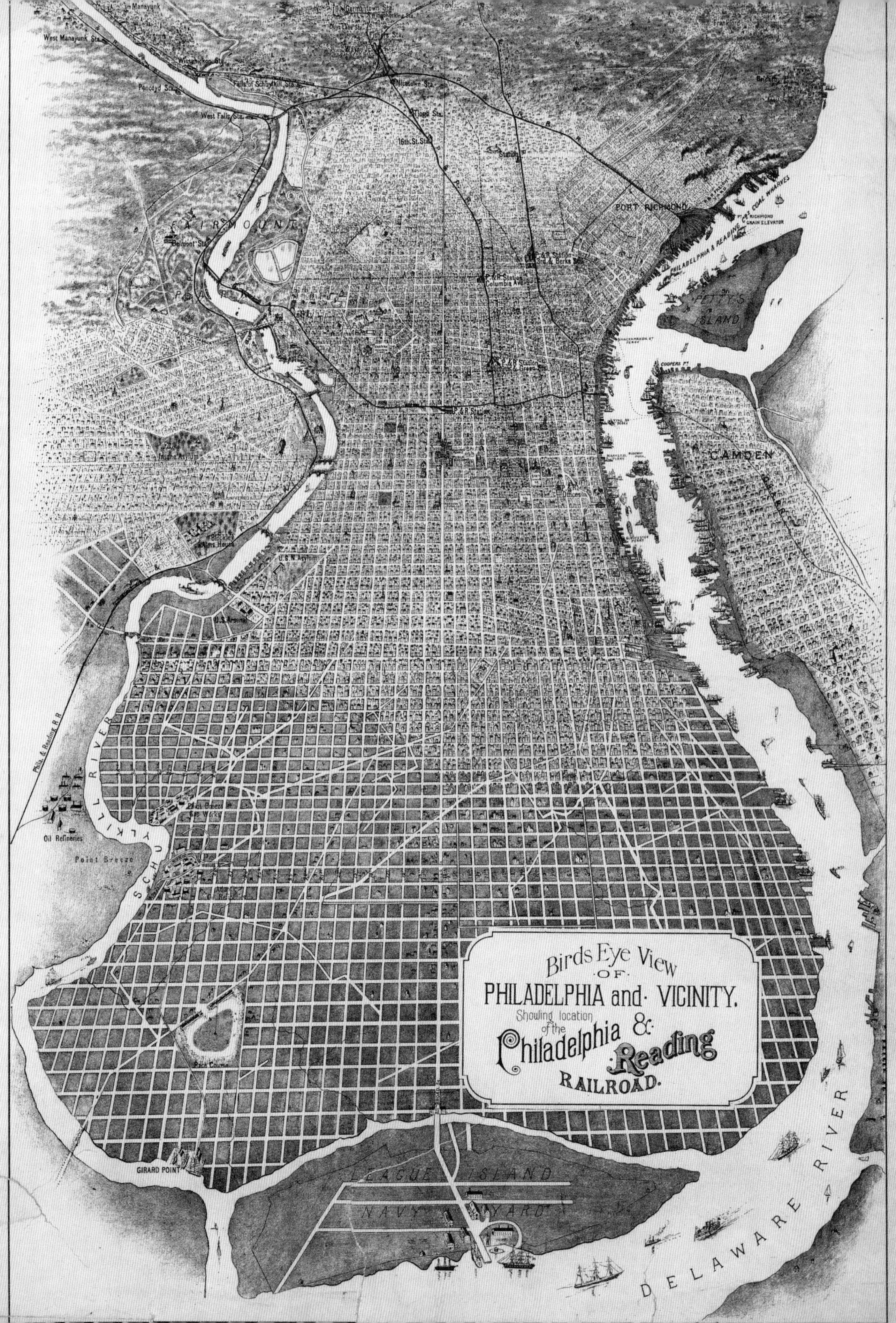
Birds Eye View
OF
PHILADELPHIA and VICINITY.
Showing location of the
Philadelphia & Reading
RAILROAD.
Manayunk
West Manayunk Sta.
Wissahickon Sta.
Pencoyd Sta.
Falls of Schuylkill Sta.
West Falls Sta.
Germantown Sta.
Nicetown Sta.
16th St. Sta.
Frankford
PORT RICHMOND
PHILADELPHIA & READING
COAL WHARVES
RICHMOND GRAIN ELEVATOR
PETTY'S ISLAND
FAIRMOUNT
Belmont Sta.
P.&R. Station Columbia Ave.
COOPERS PT.
CAMDEN
Insane Asylum
Blockley Alms House
U.S.N. Asylum
U.S. Arsenal
Phila. & Reading R.R.
SCHUYLKILL RIVER
Oil Refineries
Point Breeze
GIRARD POINT
LEAGUE ISLAND
NAVY YARD
DELAWARE RIVER

# Pennsylvania

## A Field Guide to State History

GEORGE G. SHELDON

PRC

Published in 2005 by
PRC Publishing
The Chrysalis Building
Bramley Road, London W10 6SP
An imprint of Chrysalis Books Group plc



ISBN 1 85648 729 6

Printed and bound in Malaysia

# Contents

# Introduction

It is impossible to study the history of the United States without learning about Pennsylvania. From the beginning of the colonial days, Pennsylvania contributed its share of economic and social development. It was where the determined forefathers of the United States declared their independence from the British. In its gentle, rolling hills, which turned brutally and miserably bitter cold, General **George Washington** and his rag-tag army hunkered down, somehow surviving winter's harsh grip. Pennsylvania was the site of the nation's first capital, and birthplace of its constitutions.

It was on the high ground, just south of a little town that only a few had heard of before, where two armies fought a great battle. The three days of brutal fighting at **Gettysburg** determined if the United States, formed 87 years earlier, would remain united, or divided into two countries.

Pennsylvania produced the materials, food, and manufactured products that would feed millions, and push the country into a prosperous industrialization period. Pennsylvanians provided the hard labor needed to produce steel or mine coal, and both were used to stop two world wars.

When Al-Qaeda attacked America on September 11, 2001, one of the four hijacked planes intended as a flying missile to destroy the White House or the U.S. Capital was forced down in a lonely Pennsylvania field.

It was in Pennsylvania where the first computer hummed and came to life, and through its circuits, computed its first problem to a scientific conclusion. The state was the first place where a commercial radio station broadcast its first signal, only to be followed years later with the broadcast of the first television signal. All kinds of everyday products—from **bubble gum** to **banana splits**—were developed first in Pennsylvania.

Pennsylvania has proved over the years to be more than a state of firsts. Its people are diverse, and contributed much to the history of the United States. Many important national shrines such as **Independence Hall**, the **Liberty Bell**, Valley Forge, and Gettysburg are in Pennsylvania. Each serves as constant reminders of Pennsylvania's important contributions to the United States.

Pennsylvania, officially the Commonwealth of Pennsylvania, is one of the middle Atlantic states of the United States. It is one of the 13 original colonies that declared its independence from Britain. It entered the Union under the current U.S. Constitution on December 12, 1787, making it the second state after Delaware. The second star on the U.S. Flag represents Pennsylvania. **Philadelphia** is its largest city, and **Harrisburg** is its capital.

## First Residents

Groups of American Indians, people of Mongoloid ancestry, first inhabited the area that now represents Pennsylvania. Just like the Indians found in the rest of the North American continent, they used tools, weapons, and household equipment made from stone, wood, and bark. They made their houses from branches and tree bark, and their clothing from the skins of animals. Transportation was on foot or by canoe. They spent most of their time hunting and gathering food, although the basics of a more complex civilization started, especially in the arts of weaving, pottery, and agriculture.

Some of the Indians formed confederacies, such as the League of the **Five Nations**, made up of New York-Pennsylvania groups that spoke Iroquoian. The other large linguistic group living in Pennsylvania was the Algonkian, which included the Delawares, Shawnees, and other tribes. All were unaware of European culture.

*Scenic waterfalls are found throughout Pennsylvania's mountains.*

## Colonization

In Europe, there was a desire for territorial gains beyond the seas, first by Spain and Portugal, and soon followed later by France, England, Sweden, and the Netherlands. The old system of land ownership was breaking down, and there were many looking for new homes. Trade produced commerce and personal wealth, giving capital for colonization. Pennsylvania was a simple business venture.

Several European countries claimed the land of Pennsylvania. The English founded their claim of the North America territory on the discoveries of the Cabots in 1497. The Spanish claimed land based on Columbus' discovery of the West Indies, and there is evidence that Spanish ships sailed up the coast of North America as early as 1520. The French made their claim to the territory based on the voyage of Verrazano in 1524.

It is uncertain that any of these early explorers ever touched the land that became present-day Pennsylvania. Captain John Smith sailed from Virginia up the Chesapeake Bay and into the **Susquehanna River** in 1608. There he found and named the Susquehannock

Indians. Henry Hudson, an Englishman in the Dutch service, sailed the Half Moon into Delaware Bay in 1609, which allowed the Dutch to claim the area. The Dutch explored the Delaware region and established trading posts in 1623, and later on Pennsylvania soil in 1647.

The Swedes were the first to establish a permanent settlement within Pennsylvania. After an expedition in 1637, the Swedes settled at present-day Wilmington, Delaware. In 1643, Governor Johan Printz of New Sweden established his capital on Tinicum Island within the present limits of Pennsylvania. The island, in the Delaware River, is located near present-day Philadelphia International Airport.

The Swedes were not able to maintain possession of their new territory. The Dutch, who had trading posts in the region, seized New Sweden in 1655. Governor Peter Stuyvesant of New Netherlands made it part of the Dutch colony. In 1664, the English seized the Dutch possessions in the name of the Duke of York, who was the king's brother. Once again, control of the area changed when the Dutch recaptured it in 1673. The English regained possession a year later. The Delaware region remained under the Duke of York's jurisdiction until 1681.

## The Founding of Pennsylvania

**William Penn** was born in London on October 24, 1644, the son of Admiral Sir William Penn. The Englishman was well educated and had a privileged position in British society. Penn shocked everyone when he converted to the beliefs of the Society of Friends, or Quakers, which were then a persecuted religious sect.

William Penn masterfully used his inherited wealth and social rank to benefit and protect his fellow Quakers. The society rejected rituals and oaths, and opposed war. Its followers used simple speech and their plain dress attracted attention, usually hostile. Despite the overall unpopularity of Penn's religion, he was accepted at the king's court because the Duke of York, later King James II, trusted him.

King Charles II owed William Penn £16,000, which the king had borrowed from Admiral Penn. William Penn sought refuge in the New World for his persecuted Friends. Penn asked the king for a land grant in the territory that lay between Lord Baltimore's province of Maryland and the Duke of York's

*Pennsylvania offers visitors many different museums. The Maritime Museum is on Chestnut Street in Philadelphia.*

province of New York. The land grant would repay the debt.

With support from the Duke, the king granted Penn's petition. King Charles II granted the land out of the "regard to the memorie and meritts of his late father." King Charles II signed the Charter of Pennsylvania on March 4, 1681. The king proclaimed the charter officially on April 2. King Charles II must have thought that two problems were solved: first, the debt was repaid, and second, he would rid himself of Penn and his odd Friends.

The king named the new colony in honor of William Penn's father. The king's land grant to Penn included the land between the 39th and 42nd degrees of north latitude and from the Delaware River westward for five degrees of longitude. Other provisions of the charter guaranteed its people the protection of English laws and kept it subject to the government in England. The king could annul any provincial laws. In 1682, the Duke of York deeded to Penn his claim to the three lower counties on the Delaware, which are now the state of Delaware.

Penn wasted no time starting work on his new colony. The 36-year-old Penn appointed his cousin William Markham as deputy governor of the province and dispatched him to take control.

Back in England, Penn drafted the First Frame of Government, his proposed constitution for Pennsylvania. Penn's preface that he included with the First Frame of Government became famous as a summation of his governmental ideals. In October 1682, the ship ***Welcome*** sailed up the Delaware River and the proprietor of the new colony arrived for the first time in Pennsylvania. Penn visited Philadelphia, which had just been laid out as the capital city. He created the three original counties, and on December 4, summoned a General Assembly to Upland, which he renamed as Chester.

The General Assembly was busy. The Delaware counties were united with Pennsylvania. The assembly adopted a naturalization act and, on December 7, adopted the Great Law, a humanitarian code that became fundamental Pennsylvania law and guaranteed liberty of conscience. The second Assembly, held in 1683, reviewed and amended Penn's First Frame with his cooperation and created the Second Frame of Government. Penn

*Benjamin Franklin Bridge, with Center City Philadelphia in the background. When it opened, in July 1926, it was the world's longest suspension bridge.*

returned to England late in 1684, and by that time, the foundations of the Quaker Province were well established.

## Penn and the Indians

Although he had received a land grant from the king, **Penn** decided not to grant or settle any part of Pennsylvania without first buying the claims of Indians who lived there. His heirs also continued the practice after his death. All of Pennsylvania, except the northwestern third, was purchased from the Indians by 1768. The Commonwealth bought the **Six Nations**' claims to the remainder of the land in 1784 and 1789, and the claims of the Delawares and Wyandots in 1785. Despite many attempts, the Indians and colonists failed to live side by side peacefully, which eventually led the remaining Indians to migrate westward, gradually leaving Pennsylvania.

## Pennsylvania Settlers

The new proprietor advertised for settlers to come to his new province. He called them "adventurers." He sought farmers, day laborers, carpenters, masons, smiths, weavers, tailors, tanners, shoemakers, shipwrights, merchants, and good men of administrative capacity to set the new community on its feet. **Penn** drafted a letter at the same time, where he reassured the Swedish, Finnish, and Dutch settlers who were already in the Province. Penn told them not to he disturbed at the change of government. Penn assured them that he was not a grasping and tyrannical governor, and he promised them freedom. "You shall be governed by laws of your own making...," he is quoted to have said. Penn knew he needed the support of the present occupiers of his land for the expected surge in population.

Soon waves of new settlers arrived in Pennsylvania from many different origins. Many English settlers were Anglican, but English Quakers were the dominant group from Britain. The English settled mostly in the southeastern counties, which soon lost its frontier characteristics.

Thousands of Germans were also attracted to Penn's new colony and, by the time of the Revolution, comprised a third of the population. Most came largely from the Rhineland. The Pennsylvania Germans settled

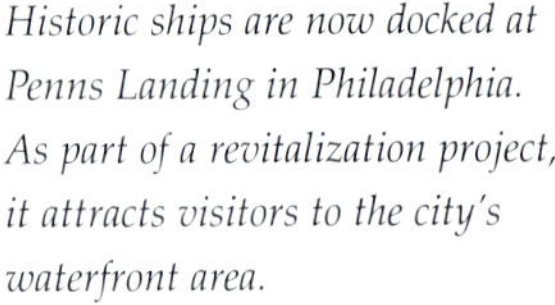

*Historic ships are now docked at Penns Landing in Philadelphia. As part of a revitalization project, it attracts visitors to the city's waterfront area.*

further west, most heavily in the interior counties of Northampton, Berks, Lancaster, and Lehigh. German immigration markedly increased after 1727. Their varied skills and industries transformed this region of Pennsylvania into a rich farming country, and contributed greatly to the expanding prosperity of the province.

Hardships in Ireland caused many Irish people to emigrate to Pennsylvania. Most were primarily frontiersmen, and they pushed first into the Cumberland Valley region and then farther into central and western Pennsylvania. By 1776, the Irish made up about one-fourth of the state's population.

Quakers opposed slavery, but by 1730, about 4,000 slaves were brought to Pennsylvania. English, Welsh, and Irish colonists owned most of the slaves. The census of 1790 showed that the number of African-Americans had increased to about 10,000, and about 6,300 had received their freedom. The Pennsylvania Gradual Abolition Act of 1780 was the first emancipation statute in the U.S.

There were also Irish and Welsh Quakers and they settled in the area immediately outside of Philadelphia. Other groups, including French Huguenot and Jewish settlers, Dutch, Swedes, and others, added to the development of colonial Pennsylvania. This mixture of people in the Quaker province helped to create its non-judgmental tolerance and multiethnic outlook.

With the influx of people and their cultures and religions, Pennsylvania grew into the third largest English colony in the new world, although it was next to the last founded. Philadelphia became the center of a thriving agricultural and commercial society. Intellectual thought, fueled by unusual freedom and religious convictions, made Philadelphia an important city. By 1776, Philadelphia had become the second largest English-speaking city in the world, second only to London.

Although there were originally only three counties, Philadelphia, Chester, and Bucks, by 1773 there were 11. Westmoreland, the last new county created before the American Revolution, was the first county located entirely west of the Allegheny Mountains.

The American Revolution had its origins in urban areas, and **Philadelphia** was a center of

*Even though this picture shows the modern Pittsburgh skyline, it is clear why George Washington thought the point (where the waterfall is) would make an excellent location for a fort.*

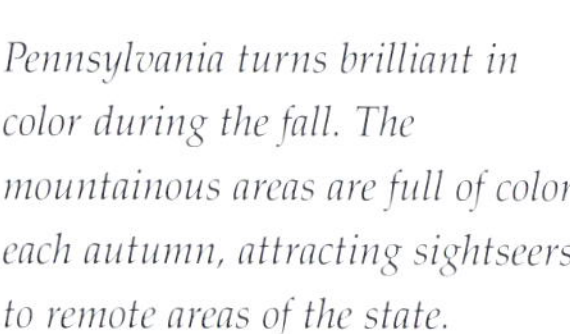

*Pennsylvania turns brilliant in color during the fall. The mountainous areas are full of color each autumn, attracting sightseers to remote areas of the state.*

upheaval. Groups of artisans and mechanics banded together in discontent. Many were loyal to Philadelphia's **Benjamin Franklin**. In 1765, Philadelphia was a center of resistance to the Stamp Act and in 1774, moved quickly to support Boston in opposition to the Intolerable Acts.

## Pennsylvania in the Revolution

Pennsylvania played a dominant role in the early development of the national government. At that same time, Pennsylvania was molding its own statehood. Pennsylvania provided leadership and a meeting place for the men dedicated to building a nation.

**Philadelphia** was the nation's capital during the American Revolution, except when the British occupied the city, which caused the capital to be moved to **Lancaster** and then onto **York**. While Congress was in session in York from October 1777 to June 1778, it approved the Articles of Confederation, which was the first step toward a national government. In 1787, the U.S. Constitutional Convention met in **Philadelphia**.

The grass-roots movement to defend American rights fermented into the movement for independence in the meetings of the **Continental Congress** at **Carpenters' Hall** and the State House (now known as Independence Hall) in Philadelphia. The spirit of independence spread quickly, as shown by spontaneous declarations of the frontiersmen in the western areas and by the political events that displaced the provincial government.

*Pittsburgh's skyline at dusk, it is easy to see the confluence of the Allegheny and Monongahela Rivers into the Ohio River.*

Troops from Pennsylvania participated in most of the campaigns of the American Revolution. A Pennsylvania rifle battalion joined in the siege of Boston in August 1775. Other Pennsylvanians fought bravely in the ill-fated Canadian campaign of 1776 and in both the New York and New Jersey campaigns.

The British considered Philadelphia of key importance. In the summer of 1777, the British Army invaded the state, and captured the city. The battles of **Brandywine**, **Germantown**, and Whitemarsh were important engagements between the British and the Americans. Following these battles, **Washington** and his army went into winter quarters at **Valley Forge** in December 1777. **Benjamin Franklin** negotiated the French alliance, and when news of the accord reached the English, the British opted to leave Philadelphia in the spring of 1778.

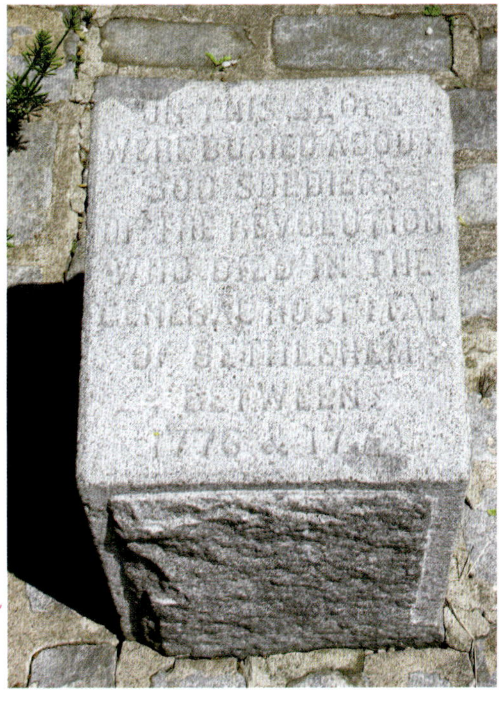

*A simple marker tells of a mass gravesite, "On this slope were buried about 500 soldiers of the Revolution who died in the General Hospital of Bethlehem between 1776 and 1778."*

Pennsylvanians in the western frontier suffered heavily from British and Indian raids until 1779. Campaigns by John Sullivan Daniel Brodhead against the **Six Nations** Indians stopped the attacks. Soldiers from Pennsylvania formed a major portion of Washington's Continental Army. Military leaders from Pennsylvania such as Arthur St. Clair,

*Pennsylvania's Amish still use horse drawn farm equipment to work the fields. Despite the old ways, their farms are the most productive in the country.*

**Anthony Wayne**, Thomas Mifflin, and Peter Muhlenberg gave valuable service in the new nation's army.

Pennsylvania also contributed to the creation of the Continental navy. Many ships were built or purchased in Philadelphia. Pennsylvanians became the ship's crews. The Irish-born **John Barry** became the first in a long list of Pennsylvania's naval heroes.

Pennsylvania farms, factories, and mines provided essential products that led to the success of the Revolutionary armies. At **Carlisle**, a Continental ordnance arsenal manufactured cannons, swords, pikes, and muskets. The state actively encouraged the manufacture of gunpowder. Pennsylvania provided extensive financial support, both from its government and from individuals. By 1780, Pennsylvania had contributed more than $6 million to Congress. When the American states had reached financial collapse, 90 Philadelphians subscribed a loan of £300,000 to supply the American army. Later, in 1782, the Bank of North America was chartered to support the fledgling government's fiscal needs. **Robert Morris** and Haym Salomon became important financial supporters of the Revolution.

During the turmoil of the American Revolution, Pennsylvanians struggled to form their own state government. Pennsylvanians disagreed with the form that their state government should take. They eventually established a Council of Safety to rule interim, and drafted the first state constitution, adopted on September 28, 1776. It provided for an assembly of one house and a supreme executive council instead of a governor. The Declaration of Rights section has been copied in subsequent state constitutions without any significant change.

*Harrisburg was not the first capital of Pennsylvania, but the city has served as the capital since 1812.*

After winning independence from British rule, the leaders of the United States found the Articles of Confederation were not working. Following the writing of the U.S. Constitution in Philadelphia, Pennsylvania became the second state to ratify it on December 12, 1787.

Over the following decades, Pennsylvania industries grew as it supplied products to an emerging nation. Coal mining and iron production offered all kinds of needed products. Leather making, shipbuilding, lumbering, tobacco, publishing, and paper manufacture also thrived in the 1800s. Pennsylvania farms fed a growing population. In the mid-1830s, Pennsylvania provided public schools to its youths. There was also a rapid establishment of academies and modern high schools. The study of literature, arts, and sciences flourished within the state's borders. As Pennsylvania prospered, transportation systems developed. Roads and canals were built to move products and supplies. Railroad lines were built to move massive loads of freight.

## Pennsylvania and the Civil War

The first (and only) Pennsylvanian to become a U.S. President was **James Buchanan**. During his term, South Carolina seceded from the Union. Buchanan did nothing to prevent the secession, and soon other southern states followed. Their disagreement centered around state rights, fueled by the issue of slavery. It marked the end of Pennsylvania's major influence on national politics. However, the state's industry contributed much toward preserving the Union. During the Civil War, Southern forces invaded Pennsylvania three times through Cumberland Valley, a natural highway from Virginia to the North. Pennsylvania's location safeguarded the other northeastern states.

*Workmen pause while constructing the Soldiers' National Cemetery at Gettysburg.*

The state's strong industrial enterprise and its abundant natural resources were essential factors in the economic strength of the Union. Pennsylvania's railroad system, iron and emerging steel industry, as well as its agricultural wealth were vital to the war effort. The state's shipbuilders contributed to the strength of the navy and merchant marine.

Many Pennsylvanian's made major contributions to the Northern cause. **Thaddeus Stevens** was an important congressional leader. Engineer Herman Haupt directed railroad movement of troops and President Lincoln personally commended him. Thomas Scott, as Assistant Secretary of War, directed telegraph and railway services. Simon Cameron was the Secretary of War until January 1862. Jay Cooke helped finance the Union cause.

Perhaps one of Pennsylvania's greatest contributions was the state's governor during the Civil War. Governor **Andrew Curtin**, at his first inaugural, denied the right of the South to secede and throughout the war was active in support of the national draft. In September 1862, he was the host at **Altoona** to a conference of northern governors, which pledged support to Lincoln's policies.

Almost 350,000 Pennsylvanians served in the Union forces, including 8,600 African-American volunteers. At the beginning, Lincoln's call for 14 regiments of volunteers was answered by 25 regiments. In May 1861, the Pennsylvania Assembly, at Curtin's suggestion, created the Pennsylvania Reserve Corps of 15 regiments enlisted for three years' service. They were soon mustered into the Army of the Potomac after the first Battle of Bull Run. Thousands more Pennsylvanians followed them into Federal service. **Camp Curtin**, established at **Harrisburg** was a major troop center during the war. Army leaders from Pennsylvania included **Winfield S. Hancock**,

*Each year, thousands of re-enactors return to Gettysburg to participate in a two day celebration and recreation of the Battle of Gettysburg.*

*The tomb of the Unknown Soldier in Philadelphia, where an unknown American killed in the Revolutionary War is buried. In the park, hundreds of other soldiers are buried in unmarked graves.*

John W. Geary, John F. Hartranft, George B. McClellan, George G. Meade, and **John F. Reynolds**. Rear Admiral John A. Dahlgren made innovations in ordinance, which greatly improved naval firepower, and Admiral David D. Porter opened the Mississippi River to Union forces.

In June 1863, Confederate General Robert E. Lee invaded Pennsylvania. On July 1, 1863, his Southern forces met the Federal army in **Gettysburg**. Under command of General George Meade, the Union army fought the Confederates for three days. Lee finally retreated, and the Southern army was never able again to mount a significant battle on northern soil.

## Industrialization in Pennsylvania

Following the Civil War, Pennsylvania led the nation in industrialization. In the last half of the 19th century, Pennsylvania's vast supply of **coal**, fueled the great blast furnaces of emerging industries. Mining and the use of the state's anthracite coal provided the key ingredient needed.

Pennsylvania's coal industry would remain dominant for more than a century. There are around 40 different beds of coal in Pennsylvania. They range from a few inches in height to over eight feet thick, are relatively flat and hence easy to extract. Interspersing the coal strata are layers of shale, sandstone, and limestone. Three quarters of the state's coal is mined from five key beds: the Pittsburgh, the Upper and Lower Freeport, and the Upper and Lower Kittanning. Some ten billion tons of bituminous coal have been produced in Pennsylvania during over 200 years of mining. It helped form a distinctive culture in the state's coal mining regions that still exists to this day. The coal was the foundation for the growth of transport and manufacturing, and allowed for cultural and social changes throughout the state.

The massive and ever-growing railroad provided the necessary transport of coal from the mines deep in the Pennsylvania Mountains to the industrial centers. Industry developed throughout the state, including locations in Philadelphia, along the Susquehanna, the Northeast, and in and around Pittsburgh.

As the miners chipped the black rock loose from deep in the mines, it was quickly extracted through a shaft to a waiting railroad car. Soon the car was coupled to others. Then it snaked through the valleys, en route to its final destination. The energy extracted from coal fueled electric power generation plants and large furnaces that produced iron, steel, or other malleable products. Factories produced everything from plates of steel to cast iron pots. Some produced railroad track, while others produced railroad cars that used the track. As automobiles were developed, Pennsylvania factories produced auto parts. The United States military relied on the **Keystone State**'s factories to produce needed supplies and materials. Fuel tanks, kitchen utensils and appliances, furniture, farm equipment, and machinery were just some of the many items that Pennsylvanians produced for the nation.

Throughout Pennsylvania, new factories sprung up, ready to produce a vast array of products. Many of those factories were located in the state's southwest, where **Pittsburgh** was the hub of this manufacturing. With the Pennsylvania Railroad in full operation, pulling tons of coal over the Appalachian Mountains was all in a day's work. With a seemingly never-ending supply of available fuel, the factories prospered for decades. Pennsylvania's plentiful energy supply, coupled with the

*An early Pennsylvanian coal shaft draws coal up from the deep mine to the surface ready for transportation.*

*In the early years of the 20th century children were often employed in factories.*

influx of newly arrived immigrants eager for work, further expanded the state's industrial growth.

## Pennsylvania and Reconstruction

Once again, the nation relied on Pennsylvania products, materials, and labor after the Civil War. The country needed to rebuild in the east, and it was expanding west. Miners worked in the state's coalmines for fuel to fire the state's iron and steel furnaces. More immigrants arrived in Pennsylvania, to work and build new lives for their families. There were increased numbers of Slavic, Italian, Finn, Scandinavian, and Jewish immigrants adding to the population of Pennsylvania. With the arrival of new groups of future U.S. citizens flowing into the state, the diversity of the population continued.

It was just a matter of time until the workers of the state sought better working conditions and higher pay. Pennsylvania led the way in labor reforms and unionization. The United Mine Workers and the Steel Workers of America union have deep roots in Pennsylvania. Some companies established

*Young miners pose for a photograph at the Pennsylvania Coal Company in South Pittston.*

Gettysburg, the site of the decisive American Civil War battle, won by the North in 1863.

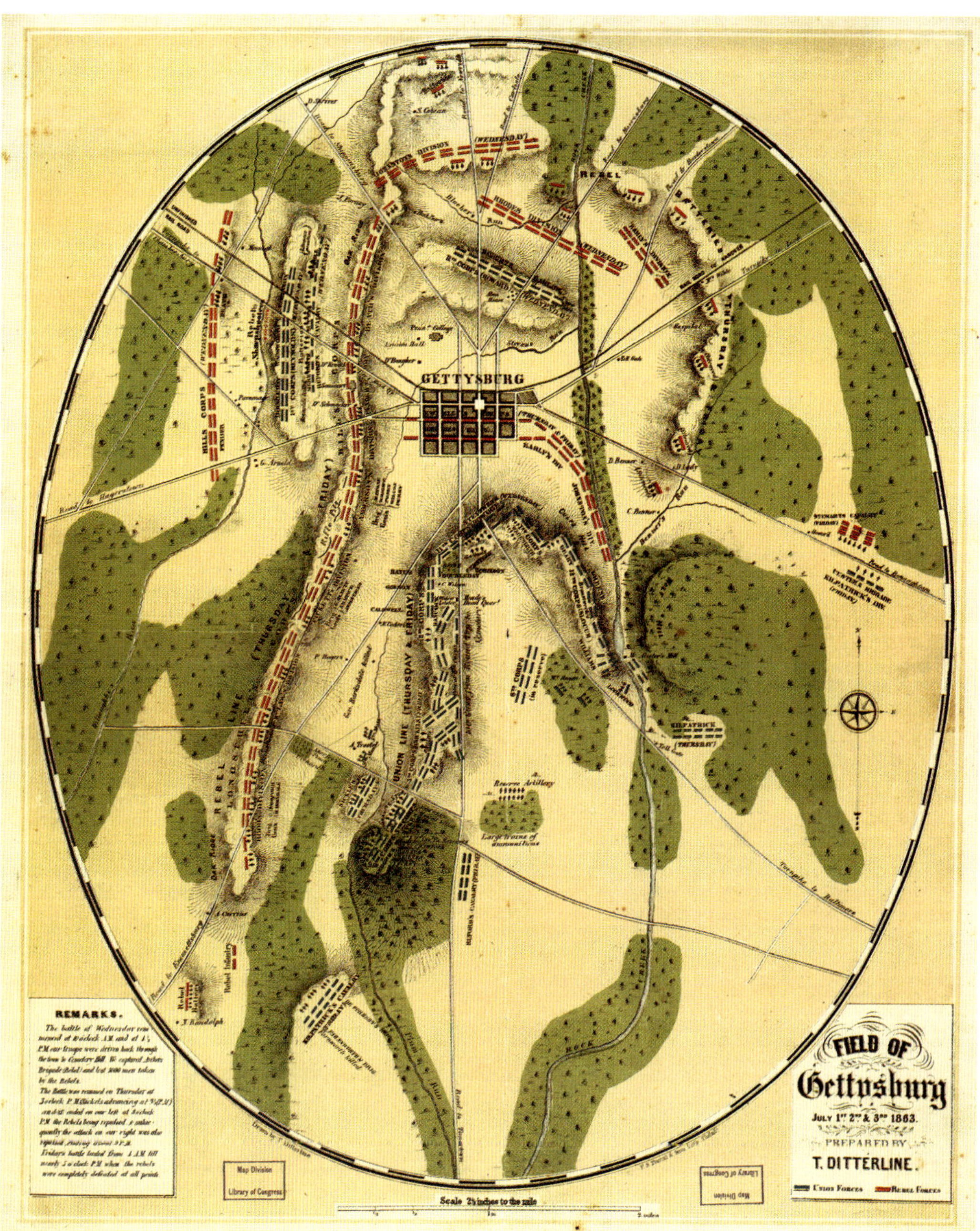


private police forces, to enforce tough work rules. Attempts by the labor force to gain reform were crushed by employers, often labeling any defying worker as a "Molly Maguire." Clashes occurred between workers and the management, some becoming violent, resulting in fatalities.

Transportation links improved. Railroads expanded their lines and over 1,700 bridges were built. Horse-drawn trolley cars were introduced in Philadelphia and Pittsburgh.

The use of the telegraph became a reliable means of communication with the rest of the country. When the telephone was invented, Pennsylvanians were quick to utilize it.

The University of Pennsylvania's Medical School, the Hahnemann Medical College, and Jefferson Medical College gave Philadelphia the reputation as an outstanding medical center. Both the **University of Pittsburgh** (in 1885) and the Temple University (in 1901) opened medical colleges.

## Pennsylvania in the 20th Century

During the last century, Pennsylvania continued its role as a leader among the states. Pennsylvania was the first state to form a statewide police department, the Pennsylvania State Police. The state built the first superhighway, the Pennsylvania Turnpike. The state legislature passed labor law reforms. Pennsylvania's prosperous farms continued producing food for the nation. With easier transport of the agriculture products, Pennsylvania farmers shipped their food outside of the state's border.

Over 1.25 million Pennsylvanians served in the armed forces during World War II, or about one-eighth of the state's population. One out of every seven members of the U.S. armed forces was a Pennsylvanian. Once again, Pennsylvania contributed heavily to support the country during the national crisis.

Pennsylvania's industries produced needed war goods. Planes, tanks, armored vehicles, guns, and ammunition streamed out of its factories. Ships were launched from Pennsylvania

*Fishing in Pennsylvania lakes and streams is a favorite pastime for many Pennsylvanians.*

*One of Pennsylvania's lush and prosperous farms. Although the state moved from an agricultural-based economy of the colonial days, farming is still an important part of the state's economy and business.*

*The Crayola Crayon Factory Outlet in Easton is one of Pennsylvania's favorite tourist destinations.*

shores along the Delaware and Ohio rivers, and on Lake Erie. A constant flow of war supplies moved over its railroads and highways. Pennsylvania's oil lubricated the modern machines of war, and its coal kept fueling the steel mills. Food from its productive farm fields fed both hungry workers and soldiers. Pennsylvania's factories operated around the clock. Women were recruited to fill positions and unemployment was non-existent within the state.

Today the state remains as diverse as ever. Certain areas have now been assigned unflattering descriptions, such as "Rust Belt," indicating that the coalmines and steel foundries are closed and rusting. While it is true that both industries had declined significantly since World War II, there are still working coalmines, and steel is still produced in Pennsylvania.

The decline of heavy manufacturing within the state has allowed the state to undo the environmental damage that those industries caused. The result has been increased tourism and a development of agricultural industries.

While Pennsylvania's population ages, high-tech companies flourish within the state. Pennsylvania struggles today with the same sort of problems that all states do, such as educational opportunities, public safety, health care, race relations, changing economy, and tax structures. Pennsylvanians are concerned about another label assigned to the state, the current "brain drain" where the young people are leaving the state for careers and opportunities in other areas. **Philadelphia** and **Pittsburgh** still offer much, including top universities and excellent research centers. Biotechnology, robotics, and software development are some of the new industries that are now established in Pennsylvania.

Being able to change, adapt, and move forward is the state's greatest attribute. It is an historic fact. The citizens of this state did play a key role in establishing the country, in fine-tuning its government, and holding it all together repeatedly at places like **Valley Forge** and **Gettysburg**. If history can predict future performance, Pennsylvanians have what it takes to meet many new challenges, no matter what they are.

## Abolition Hall

The antislavery meeting hall in Montgomery County brought many leading abolitionist speakers to the Philadelphia area. Opened in 1856 by George Corson and his wife, Martha, the hall was built over a carriage shed. It could accommodate up to 200 visitors. The family's 1767 home was also used as part of the **Underground Railroad** organisation's network.

## Abolition Society

By the 1770s, the issue of slavery and its abolition, became a full-scale movement in Pennsylvania. Quaker activists Anthony Benezet and John Woolman led the reform, and many Philadelphia slaveholders of all denominations began bowing to pressure to emancipate their slaves on religious, moral, and economic grounds.

In April 1775, Benezet called the first meeting of the Society for the Relief of Free Negroes Unlawfully Held in Bondage at the Rising Sun Tavern in **Philadelphia**. Thomas Paine was one of the ten white Philadelphians who attended. Often referred to as the Pennsylvania Abolition Society, the group focused on the intervention in the cases of blacks and Indians who claimed they were illegally enslaved. Of the twenty-four men who attended the four meetings held before the Society disbanded, seventeen were Quakers. The Abolition Society sought social, educational, and employment opportunities for those illegally enslaved.

## Accordion

In 1854, Anthony Faas received a patent for his new musical instrument, the accordion. The Philadelphian made two important improvements to his musical contraption—one to the keyboard and another to enhance the sound. Sometimes called a squeezebox, the person playing the accordion pushes and pulls on its bellows to force air through its reeds. Popularized by different cultures with different designs to make unique sounds, the accordion became highly recognized in America by bandleader Lawrence Welk.

## Accuweather

On November 15, 1962 Joel N. Myers, at the time a graduate student, began forecasting the weather for a gas utility company in Pennsylvania. It was his first client. He went on to build the world's best-known weather forecasting business. Myers went on to earn a Doctorate in Meteorology at the State College. The company he set up grew to provide services for over 15,000 clients. Today Accuweather employs over 400 people—the greatest number of meteorologists in one location. Dr. Myers innovations are widely used in broadcasting and the Internet today, and have been credited with saving hundreds of lives by providing early warnings of severe weather.

## African Zoar Methodist Episcopal Church

In 1794, the African Zoar Methodist Episcopal Church was founded in Philadelphia at 4th and Brown Streets by 15 men and three women from St. George's Church, led by Reverend Harry Hosier. They became active in the **Underground Railroad,** a secret network of black and white antislavery Northerners and safe houses. This church is the United Methodism's oldest black congregation. It moved to 12th and Melon Streets in 1883.

## Alcott, Louisa May

The author of *Little Women* was born in **Germantown**, near **Philadelphia** on November 29, 1832. A Civil War nurse and suffragist, she wrote books for children and numerous gothic thrillers. Her parents, educator Bronson Alcott and his wife Abigail, lived in Pennsylvania, 1830–34. She grew up in Boston, and received tutoring by American writers Henry David Thoreau and Ralph Waldo Emerson. While serving as a Civil War nurse, Alcott wrote letters to her family that she published later as Hospital Sketches. Alcott's most famed work is *Little Women*, an autobiographical novel of her childhood, recounting family life in New England. She died in 1888.

## Allegheny Portage Railroad

The Allegheny Portage Railroad was the first railroad constructed over the Allegheny Mountains, operating between 1834–1854. It was considered a technological wonder in its day. The railroad consisted of a 36-mile system of inclined planes and levels. The trains of canal-boat sections were moved by a stationary engine at the planes, and by a locomotive on the levels. By 1835, the cost of shipping goods by the Portage Railroad and canal from **Philadelphia** to **Pittsburgh** dropped dramatically to about $20 per ton. The distance now only took a few hours, rather than 3 days. It marked the beginning of the opening of the interior of the United States to trade and settlement. Today the location, about 12 miles west of **Altoona**, is a National Historic Site.

*The temporary home of the Liberty Bell during the American Revolution was the Zion Reformed Church in Allentown, where patriots were able to safely hide their beloved symbol of freedom.*

## Allentown

Located along the Lehigh River, Allentown is sandwiched between the state's coal region to the north and the Pennsylvania Dutch region to its south. The seat of Lehigh County, in eastern Pennsylvania, is the state's fourth largest city. Founded in 1762 by the noted colonial leader and jurist, William Allen, it was known until 1834 as Northamptontowne. American Patriots hid the **Liberty Bell** in the Zion Reformed Church from the British during their occupation of **Philadelphia** in 1777. Allentown was also where soldiers wounded in the American Revolution were hospitalized.

Today it is a major manufacturing and distribution hub, whose products include chemicals, cement, communications and transportation equipment, electrical goods, clothing, shoes, processed foods, cigars, and fabricated metals. Allentown is the home of Cedar Crest College (1867), Muhlenberg College (1869), and United Wesleyan College (1921). According to the U.S. Census Bureau, its population in 2001 was 106,632.

*Allentown is one of Pennsylvania's larger cities. Its downtown is marked by a center square, a popular feature of many of the state's communities.*

## Altoona

The city of Altoona is located in central Pennsylvania on the eastern slopes of the Allegheny Mountains. The first settlers arrived in the area in the 1750s. They constructed a series of stockades in the region as a defense against Indian raids, which included Fort Roberdeau. In 1811, iron making began at the Allegheny Furnace. By 1831, the Main Line of the Pennsylvania **Canal** was extended to Hollidaysburg. The canal was linked to the **Allegheny Portage Railroad** in 1834, which hoisted canal boats over the Allegheny Ridge on primitive rail cars.

The Pennsylvania **Railroad** designed Altoona, which was strategically located east of **Pittsburgh**, in 1849. Located in Blair County, it was used by the railroad as a switching point for the locomotives that were used to cross the mountains. The Allegheny Mountains remained a major barrier to the completion of an east–west railroad across the state. In 1854, through innovative engineering, thousands of workers completed the **Horseshoe Curve** west of Altoona. This engineering marvel provided a westward passage at a grade that was gradual enough for heavy trains.

Following World War II, Altoona's economy suffered as a result of the demise of the railroad business. Recently Altoona was connected to the nation's interstate system with the completion of route I-99. According to the U.S. Census Bureau, Altoona's population in 2001 was 49,523. Altoona is Pennsylvania's ninth largest city.

## America's Continental Congress

America's Continental Congress was a group of delegates from the original thirteen colonies. It evolved into the revolutionary government that directed the war for independence. On September 5, 1774, the first Continental Congress convened in **Carpenters' Hall**, Philadelphia, Pennsylvania. The delegates met to discuss joint action on the situation arising from the so-called Intolerable Acts, passed by the British Parliament. There were about 50 delegates, who represented the 13 colonies except Georgia.

The Congress petitioned the king of Great Britain, appealing to him to help restore harmony between Britain and the colonies. Before adjourning in October, the delegates summoned a second Congress to assemble in Philadelphia on May 10, 1775.

When the Second Continental Congress convened the following year at the state house, known now as **Independence Hall**, the delegates formed committees and assumed governmental duties that had previously been exercised by the king of England. Congress authorized **George Washington** to organize the Continental Army. The Congress directed the colonies to form their own governments and

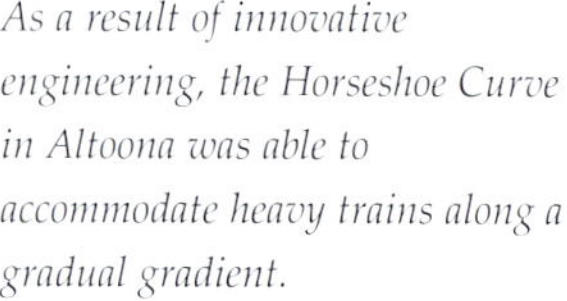

*As a result of innovative engineering, the Horseshoe Curve in Altoona was able to accommodate heavy trains along a gradual gradient.*

began debating a resolution in favor of independence. It approved the resolution on July 2, 1776, and on July 4, it adopted the **Declaration of Independence**.

On November 15, 1777, the delegates finally agreed on the **Articles of Confederation** while meeting in **York**, which codified their procedures and stipulated their powers. When the states approved the Articles of Confederation on March 1, 1781, the Congress of the Confederation replaced the Continental Congress. After the states approved the Constitution of the United States in 1789, the present Congress of the United States succeeded the Congress of the Confederation.

## America's First Bank Heist

A huge sum of money was taken from vaults of the Bank of Pennsylvania at **Carpenters' Hall** during the night of Saturday, August 31 or the early morning hours of Sunday, September 1, 1798. Someone had stolen $162,821. Philadelphia blacksmith Patrick Lyon became the chief suspect, because he had worked on the bank's locks. Bank officials were certain Lyon made a duplicate key and stole the money. When he learned he was the chief suspect, Lyon returned to Philadelphia to clear his name. (He had left the city because of an outbreak of yellow fever.) The constable quickly arrested him and threw him in the Walnut Street jail. While Lyon's awaited a trial, a suddenly richer (but not the brightest) Isaac Davis began depositing large sums of money in the same bank he had robbed. When questioned about his sudden wealth, Davis confessed to the crime and made a deal to return all the money. The governor of Pennsylvania promised a pardon in return for full disclosure and full restitution. Davis seemingly never served a day in prison. Even after the confession, the bank and law officers stubbornly insisted that Lyon was somehow involved in making a false key to the vault. Finally, he was released weeks later when the charges were dismissed. After writing a book about his false arrest, Lyon successfully sued and won a verdict of $12,000 for false imprisonment.

## America's First Cement

It is everywhere in America now, but cement was not always here. In 1871 at Coplay in Lehigh County, David Saylor was the first to create Portland cement in the United States. Later, the first use of the rotary kiln to make cement on a commercial scale occurred at Coplay in November 1889.

## America's First Commercial Telegraph

"Why don't you write, you rascals?" was the first message sent on January 8, 1846 by the telegraph operators at the newly installed telegraph offices in **Lancaster** and **Harrisburg**. This

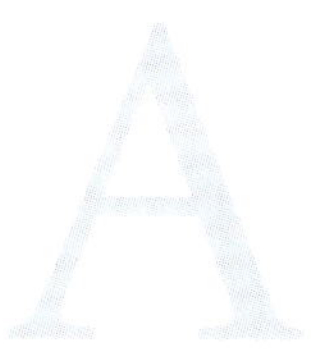

was the first commercial telegraph line in the United States and ran along the railroad right-of-way between the two cities. It was completed in 1845.

### America's First Daily Newspaper

In 1783 in Philadelphia, the *Pennsylvania Post and Daily Advertiser* became the nation's first daily newspaper. Pennsylvanians have been reading newspapers since 1719, when the state's first newspaper—and the fourth newspaper in the American colonies—debuted. It was called the *American Weekly Mercury*. By the time of the revolution, six newspapers were published in the Commonwealth, including four in Philadelphia.

### America's First Electric Street Cars

America's first streetcar system built for electric power operation was in **Scranton**. While other cities have made the same claim, Scranton has the nickname "The Electric City." It began operation on November 30, 1886. The initial run was from the Green Ridge section to central Scranton.

### America's First Flag Day

In 1893, the Society of Colonial Dames in **Philadelphia** succeeded in getting a resolution passed to have the U.S. flag displayed on all the city's public buildings. Elizabeth Duane Gillespie, a direct descendent of Benjamin Franklin and the president of the society, tried to get the city to call June 14, "Flag Day." This resolution was not taken seriously at the time. Years later, on May 7, 1937, Pennsylvania became the first state to establish Flag Day as a legal holiday. June 14 was chosen as Flag Day because of Congress' approval of the design of the U.S. flag on June 14, 1777. Flag Day is a nationwide observance today. However, Pennsylvania is the only state that recognizes it as a legal holiday.

### America's First Gas Station

With improvements to existing roads, travel on Pennsylvania's main highways was becoming easier during the decade of 1910. Cars were reaching a top speed limit of 25 mph. As more people were getting cars, one of the things these early motorists needed was fuel. The world's first "drive-in" gas station opened in **Pittsburgh** in 1913. Built by the Gulf Refining Company at Baum Boulevard and St. Clair Street in East Liberty, motorists now had an easy way to fill up their fuel tanks.

### America's First Iron Steamboat

The *Codorus*, built in **York** by Quaker John Elgar, was launched on the **Susquehanna River** at Accomac on November 22, 1825. Elgar's 6,000 lb boat, complete with a metal hull, rolled through the streets of York to its launch site. The following spring, the coal-burning steamship chugged up the Susquehanna River. The three-month voyage to Binghamton, New York proved that upstream navigation on the sometimes shallow, rocky Susquehanna was possible, but impractical. The *Codorus* returned to York Haven, and later two other steamboats tried to defy the Susquehanna River. Another boat, *The Susquehanna*, exploded near Berwick, killing several passengers, including a Maryland state legislator. Elgar's boat, and others that followed, proved the Susquehanna navigable only for flatboat river traffic heading downstream during high water. Pennsylvania's canals were developed to promote more commerce by enabling traffic to travel both ways.

### America's First Memorial Day

In 1864, three women in Boalsburg placed flowers and ferns on the graves of several of the town's Civil War dead. Decorating those graves, according to Boalsburg residents, gave them the right to declare their town as the first to establish Memorial Day. Originally called

*Boalsburg claims to be the birthplace of Memorial Day. When local women decorated soldier's graves, the ritual became known as Decoration Day, and then Memorial Day.*

Decoration Day, America observes the legal holiday yearly on the last Monday in May in honor of the nation's armed services personnel killed in wartime. The holiday is traditionally marked by parades, memorial speeches and ceremonies, and decorating graves with flowers and flags.

## America's First Paper Mill

In 1690, along the Monoshone Creek near Germantown, outside Philadelphia, William Rittenhouse founded the first paper mill in the United States. Rittenhouse, born in Germany in 1644, learned his papermaking skills in Holland. With his children, Rittenhouse settled in **Germantown** in 1688. William was a Mennonite, the first minister of that church in Germantown, and the first Mennonite bishop in America.

To make his paper mill successful, Rittenhouse teamed up with the first printer in Pennsylvania, **William Bradford**. The Rittenhouse mill produced about 1,200 reams of paper. A spring flood destroyed the original mill in 1701. Fire destroyed the second mill built by Rittenhouse. A third mill that Rittenhouse built stood until the late 1800s.

One of the watermarks used in Rittenhouse paper featured the monogram WR, the founder's initials. Another watermark

was a cloverleaf inside a crowned shield. The cloverleaf design was the mark of the village of **Germantown**. Under the shield, in outlined letters, was the word "Pensilvania."

## America's First Public Crematorium

The Funeral Reform Society in 1884 constructed and ran the first public crematorium in the United States at the Greenland Cemetery on Highland Avenue in **Lancaster**. Known as the Lancaster Crematorium, it went out of use in 1900, but just recently, began operation again.

## America's First Radio Station

When you manufacture radios and want to sell them, you have to give the people a reason to buy them. This was the simple logic behind the Westinghouse Corporation's decision to start broadcasting. On November 2, 1920, KDKA radio in **Pittsburgh** produced the first commercial radio broadcast. The first broadcast was to coincide with the presidential election of Harding-Cox. The idea was to provide listeners with the information about the election results before they could read about it in the newspaper.

Dr. Frank Conrad was the Assistant Chief Engineer of Pittsburgh's Westinghouse Electric Company. He first became interested in radio in 1912, and as a hobby, transmitted music from his home during the evenings several times each week. His boss at Westinghouse noticed a department store advertisement for radios that could receive Dr. Conrad's broadcasts. The switch was flipped at 6pm to broadcast the first commercial radio show (a term Dr. Conrad invented) in the nation. The experiment was successful.

Within several years, over 500 stations were broadcasting daily. Conrad was not present when KDKA began broadcasting—he was standing by at his home in Wilkensburg to broadcast from there, should something have gone awry at the station in downtown **Pittsburgh**.

The call letters of KDKA do not stand for anything. KDKA's license— the first radio station license—was issued on October 27, 1920. The call letters KDKA were routinely and randomly assigned from a roster kept to provide identification for ships and marine shore stations. At the time, these were the only regular radio services then in operation under formal license by the Federal Government. When it came time to issue the license, KDKA was simply the next set of call letters on the list.

This first broadcast from KDKA that originated in a tiny, makeshift shack atop one of the Westinghouse Electric and Manufacturing buildings in East Pittsburgh was the beginning of the new radio industry, and another first for Pennsylvania.

## America's First School Slate Factory

A standard in school classrooms, the first factory to produce the common blackboard and school slates opened in present-day Slatington in 1847. Slate production topped over one million pieces early in the 1900s. Slatington became the nation's top slate and classroom blackboard producer.

## America's First Stars and Stripes in Battle

Congress approved the design of the flag in a resolution adopted on June 14, 1777 stating that the flag of the United States "shall be of thirteen stripes of alternate red and white, with a union of thirteen stars of white in a blue field," representing the new constellation.

The resolution was passed following a special committee's report, which had been assigned to suggest the flag's design. American soldiers first carried a flag of this design into battle on September 11, 1777, at the **Battle of Brandywine**.

## America's First Toilet Paper

There was a time when American's did not have toilet paper. Joseph Gayetty invented toilet paper in 1857. His invention was composed of flat sheets. Before Gayetty's invention, people tore pages out of mail order catalogs. Unfortunately, Gayetty's invention failed.

Ten years later, along came Thomas, Edward, and Clarence Scott, three brothers from Philadelphia. They began selling toilet paper that consisted of a small roll of perforated paper. They sold their new paper product from a pushcart. This was the beginning of the Scott Paper Company. The company also developed and sold the first paper towels. In 1995, the company merged with Kimberly-Clark. The company still produces its paper products in Pennsylvania, south of Philadelphia at Chester.

## America's First Zoo

The **Philadelphia** Zoo was America's first public zoo. Today the Zoo exhibits more than 1,600 animals from around the world. With its picturesque Victorian gardens, outstanding art, and historical architecture, the zoo hosts thousands of visitors each week. The Zoological Society of Philadelphia was chartered on March 21, 1859 but the pending Civil War stalled its opening. Finally, the Zoo opened its gates to the public on July 1, 1874. Visitors of the 42-acre garden explore design elements of various continents and historical periods. The grounds include Solitude, the country home of John Penn, grandson of **William Penn**.

## America's Oldest Brewery

In 1829, David G. Yuengling, an immigrant from Wurtemburg, Germany, settled in Pottsville, and started a brewery. He set up his brewery on Centre Street, at the site of the present-day city hall. Yuengling called his new venture "The Eagle Brewery."

Two years later, a fire destroyed the plant. Yuengling built a new brewery on Mahantongo Street. In those early days, Yuengling had malt from Philadelphia transported more than 100 miles to Pottsville by means of the Schuylkill **Canal**. His final brew was then delivered throughout the region by horse-drawn wagons.

The brewery survived the Prohibition Era by brewing "near-beer." The family-owned business gambled correctly that Prohibition would be repealed. They managed to stay in business until brewing beer was legal again. Many other breweries went out of business.

Today, the D.G. Yuengling and Son Brewery still successfully operates from

*The Yuengling Brewery in Pottsville is the oldest brewery in America.*

Pottsville, nestled among the rolling Appalachian foothills. The company holds a record of continuous operation since 1829 and the longest uninterrupted history of management by a single family in the country.

## American Bandstand

It started as a small, local daily show, and featured real **Philadelphia** teenagers, who would show up at the small studio, decorated with records, a dance floor, and wooden bleachers. It was the first Tuesday in October 1952. Hundreds of teenagers jammed WFIL's Studio B, located at Forty-Sixth and Market Streets in Philadelphia. The new television show would have a major impact on the music, dance, and lifestyles of American teenagers.

When it started, the show was simply called *Bandstand*, and its first host was Bob Horn. The format was simple, and remained the same throughout the history of the show. Horn introduced the performers on each show by saying, "We've got com-pa-nyyyy!" after which Lee Stewart would play records, and the singers would lip-sync their songs as the local youths danced for the cameras. However, in 1956, police arrested Horn for DWI (Driving While Intoxicated) amid an anti-drink driving campaign by WFIL's owner, the *Philadelphia Inquirer*. TV executives fired Horn immediately, and replaced him with a 25-year-old Dick Clark. He had a youthful appearance, and knew how to communicate with teenagers.

Clark earned the nickname as America's youngest teenager. He promoted the show in New York, and finally sold it to a network. On August 5, 1957, *American Bandstand* debuted on the ABC network. It broadcast the show in the 3.00–4.30pm time slot. It was the perfect time to reach teens coming home from school.

The first song played on the national program was Jerry Lee Lewis' "Whole Lotta Shakin Goin' On." Until 1964, the network broadcast the show nationwide from the WFIL TV studio in Philadelphia. At one point, Dick Clark was receiving more weekly mail than any other celebrity was. Teens would tune in to see the latest fashions and dance steps. Strict rules governed the teenager's appearance and behavior. The show's producers did not allow girls appearing on the show to wear slacks or tight sweaters. Boys had to wear a coat and tie. TV producers banned smoking and chewing gum. The show grew in popularity around a regular group of Philadelphia high school students who developed their own national following. Unfortunately, in the beginning, producers allowed only white teenagers on the show, despite the thousands of black teenagers that lived so close to the TV studio.

There were performances by top music personalities, dancing contests, and undiscovered professional talent. Much of that new talent was from the Philadelphia region. "Rate-A-Record" (where selected studio audience members are asked to rate a record from 35 to 98) became one of the shows most popular segments. The series had a short run on prime time television in the fall of 1957 on ABC. The daytime network version continued until 1963,

*"Tom and Jerry" or as they were later to become, Simon and Garfunkel, who made their TV debut on* American Bandstand *November 22, 1957.*

and then became a once-a-week Saturday afternoon show.

Over the years, almost every rock star was a guest on the program, apart from two exceptions. Elvis Presley and Rick Nelson never appeared on the show. In 1957, two boys, calling themselves Tom and Jerry, made their debut singing with their song, "Hey Schoolgirl." The singing duo was Paul Simon and Art Garfunkel. In 1987, the show that influenced so many American teenagers and that started so simply in Philadelphia made a final broadcast, marking the end of the era of Rock and Roll music.

## American Federation of Labor

On November 15, 1881, in Turner Hall, a convention was held that formed the organization which became the American Federation of Labor. In a short time, it was the nation's largest labor federation.

On November 14, 1938, the first convention of the Congress of Industrial Organizations was held, representing 34 international unions. In 1955, both the American Federation of Labor and the Congress of Industrial Organizations merged into what was known as the AFL-CIO.

## Amish

Often called the "plain people," Pennsylvania's Amish population is concentrated in **Lancaster** County. The Amish have upheld their unique and conservative agricultural way of life despite the pressures and influences of the modern industrial society that surrounds them.

*Pennsylvania's Amish still use horse drawn farm equipment to work the fields. Despite the old ways, their farms are the most productive in the country.*

They are a protestant group from **Mennonite** origin; the name Amish is derived from Jakob Amman, a Swiss Mennonite bishop that founded the sect in the late 1600s. Amman insisted that a strict discipline was maintained within the church by shunning those that disobeyed before excommunicating them.

The Amish were subject to persecution in Europe. They emmigrated in the 18th century to Pennsylvania, settling in Lancaster County and the surrounding areas in the 1720s and 1730s. The Amish have since spread into Ohio, several other midwestern states, and Canada.

Lancaster's Amish, now the second largest population compared with Ohio, have a greater visible presence because of their closer proximity to the larger urban areas. While the Amish live in other areas of the state, hundreds of thousands of curious tourists visit Lancaster each year to see their unique lifestyle. Because of its location, Lancaster is a day trip away from many major population centers, such as New York City, **Philadelphia**, Baltimore, Washington D.C., and others. Its closeness to major cities makes it an attractive place for visitors escaping from urban areas to witness the slow pace of Amish life.

The commercialization of the Amish way of life is a double-edged sword. For some members of the Amish community, tourism was resented and many moved away. But tourism has brought them great economic advantages. Tourism lessens the cultural gap between the Amish and the outside world. Public interest in Amish culture has promoted sympathy for them, which discourages government intervention in their everyday life.

The Old Order Amish are quite conservative. They use horse-drawn buggies. They dress in a plain and distinctive style, using hooks and eyes instead of buttons to fasten their clothes. Amish girls and women wear only modest dresses made from solid-colored

*Hundreds of visitors visit Pennsylvania every year to witness the slower pace of the Amish life, such as the horse-drawn equipment shown here.*

fabric with long sleeves and a full skirt that is never shorter than halfway between the knee and the floor. Their dresses are covered with a cape and apron and are fastened with straight pins or snaps. They never cut their hair, which they wear in a bun on the back of their head. They wear a white prayer covering on their head if they are married, and a black one if they are single. Amish women never wear jewelry. Amish boys and men only wear dark colored suits, straight-cut coats always without lapels, trousers, suspenders, a plain shirt, black socks and shoes, and a black or straw broad-brimmed hat.

*Amish buggies still maneuver in Pennsylvania on busy roads and through congested intersections.*

Married adult males wear beards but shave under their nose so they do not have mustaches. Marriage with outsiders is forbidden. The Amish refuse to take part in civil affairs, such as voting or serving in the military. Estimates of the population of the Old Order Amish vary, but their numbers are believed to be around 100,000.

While loyal to the government, the Amish sometimes run into conflicts with it. Education issues, work rules, and even the requirement to place lights on their horse-drawn buggies at night cause controversies and dissent. Some are in the local news for being charged with violating laws about animal cruelty, professional licensing requirements, or complying with health regulations.

The Amish also struggle with the basic ideas of modernity. While they try to avoid it, technology creeps into the Amish way of life. They have conflicts with the use of motor vehicles and telephones, as well as "luxuries" in the home. The Amish still do not allow electricity in the home, but do use mechanical or gasoline-powered machines. As additional farmland is no longer available, many Amish have started businesses, and must use computers, fax machines, or other such modern technology to survive. Today's Amish struggle with how to limit themselves and can keep a distance from the outside world. It is not uncommon to see an Amish family shopping at Walmart for groceries and supplies.

The Amish that have farms use horse-drawn equipment with metal wheels (no rubber tires.) They produce various crops, including corn, hay, wheat, tobacco, soybeans, barley, potatoes, and other vegetables. They also maintain dairy herds, and grow grasses for grazing.

Although in many ways, they may seem stuck in the past, the Amish do use modern medical facilities and seek care from doctors. Many Amish women deliver their babies in a hospital, while others birth their children in homes with the assistance of a midwife.

The Amish community still organizes barn raisings, a daylong event where everyone gathers to build a barn for their neighbor. They send their children to private, one-room schoolhouses, and their children attend until the eighth grade. From there, they work on the family farm or in a business.

While the Old Order Amish are the most prevalent, other groups are not as restrictive or conservative. As in many religions, they have formed into separate factions.

## Anthracite Coal Strike of 1902

In May 1902, over 150,000 anthracite coalmine workers went on strike for six months. The miners sought union recognition, higher wages, and shorter hours. President Theodore Roosevelt set up the Anthracite Coal Strike Commission. The commission held hearings at the Lackawanna County Courthouse in **Scranton** and granted some demands in March 1903. The strike was one of the longest in U.S. history. It is notable in that it introduced unbiased federal intervention in labor disputes.

## Appalachian Trail

From Maine to Georgia, the Appalachian National Scenic Trail wanders the ridges, hills, and valleys of the Appalachian mountain ranges for more than 2,174 miles—230 of those miles arc through Pennsylvania. A walk along the trail gives the hiker a small sense of what early Pennsylvania must have been like to the hardy pioneers that first settled there. The rocks along the trail are known to ruin hiker's boots. Many hikers hobble away from the trail with sore feet, blisters, and bruises. Pennsylvania's portion of the Appalachian Trail is rugged. It avoids historic places, and many of the state's most beautiful vistas. Hikers should beware of rattlesnakes or copperheads on this length of the trail. Water supplies along the trail are known to be unreliable, especially in the summer months.

The Appalachian Trail was the idea of Benton MacKaye, a federal employee, educated as a forester and self-trained as a planner, who proposed it in 1923 as the connecting thread of "a project in regional planning." The trail opened in 1934.

## Appleseed, Johnny

John Chapman lived along French Creek near Franklin, Venango County, between 1797 and 1804. Early records point out he had set up a nursery there and another one near Warren. An American pioneer and folk hero of many legends, he later traveled throughout the Ohio

*Signs mark the Appalachian Trail throughout Pennsylvania.*

*Through an elaborate State Park system, Pennsylvania maintains scenic hiking and walking trails. The Appalachian Trail also arcs through Pennsylvania.*

Valley, pruning and planting apple trees. Chapman was born in 1774 in Massachusetts, and died in Indiana, 1845.

## Articles of Confederation

There were three phases in developing the United States government, and Pennsylvania provided the site for each phase. The second phase, following the Declaration of Independence, was to create the Articles of Confederation. It was the colonists' first try at developing a constitution and was the first constitution of the United States. Although there was a need for unity among the states, the Articles of Confederation failed to create a strong federal government. The problem of

creating a new government for a new nation weighed heavily on those that sought independence from Britain.

A committee of the Second Continental Congress wrote the Articles of Confederation. The head of the committee, John Dickinson, presented a report on the proposed articles to the Congress in July 1776. In that report, Dickinson proposed a strong central government, with control over the western lands, equal representation for the states, and the power to levy taxes. The representatives from the 13 states feared a powerful central government similar to the British rule that they were fighting to gain independence from. Congress worked on the Articles of Confederation in **Philadelphia**, and then in **Lancaster** and **York** after fleeing the British army. Congress changed Dickinson's proposed articles before sending them to the thirteen states for acceptance. Congress adopted this first constitution, which included a preamble and 13 articles, on November 15, 1777.

It would take years before all the states ratified the articles. Caused by the preoccupation with the American Revolution, the delay allowed disagreements among the states to fester. Those differences included quarrels over boundary lines, differing tariff laws, conflicting decisions by state courts, and trade restrictions between the states. The smaller states wanted equal representation compared with the larger states in Congress, and the larger states were concerned they would pay too much money to support the federal government.

Another major disagreement among the states was the control of the western territories. Some states had no frontier borders, while others did. The states with no frontier borders wanted the government to control the sale of these territories so all the states profited, while the states bordering the frontier wanted to control as much land as they possibly could. Eventually the states agreed to give control of all western lands to the federal government. The articles were finally approved on March 1, 1781 when Maryland agreed to it.

The Articles of Federation created a loose union of independent states that granted limited powers to a central government. The national government consisted of a single

*Austin shown after a dam burst in 1911. The flood caused major devastation in the area.*

house of Congress, where each state had one vote. Congress had the power to set up a post office, to estimate the costs of the government and ask donations from the states, to develop armed forces, and to control the development of the western territories. It took the consent of nine of the 13 states before Congress could coin, borrow, or appropriate money, as well as declare war and enter treaties and alliances with foreign nations. There was no independent executive and no veto of legislation. Judicial proceedings in each state were to be honored by all other states. The federal government had no judicial branch, and the only judicial authority Congress had was the power to mediate disputes between states. Under the Articles of Confederation, the states denied Congress the power to levy taxes. The new federal government was financed by donations from the states based on the value of each state's lands. Any amendment to the Articles of Confederation required the unanimous approval of all 13 states.

In trying to limit the power of the central government, the Second Continental Congress created a weak Federal government, one without the power to govern the nation effectively. With its inability to regulate trade and levy taxes, the Federal government was often broke. Sometimes the states refused to give the Federal government the money it needed.

Tariff wars broke out between the states, nearly paralyzing interstate commerce. Congress did not have the power to pass needed legislation, and did not have the power to enforce cooperation.

Congress lacked the power to force the states to adhere to the terms of the Treaty of Paris, which officially ended the American Revolution in 1783. Soon, some states started their own negotiations with foreign countries. The new nation was unable to defend its borders from British and Spanish encroachment because it could not pay for an army when the individual states refused to contribute the necessary funds.

*A railroad train that was caught in the flood in Austin, 1911.*

Because of its inherent weaknesses, the new United States government, created by Congress in Pennsylvania, commanded little respect, and its prestige was further diminished by its inability to cope with internal uprisings. As it became clear the new government was not working, Congress called for a Constitutional Convention to be held in May 1787 to revise the articles. Between May and September, the convention met in Philadelphia and wrote the present U.S. Constitution.

## Austin Flood Disaster

On September 30, 1911, the Bayless Pulp and Paper Co.'s dam broke in Potter County. The concrete dam, built two years earlier, was nearly 50 feet high and 534 feet long. The dam's failure released torrents of water and debris down Freeman Run into Austin and Costello, causing massive destruction, killing at least 78 people. It was the second worst single-dam disaster in Pennsylvania. Only the **Johnstown Flood** caused more devastation.

*Austin after the flood in 1911.*

# B

## Baldwin Locomotive Works

*A mallet locomotive built by Baldwin and used here by the Duluth and Iron Range Railway.*

In 1831, Matthias Baldwin, a Philadelphia jeweler and abolitionist, opened a machine shop and decided to enter the locomotive manufacturing business. A year later, on November 23, 1832, the company successfully ran its first locomotive, *Old Ironsides*, on the Philadelphia, Germantown & Norristown Railroad. The Baldwin Locomotive Works was to become the largest and most successful locomotive building firm in the world.

Within a few years, the company produced two new locomotives a month and employed 240 men at its Broad Street location. By 1861, the Baldwin Locomotive Works had produced 1,000 locomotives. In its heyday, it employed about 1,700 men. In 1906, Baldwin began construction of a large auxiliary plant in the Philadelphia suburb of Eddystone. In 1928, the Broad Street plant closed and the company transferred all work to the Eddystone Plant. Tough financial times caused Baldwin to take on partners, and in the early days, the firm's name changed often. Matthias Baldwin died in 1866, but his company continued to do business.

The company's growth slowed in the mid-1920s as the U.S. railroad industry began its long decline. Despite mergers and acquisitions—and the development of diesel engines—the company's business declined. Baldwin declared bankruptcy in 1935. World War II brought a short-term reprieve, but following the war the steam locomotive was obsolete and orders dwindled. The Westinghouse Corporation bought Baldwin in 1948, but was unable to revive the company. In 1950, the Lima-Hamilton Corporation and Baldwin merged, but the end was near. In 1956, Baldwin manufactured the last of its 70,541 locomotives.

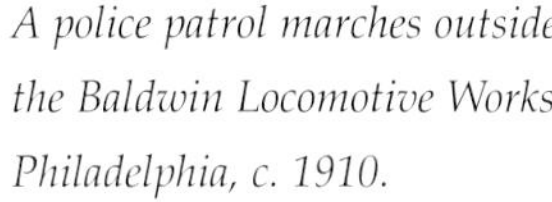

*A police patrol marches outside the Baldwin Locomotive Works, Philadelphia, c. 1910.*

## Banana Splits

Optometrist Dr. David Strickler invented the banana split at his downtown pharmacy on Ligonier Street in Latrobe, Pennsylvania. According to local legend, Dr. Strickler received his inspiration while watching soda jerks work during his visit to Atlantic City, N.J. He returned home to create the banana split in 1904. It contained several scoops of ice cream and flavored syrups, sauces, nuts, and fruit, with whipped cream on top served on a banana split lengthwise.

Dr. Strickler hoped his banana split would draw students from nearby St. Vincent College. His invention worked. The college students loved his decadent sundae and spread word about it when they returned home, mostly on the East Coast. As the banana split became popular, Dr. Strickler commissioned a local glass company to custom-make a long, narrow dish to hold his ice cream creation. Sometimes called a houseboat, the banana split remains a favorite dessert.

## Barry, John

An Irish-born naval officer who made Philadelphia his home port, Commodore John Barry is known as the Father of the American Navy. As a Roman Catholic, he was obviously attracted to William Penn's city that promised religious freedom. Although he lived only 58 years, this son of a poor Irish farmer rose from a humble cabin boy to the senior commander of the entire United States fleet. Barry commanded the *Lexington* in the capture of the *HMS Edward*, the first British ship taken during the war. On February 22, 1797, President **Washington** presented Barry with Commission Number One in the Navy which was dated June 4, 1794, the date of his original selection. The formal ceremony took place on Washington's birthday. Barry died September 12, 1803, from lifelong complications of asthma.

## Bartram, John

Born in Marple, Pennsylvania in 1699, John Bartram is known as the founder of American botany. A Quaker, he taught himself botany and planted the first botanical garden in America along the banks of the Schuylkill River in Philadelphia. He made many dangerous expeditions into America's frontier to collect plant samples. Throughout his life, he corresponded with distinguished naturalists in Europe, and in 1765, King George III of England appointed him "Botanist to the King." Bartram also distinguished himself by performing important plant hybridization experiments. He died in 1777. His world-renowned garden still exists as a public park and museum by the Fairmount Park Commission in West Philadelphia, at 54th and Eastwick Streets.

## Baseball in Pennsylvania

Two major league baseball teams call Pennsylvania their home, the Philadelphia Phillies and the Pittsburgh Pirates. The Phillies started playing in Pennsylvania in 1880, while

*Moving from Three Rivers Stadium, the Pittsburgh Pirates are now playing at PNC Park.*

*Baseball is part of Pennsylvania. The Philadelphia Phillies and the Pittsburgh Pirates are the state's two major league teams. Other cities are home to minor league teams.*

the Pirates started in 1882. The Phillies and the Pirates are currently a part of the National League. Both teams have played in and won the World Series. The Pirates last won the Series in 1971, while the Phillies won in 1980.

In 1903, the Pirates played in, and lost, the first World Series. In 1909, the first baseball stadium in the United States, Forbes Field, was built in Pittsburgh. It was soon followed by similar stadiums in Chicago, Cleveland, Boston, and New York.

Forbes Field finally closed in 1970 when the Pirates moved to the newly opened Three Rivers Stadium. On October 13, 1971, at the Three Rivers Stadium, Pirates defeated the Baltimore Orioles in Game Four of the first night World Series game in baseball history.

Many cities in Pennsylvania host minor league baseball teams affiliated with the major leagues. Their level of play as a minor league vary. **Allentown**, **Altoona**, **Erie**, **Harrisburg**, **Reading**, **Scranton**, and **Williamsport** currently are the hometowns of the minor leagues. Other cities are trying to attract the minor league teams to their communities. Pennsylvania is also the home of the Little League.

## Beaver

The present-day town of Beaver was not named for the furry critter that gnaws trees. Beaver was the name of the Delaware Indian chief and of his village that was located near there. Its location along the Ohio-Beaver River trails made it important in the fur trade.

## Bedford Springs

Around 1796, the medicinal value of the springs in present-day Bedford County was discovered. Deep in the Appalachian Mountains, Bedford Springs became a leading resort visited by many dignitaries.

**James Buchanan** used the Bedford Springs Hotel as his summer residence while he was president. It was here the president received the first trans-Atlantic telegram, sent from England by Queen Victoria. Construction of the hotel began in 1804, which at the time was equivalent to one of today's spas, and it expanded into a grand facility. The United States Supreme Court also convened at the Bedford Springs Hotel, the only time the Justices have met outside their Washington chambers. Because of the timing of their stay, they were likely to have discussed the historic Dred Scott case at the hotel. Presidents Hayes, Garfield, and Harrison also stayed at the Bedford Springs Hotel. It has been closed since the 1980s, and is decaying rapidly.

## Bethlehem

Pennsylvania's city of Bethlehem is unique in that it is located in both Lehigh and Northampton counties. Strategically positioned on the Lehigh River, Bethlehem borders with **Allentown** and Easton, forming an important industrial and manufacturing center. It is Pennsylvania's 7th largest city.

*Over 500 American soldiers from the Revolutionary War were buried on a hillside in Bethlehem.*

*Bethlehem has well-preserved historic buildings.*

Early immigrants, who belonged to the Unitas Fratrum (now known as the Moravian Church), founded Bethlehem in 1741. They named it on Christmas Eve to commemorate Jesus Christ's birthplace. The city's Christmastime celebrations and restored 18th-century buildings attract many tourists each year.

For years, the city was the home of the Bethlehem Steel Corporation, one of the largest producers of steel in the United States. While most of its operations were located out in other cities, the corporation's headquarters were in Bethlehem. In November 1995, the company closed its last operating blast furnace in its original plant, ending an era of more than 100 years of continuous steel production in Bethlehem. This resulted in 1,800 workers losing their jobs.

The city's other manufacturers include textiles, foundry products, machine parts, chemicals, electrical equipment, and food products. The city is the home of the **Lehigh University** (1865), Moravian College (1742), and a community college. Bethlehem's population, according to the U.S. Census Bureau, was 71,329 in 2001.

## Birthplace of the U.S. Constitution

The **Articles of Confederation** governed the United States through the final years of the Revolutionary War, through the peace negotiations, and into the beginning of a sovereign nation. Ratified on March 1, 1781, the Articles of Confederation were more a congenial league among America's independent States rather than a true Union. The founders of the nation were, understandably, against creating a strong, central national government, as they were already fighting a costly war for independence against a British government who had this kind of control.

The newly formed government, who were functioning under the Articles of

Confederation, did not work. In 1781, there were major developments. American finances were in such a crisis that Congress created a separate department of finance. The year before, when the value of Continental currency plummeted, Congress could not supply the American Army. Shortages of food led some Connecticut soldiers to mutiny at Washington's camp in New Jersey. Congress responded by appointing **Robert Morris** as superintendent of finance.

With the ratification of the Articles of Confederation, under discussion since 1777, Congress assumed a new title, "The United States in Congress Assembled." French and American forces joined at Yorktown, Virginia, on land and at sea, and attacked British fortifications. The Americans and French soon held British strongholds. British General Cornwallis surrendered, giving up almost 8,000 men. There was no hope that Britain could win the war in America. Now the American forefathers would have to run their new country.

Their failure to establish a strong central government caused yet more problems. When a delegation of army officers complained to Congress about their unpaid salaries and pensions, Congress had no solution. An anonymous letter urged officers to unite and attempt one last appeal to Congress, and if ignored, they were to revolt against Congress. Washington, addressing the army in person at its headquarters in Newburgh, New York, passionately convinced his officers to be patient, and not to dishonor themselves after their victory. They were visibly moved, and the officers adopted resolutions to present to Congress. They pledged not to threaten violence or rebellion. In another incident, soldiers from Pennsylvania marched on Congress, demanding their back pay. Armed and angry, they surrounded **Independence Hall**. The members of Congress eventually left the building and fled to Princeton, New Jersey.

A dissatisfied army was not Congress's only problem. When American commissioners attempted to make trade arrangements with Britain, the British Ambassador refused, because any state could ignore Congress's trade regulations. The Congress did not have the power to regulate commerce on a national scale. This led to the formation of a committee dedicated to appealing to the states to grant Congress enlarged powers over commerce. Despite these attempts, the states took no effective action.

Britain had given up its territory between the Mississippi River and the Allegheny Mountains, doubling the size of the new nation. This new land area became the subject of many squabbles among the states. Robert Morris soon realized he had no power to handle the financial problems, and he resigned.

In 1784, Congress decided to leave **Philadelphia**, and moved to New York. But many of its members were soon to return to the city to make tough decisions about the future of the country.

The founders realized the problems of a weak central government. Several commissioners from Virginia and Maryland met in 1785 at the home of George Washington in Mount Vernon, to discuss the regulation of trade between the two states. At the meeting's conclusion, the commissioners agreed that all the states should meet at a convention in Annapolis to discuss common commercial problems. The following year, there were attempts in Congress to amend the Articles of Confederation. They all failed. Nine states had agreed to send delegates to Annapolis to discuss commerce, but only five state delegations arrived on time. Because of the poor attendance, the delegates decided to invite the states to another convention.

Alexander Hamilton drafted an address to the states, inviting them to a convention to be held in Philadelphia in 1787, to discuss not only commerce, but all matters necessary to improve the federal government. After a lengthy debate, on February 21, 1787, Congress endorsed the plan to revise the Articles of Confederation.

On May 25, 1787, delegates from every state except Rhode Island met in Philadelphia. The delegation included the most respected and talented men in America. The delegates selected **George Washington** to serve as president of the Constitutional Convention.

Both the weather and the debate heated during the summer. There were many tough topics to tackle. Some of the major issues were representation, and whether it should be equal based by each state regardless of population, or totally based on the state's population. Slavery became an issue. Alexander Hamilton suggested the creation of a strong executive branch, including a president that was elected for life. Receiving little support for his plan, he left the convention.

Their work continued during the summer. They debated, discussed, and formulated the framework of a new national government. Washington controlled the discussion, and formed committees to draft a constitution, and others to address topics such as navigation and the slave trade.

On September 12, 1787, the Committee on Style and Arrangement presented a completed draft to the Constitutional Convention. On September 15, 1787, the Convention adopted the U.S. Constitution. Two days later, all delegates except three signed the Constitution. As an aged, eighty-one year-old, **Benjamin Franklin** inscribed his signature on the parchment, tears streamed down his cheeks. Just before signing, he had said, "It ... astonishes me ... to find this system approaching so near to perfection as it does; and I think it will astonish our enemies." The *Pennsylvania Packet* printed the first public copy of the Constitution on September 19, 1787.

*Known first as the Pennsylvania State House, the building fell into disrepair until Philadelphians later realized how important and significant it was to the nation's history.*

Congress then formally submitted their new Constitution to the States on September 28, 1777. Delaware was the first state to ratify it on December 7, 1787. Five days later, on December 12, Pennsylvania was the second state to ratify the U.S. Constitution with a vote of 42-23. New Jersey followed, as did Georgia, Connecticut, and Massachusetts. With six states ratifying the constitution, on March 24, 1788, Rhode Island was the first state to reject it. On April 28, 1788, Maryland was the seventh state to ratify it. South Carolina, which was followed by New Hampshire, ratified the Constitution. With New Hampshire's acceptance, the U.S. Constitution was formally accepted. A Committee was appointed on July 2, 1788, to plan the transition to the new government. New York voted for ratification and became the eleventh state to accept the new Constitution on July 26, 1788.

The following year, on March 4, 1789, the new U.S. Government under the U.S. Constitution formally went into effect. On April 1, a quorum was reached in the House of Representatives and it began its first session. On April 6, George Washington was elected president. He was inaugurated in the temporary capital in New York City on April 30, 1789.

The U.S. Constitution, still in effect today, was proposed, debated, deliberated, designed, and approved by the Constitutional Convention, during the summer of 1787 in strict secrecy in Philadelphia, the second time the city was the host to the beginnings of an independent America.

Anxious citizens gathered outside Independence Hall when the proceedings ended in order to learn what had been produced behind closed doors. A Mrs. Powel of Philadelphia asked Benjamin Franklin, "Well, Doctor, what have we got, a republic or a

monarchy?" With no hesitation whatsoever, the elderly Franklin quickly answered, "A republic, if you can keep it."

## Bituminous Coal

Pennsylvania's bituminous coal industry started around 1760 on Coal Hill, now Mt. Washington, in Allegheny County. The Pittsburgh coal bed was mined to supply Fort Pitt with coal. The coal bed was eventually judged the most valuable individual mineral deposit in the nation.

## Black Cherry Capital

Pennsylvania is the home to the little town known as the Black Cherry Capital of the World. Located along scenic Route 6 in McKean County, the Borough of Kane harvests such a large crop of black cherries each year that it earned the nickname. Each July, the borough celebrates with a Black Cherry Festival.

## Black Hand Society, The

The Black Hand was a symbol and name for a criminal and terrorist secret society. The Black Hand flourished in Sicily in the late 19th century, and in the United States it was especially active in New York City at the beginning of the 20th century.

On September 2, 1906, John F. Henry, a member of the newly formed Pennsylvania State Police was at Florence, Jefferson County. Henry and several other troopers tried to arrest several, heavily armed Black Hand Society fugitives that afternoon. As Henry advanced toward the house where the criminals were hiding, he was shot and killed. He was the first member of the Pennsylvania State Police killed in the line of duty. Two other troopers, trying to rescue Henry, were seriously wounded before they could reach him. A second detachment of 15 Troopers arrived at 6.30 pm. Covered by heavy gunfire, Trooper Francis Zehringer and two other troopers rushed to the house, battered in a side door, and entered. The killers fired from a stairway and killed Zehringer, the second trooper to die in the line of duty. The troopers decided not to sacrifice any others. Using the cover of darkness and a rainstorm, they placed dynamite at the base of the house. At dawn, they detonated the explosive. The house was destroyed and the fugitives killed.

## Blue Mountain Forts

In Dauphin County north of **Harrisburg**, the Paxton Rangers defended settlers against Indian raiders. By 1763, the rangers operated from six loghouse stations along the Blue Mountains. The small forts were scattered from the Swatara to the **Susquehanna**. The Paxton Rangers were a casually organized group of volunteers from the region. The Paxton Rangers were also known as the Paxtang Boys, who massacred the Conestoga Indians in Lancaster.

## Boehm's Chapel

Built in 1791, the "Temple of Limestone" is the oldest existing structure designed for Methodist use in Pennsylvania. Located in Willow Street, Lancaster County, Boehm's Chapel is one of the oldest Methodist chapels in America. It was erected on land owned by Bishop Martin Boehm, the co-founder of the United Brethren in Christ. Bishop Francis Asbury, the "Father of American Methodism," often visited Boehm's Chapel.

## Boone, Daniel

Born to Quakers in Pennsylvania, Daniel Boone became an American pioneer, woodsman, and a subject of much folklore. He named his **Kentucky rifle** "Tick-Licker." He wore a coonskin hat and buckskin clothes with fringes and never spent a day of his life in a school. He never admitted to being lost but confessed that he once was "confused for several weeks." Chief Black Fish of the Shawnee Indians captured him, but Boone escaped when he learned of a British and Indian plot to attack Boonesborough in Kentucky.

Boone was the fourth son and sixth child of Squire and Sarah Boone. Born in a log cabin in Oley (east of Reading), then Philadelphia County but now Berks County, on November 2, 1734, Boone grew up in the frontier of Pennsylvania. Some of his earliest childhood memories included visits by Indians to the Quaker farms in Pennsylvania.

When he was 14, his family migrated to South Carolina. From his earliest days in Pennsylvania, Boone became a skillful hunter and trapper. In 1756, he married Rebecca Bryan. He eventually fathered ten children, several of which would die during Indian attacks. Boone set out to explore the wilderness around the Kentucky River, making the first of many trips into the region starting in 1767. In 1775, a Carolina trading company hired him to establish a road so settlers could reach Kentucky. He built a fort on the site of

*A historical marker gives information about the Daniel Boone Homestead.*

*The Daniel Boone Homestead near Douglassville where he lived as a child.*

Boonesborough. The road Boone established is the Wilderness Road. He faught against the British and the Indians in the American War of Independence.

Boone lost most of his land claims in Kentucky because of faulty titles. He never stayed in one location long. Boone's love of the wilderness from his childhood years in Pennsylvania continued to the end of his life. He was often away on a hunting expedition or exploring unsettled country. His skill in the woods and with the Indians was so outstanding that he became the most famous pioneer of his time. His wife died in 1813. Boone died on September 26, 1820 in Defiance, Missouri.

Boone has two graves, one in Defiance and the other in Frankfort, Kentucky. Twenty-five years after his death, the body of the native Pennsylvanian was reportedly dug up and moved to Kentucky. His family claimed that the wrong grave was dug up.

His Pennsylvania birthplace has been restored and is open for tours.

## Borders of Pennsylvania

Pennsylvania is often referred to as one of the Middle Atlantic States, even though none of its borders touches the Atlantic. The state's eastern border is with New Jersey, just across the Delaware River. To the south, Pennsylvania shares its border with Delaware, Maryland, and West Virginia. The unusual arc border between Pennsylvania and Delaware was created as a court decided compromise. West Virginia actually shares Pennsylvania's southwestern corner. The western border is shared with Ohio. Pennsylvania's northern border is shared with New York. Lake Erie also forms the northern border of the state.

Over the years, several other states made claim to the territory that now comprises Pennsylvania. The states that disputed Pennsylvania's borders were Connecticut, Maryland, and Virginia.

*Pennsylvania borders include the scenic Delaware Water Gap.*

## Boscov, Solomon

Solomon Boscov, an immigrant who came from Russia in 1911, began at Reading as a peddler. He went on to establish a large, family-owned department store chain. His first store started after World War I and gradually expanded into a larger one. New stores opened starting in 1962. In 1969, Solomon Boscov died. His family continued the department store business, expanding and opening dozens of stores both in Pennsylvania and other states.

## Boulder Field

Located in Hickory Run State Park, near White Haven in Carbon County, Boulder Field is an area 400 by 1,800 feet that consists of nothing but rocks and boulders. Produced by periglacial activity during the Ice Age, it is the largest glacier-made rock field of its kind.

Some boulders in Boulder Field are nearly 26 feet long, and the depth of the boulders measure one to 12 feet. The main rock types include red sandstone and conglomerates. This area has remained unchanged for more than 20,000 years and was declared a National Natural Landmark.

## Bower Hill

A large crowd of insurgents burned General John Neville's mansion to the ground during a major escalation of violence in the **Whiskey Rebellion**, on July 16 and 17, 1794. Neville was the Inspector of Revenue under President Washington. In the two-day battle, Neville with his slaves and small federal detachment faced a force of over 500 rebels. Several opposed to the tax died in the violence on Bower Hill in Allegheny County.

## Bowman Field

Bowman Field is Pennsylvania's oldest operating minor league baseball park. Over the years, this Williamsport park became home to successive Williamsport teams and hosted many major league teams for exhibition games. The first professional game was played in the park on April 27, 1926, between the Williamsport Grays and the Harrisburg Giants, a Negro league team.

## Bradford, William

A Quaker recruited by **William Penn** in 1682, William Bradford (1663–1752) settled in the middle of the forest in **Philadelphia**. In 1685, he set up his printing press, the first one south of New England, and only the third one in the colonies. He used paper produced by William Rittenhouse in **Germantown**. He later setup a press in New York. His grandson, also William Bradford (1722–1791), became a printer and was active in the American Revolution.

## Brady, Captain John

Captain John Brady, born in 1733 in Newark, Delaware, was killed by Indians in an ambush on April 11, 1779 near Muncy. The hero of the colonial wars was in charge of Fort Brady. He was returning to the fort with supplies for other hardy settlers when he was murdered.

## Brady, Samuel

Born near Shippensburg on the edge of the Pennsylvania frontier and Indian lands in 1756,

The TIMES are Dreadful, Dismal Doleful Dolorous, and DOLLAR-LESS.

An Emblem of the Effects of the STAMP

O! the fatal Stamp

Thursday, October 31, 1765. THE NUMB. 1195.

PENNSYLVANIA JOURNAL;

AND

WEEKLY ADVERTISER.

EXPIRING: In Hopes of a Resurrection to LIFE again.

I AM sorry to be obliged to acquaint my Readers, that as The STAMP-ACT, is fear'd to be obligatory upon us after the *First of November* ensuing, (the *fatal To morrow*) the Publisher of this Paper unable to bear the Burthen, has thought it expedient TO STOP awhile, in order to deliberate, whether any Methods can be found to elude the Chains forged for us, and escape the insupportable Slavery, which it is hoped, from the last Representations now made against that Act, may be effected. Mean while, I must earnestly Request every Individual of my Subscribers many of whom have been long behind Hand, that they would immediately Discharge their respective Arrears that I may be able, not only to support myself during the Interval, but be better prepared to proceed again with this Paper, whenever an opening for that Purpose appears, which I hope will be soon. WILLIAM BRADFORD

*The second William Bradford published the* Pennsylvania Journal, *which helped promote the Revolutionary cause.*

Samuel Brady became a famed frontier scout and the subject of many local legends. At age 18, Brady joined the Pennsylvania First Regiment and rose to the rank of Captain. He became well-known for his many narrow escapes. Brady was nearly killed during a retreat during the Paoli Massacre.

The following year, he escaped from pursuing Indians by jumping off a cliff 500 feet down into the Allegheny River at a place known as the Narrows in Armstrong County. He escaped again from Indians in Ohio when they were preparing to burn him at the stake. He ran 100 miles to return to Fort Pitt.

In June 1779, in what was then Seneca territory and today Clarion County, Brady led a force seeking the Indians that killed a settler and her four children, taking two children as prisoners. Brady's force surrounded a war party of seven Indians—seemingly both Seneca and Munsee—killing their leader and freeing the two children. Brady died Christmas Day, 1795 in Ohio, while serving with General "Mad" **Anthony Wayne**.

## Brandywine, Battle of

British General Sir William Howe led his army of 18,000 British and Hessian troops toward Philadelphia. As the Commander-in-Chief of the powerful British army in America, he was determined to capture the capital city of the rebellious Americans.

In July of 1777, Howe and his army sailed aboard 264 British ships south toward Philadelphia from their encampment in New Jersey. As they approached America's largest city, Howe learned of the defender's fortifications. There was also a small navy force in and along the Delaware River, blocking his path. General Howe changed his course to the Chesapeake Bay. There he landed at Elk Ferry (about 8 miles below present-day Elkton, Maryland) and marched his 5,000 German Hessians and 13,000 British troops about thirty miles northeast into **Philadelphia**.

Standing in his way was General **George Washington**, and the 11,000 troops of the Continental Army. Over the previous winter, Washington had successfully defeated the British army at Trenton on December 26, 1776, and again in Princeton on January 3, 1777. Washington moved his army into camp near Morristown, New Jersey. The Continental Army spent the summer of 1777 encamped in the security of the Watchung Mountains of New Jersey, descending only to fight with the British army when there were military opportunities. When Washington learned of Howe's movement, he moved his army to Wilmington.

General Howe decided to move his army. Howe's men were ready for the march, having recovered from malnutrition from sailing for over a month. General Washington was convinced that his army was capable of stopping the advancing British. In early September, the two generals, in anticipation of a battle, positioned their armies, but neither engaged the other. Washington had expected Howe to march toward him in Wilmington, but Howe decided that was not the place to fight the Americans. Washington's position gave him the advantage, and Howe knew it. Instead, Howe marched his troops further north, toward the Brandywine River. It was a peaceful area, primarily populated by Quaker families.

Howe's movement made Washington move from his advantageous position in Wilmington to the eastern side of the Brandywine River. It was a natural barrier and an excellent defensive position, providing an advantageous high ground behind the army, and thickly wooded slopes that offered an area of concealment for the American troops. Washington positioned his troops at the main fords along the river. These were shallow places where an army could cross the

*General Sir William Howe led the army of British troops at the Battle of Brandywine.*

B

Brandywine River, including Buffington's Ford (about a mile above today's bridge at Lenape), Chadds Ford, and Pyle's Ford (south of modern day Route 1). Washington believed the main attack of Howe's army would occur at Chadds Ford. He positioned his main regiments and brigades there.

Howe sent about 8,000 troops straight to Washington at Chadds Ford. The force, led by Hessian general Wilhelm von Knyphausen, was a decoy. The remainder of Howe's army marched north about 17 miles, and then crossed the Brandywine River above the fords that Washington had guarded. Howe marched that half of his army south, down what is today Birmingham Road, to launch a surprise attack on Washington's right flank.

Howe's plan worked. In the confusion, Washington was unable to reform his lines. They ran low on ammunition. Overrun by the advancing British army, the Continental Army retreated to Chester, about 12 miles away. They abandoned their dead and wounded, along with equipment. The British, thoroughly exhausted, did not pursue the retreating Americans. They camped on the battlefield.

Despite their defeat, the Americans were not demoralized. They blamed their loss on bad intelligence reports rather than on a lack of fighting skill. "Notwithstanding the misfortune of the day, I am happy to find the troops in good spirits, and I hope another time we shall compensate for the losses now sustained," Washington wrote to Congress.

Scholars cannot agree on the exact losses each side suffered that day. American losses were about 300 taken prisoner, 800 killed, and 800 wounded. British losses were heavier, as high as 2,000 killed or wounded.

## Brig *Niagara*

The United States Brig *Niagara* in Erie is a reconstruction of an early 19th-century warship of the United States Navy. On September 10, 1813, nine small ships defeated a British squadron of six vessels in the Battle of Lake Erie. The *Niagara* is a squared-rigged, two-mast warship. She was originally armed with eighteen carronades and two long guns. After the War of 1812, *Niagara* was scuttled in Misery Bay within Erie Harbor. In 1913, the wreck of the *Niagara* was salvaged, and the ship was reconstructed on her keel. The *Niagara* is today open for guided tours and offers an active day sailing program from her port in **Erie**.

## British Capture of Philadelphia

The British forced the American army to retreat after the **Battle of Brandywine** in 1777. The defeat did not demoralize the troops of the Continental Army. They believed that it was not the result of poor fighting ability but rather their unfamiliarity with the landscape and poor reconnaissance information.

During the next several days, the British ransacked houses and property at Chadds Ford, looting books, furnishings, livestock, food, clothing, and money. The peaceful Quakers, who occupied this area, did not oppose them.

General Howe and his Army moved closer to Philadelphia with little opposition from **Washington**. The two armies maneuvered, hoping to find the other at a disadvantage. There were no decisive military actions during the next two weeks. The British moved north toward Paoli and marched into Philadelphia unopposed on September 26, 1777. The British occupied the city throughout the winter while the Americans languished at Valley Forge.

As word spread about the American defeat at Brandywine, Congress fled **Philadelphia** and moved to **Lancaster**, and then to **York**. They knew they had to escape before the British occupation. The Americans

*The rebuilt United States Brig* Niagara *sails from Erie on regular day cruises.*

B

moved military supplies out of the Philadelphia area to Reading. Washington responded cautiously after the battle. The impending loss of Philadelphia hurt the patriot cause. Washington's army had dropped from a high of nearly 15,000 prior to the battle to only 6,000.

## Bubble Gum

"It was an accident," Walter E. Diemer recalled years later. It all began when he sold a batch of the bubble-laden compound to a local grocery store. They sold out that afternoon, and ordered more. Diemer taught the company's salespeople to blow bubbles, and so the bubble gum business was launched.

Working for the Fleer Corporation, Diemer accidentally invented the confection, which traditionally gets flavor from a mix of wintergreen, peppermint, vanilla, and cinnamon. From its humble and unintentional beginnings in Philadelphia, it quickly spread around the world. The only color Diemer had—pink—is what he used. It became the standard color for bubble gum, and is still used today.

## Buchanan, James

The only Pennsylvanian to become president of the United States, James Buchanan was born in a log cabin deep in the mountains of what was then Pennsylvania's frontier, Cove Gap near Mercersburg, on April 23, 1791. He was the only U.S. President to remain a lifelong bachelor. He was tall and stately, and often looked stiff, probably from the style of the high collars he wore.

The eldest of 11 children, Buchanan was a graduate of nearby Dickinson College in Carlisle. A gifted debater, he studied law. He was admitted to the Bar in 1812, and went on to become a prosperous lawyer in **Lancaster**.

Buchanan did become engaged, but his fiancée, Ann Coleman, died suddenly after breaking off the engagement, and he vowed never to marry.

Buchanan served as a volunteer for the defense of Baltimore against the British during the War of 1812. He was elected to the Pennsylvania state legislature at the age of 23. His career in politics and law continued, and he won election as a U.S. representative in 1820. He soon become a supporter of General Andrew Jackson, and later, a leader in the Democratic Party. He was reelected four times to the House of Representatives.

When Jackson was elected president, he persuaded Buchanan in 1831, who was ready to retire from politics, to agree to the post of U.S. diplomatic representative in Russia. Buchanan served at Saint Petersburg (then the Russian capital) from 1832 to 1833.

During his service, Buchanan negotiated an important commercial treaty with Russia. After returning to the United States, Buchanan was elected to the U.S. Senate by the Pennsylvania legislature. He remained in the senate for the next decade.

It was during this time that Buchanan took his stand on slavery, the most controversial and divisive issue of the day. Buchanan argued that slavery was morally wrong, but he firmly believed the federal government had a duty to protect it in the Southern states.

Buchanan supported James Polk, and after his election in 1844, the new president appointed Buchanan as secretary of state. Buchanan, who had just won reelection to the senate, resigned and took the position. Buchanan achieved significant accomplishments for U.S. foreign affairs. He successfully negotiated a treaty with Britain that gave the United States most of the Oregon territory south of the 49° north latitude.

In a lasting dispute with Mexico, Buchanan insisted that Mexico recognize the annexation of Texas, Mexico's former province,

*James Buchanan, the 15th President of the United States, is the only president that came from Pennsylvania. Born in a log cabin in the Pennsylvania frontier, Buchanan lived at Wheatland in Lancaster.*

by the United States and that it pay the long-standing claims of its citizens. When the American demands were not met, the Mexican War broke out in 1846.

When Polk's term ended, Buchanan retired to his home in Lancaster. He worked for the presidential nomination for the 1852 election, but it was given to Franklin Pierce. A weary Buchanan accepted President Pierce's appointment as U.S. envoy in Great Britain.

Because of his service abroad, Buchanan was well known and it helped to bring him the Democratic nomination in 1856. He had been freed from involvement in many bitter domestic controversies.

*Bottom: President James Buchanan's birthplace near Mercersburg is in a peaceful hollow in Franklin County. The log cabin in which he was born is long gone. A large permanent pyramid-style monument marks the area of his birthplace.*

*Below: Wheatland, the home of James Buchanan, in Lancaster.*

Two days following his inauguration, U.S. Supreme Court Chief Justice Roger B. Taney delivered the Dred Scott decision, asserting that Congress had no constitutional power to deprive people of their property rights of slaves in the territories. Southerners were delighted, but the court decision created a furor in the North. Buchanan had said that in his inauguration speech the pending court decision would end the slavery issue in the territories. He could not have been more wrong.

Buchanan's four-year term was, at best, difficult. Presiding over a rapidly dividing nation, he was unable to grasp the political realities of the time. Relying on constitutional doctrines to close the widening divide over slavery, he failed to grasp that the North would not accept constitutional arguments, which favored the South. Nor could he realize how sectionalism had realigned political parties. The Democrats split, and the Whigs were destroyed, opening political opportunity to the Republicans.

During the midterm election, Republicans took control of both houses. He vetoed every bill passed by the Republican majority in Congress from 1859 to 1861. His struggles to avoid the War Between the States made many enemies, so he decided not to run for a second term. Late in his term, a Civil War was imminent when the Southern states insisted they would secede. He tried to appease them, but failed. Because of Lincoln's election, South Carolina voted to leave the Union in December 1860. In 1861 Mississippi, Florida, Alabama, Georgia, and Louisiana joined South Carolina in forming the Confederate States of America. Determined not to risk a civil war by committing an overt act, Buchanan allowed the Confederates to occupy federal military installations and to take U.S. government property within the seceded states. In January 1861, Buchanan sent a merchant vessel, *Star of*

James Buchanan was known as "Old Buck" and was the nation's only bachelor president.

*the West*, to Charleston, South Carolina, with supplies for a federal fortress in the harbor, Fort Sumter. On its arrival there, Confederate shore guns fired on the ship and it withdrew. President Buchanan fervently waited for his term to expire on March 4.

Despite repeated criticism of his policy, Buchanan continued it until Lincoln's inauguration. While in the White House, his niece Harriet Lane served as his hostess and became popular as the First Lady. On Lincoln's inauguration day, James Buchanan escorted President-elect Lincoln to the ceremonies and then returned with him to the White House. Then, he traveled to the more peaceful, pleasant atmosphere of Wheatland in Lancaster. Buchanan told his neighbors that he had left President Lincoln with the comment, "If you are as happy, my dear sir, on entering this house as I am in leaving it and returning home, you are the happiest man in this country."

Buchanan lived quietly the rest of his life at Wheatland. Throughout the Civil War, Buchanan supported Lincoln's administration in its fight for the Union. During his retirement, he wrote a vigorous defense of his own administration. It was first published in 1865 under the title *The Administration on the Eve of the Rebellion*. Buchanan died at his home on June 1, 1868. He is interred at Woodward Hill Cemetery in Lancaster.

## Buck, Pearl S.

The West Virginia born author of over 300 books and other published works, Pearl S. Buck strove for better understanding between peoples. She wrote more than 65 books, many of which sympathetically portray China and its people. Her novel "The Good Earth" was awarded the Pulitzer Prize in 1932.

Her epic portrayals of life on Chinese farms won her the Nobel Prize for Literature in 1938. Following her many years in China as a missionary, she returned to the United States in 1934 and lived in Perkasie, Bucks County. Her last works were *The Kennedy Women* (1970) and *China as I See It* (1970). She died in 1973.

*Pearl S. Buck won the Nobel Prize for Literature in 1938.*

B

## Bucktails, The

On April 24, 1861, Colonel Thomas L. Kane assembled 100 volunteers at Smethport, in McKean County. From the small community in Northern Pennsylvania, the men traveled to **Harrisburg**. They wore the tails of buck deer as a distinctive insignia. The deer tails were placed on each recruit's cap. Responding to President Lincoln's call for volunteer troops to rise to the defense of the Union, these rugged men provided the name of the famed 42nd Regiment, of which they were the core. The Bucktails served with distinction in many major engagements during the Civil War, including Second Bull Run, South Mountain, Antietam, Fredericksburg, **Gettysburg**, the Wilderness, and Spottsylvania.

*The Pennsylvania Historical Marker that commemorates the Bucktails.*

## Burns, John

During the **Battle of Gettysburg**, local resident John Burns grabbed his rifle and fought with the Iron Brigade. A veteran of the War of 1812, the seventy-year-old craggy man took his place on the battlefield. Burns fired 17 shots on July 1, 1863, and according to tradition, killed three Southerners as he defended his homeland. Shot in the leg by the Rebels, he survived his wounds to meet later with President Abraham Lincoln. He became a national hero when his actions were widely reported in newspapers throughout the Northern states.

## Bushy Run, Battle of

The British army under the command of Colonel Henry Bouquet defeated the Indians on August 5, 1763. Attacked by Delaware, Mingo, Shawnee, and Wyandot Indians, Colonel Bouquet successfully defended his position. Bouquet's British and American

*The last dying moments of a Bucktail, a member of a group of volunteers during the Civil War who were distinguished by the deer tails on their caps.*

*John Burns was a national hero in the North after he took part in the Battle of Gettysburg.*

forces, en route to Fort Pitt, had used Indian style tactics during the battle to win. They fought in the woods, which included small hills, swamps, bogs, and small streams. This battle stopped the siege of Fort Pitt and led to the settlement of the West. The battlefield is now a State Park near Harrison City in Westmoreland County.

## Camp Security

Camp Security, the last remaining prisoner of war camp from the Revolutionary War, is in Springettsbury Township, just east of **York**. One of only a few to ever be setup by the Continental Army, it housed over 1,000 British and Canadian prisoners of war between the summer of 1781 and the spring of 1783. Its primary purpose was for imprisoning General Burgoyne's men, originally captured during the Battle of Saratoga (New York) in 1777. As many as 2,000 men were imprisoned at Camp Security. Many soldiers brought their families with them. In 1783, a devastating fever raced through the camp, taking the lives of many British soldiers. Prisoners stayed until the signing of the Treaty of Paris. They were then freed. Some stayed in the vicinity, while others went to Canada to receive a land grant for their service in the British army.

## Camp William Penn

Located in La Mott, just north of **Philadelphia**, Camp William Penn was Pennsylvania's only training camp for African-American soldiers during the Civil War. The largest of the 18 similar camps in the nation, over 10,000 men of the Federal Colored Troops trained here. The Black troops enjoyed pleasant relations with their white neighbors, who baked cakes for the soldiers and provided campsites for their visiting families. Parishioners of local Quaker and Episcopal churches visited the camp often to preach, conduct Bible classes, and share religious books. Recruits first arrived on June 26, 1863, and many left to fight in Virginia, South Carolina, and Florida. The camp closed on August 14, 1865.

## Camptown

Bradford County may have contributed to some of **Stephen Foster**'s well-known songs. *Camptown Races* was most likely inspired by the horse races at the village of Wyalusing. Foster's first music was completed during 1840–1841 when he was living in Towanda and Athens.

## Canals

The days of canal transportation in Pennsylvania are over. The mule teams are gone. The shallow-bottom canal boats have rotted and decayed. Throughout the state, historic markers are the only signs left to show the way to former canal beds and the remnants of ruined locks. Now nearly a forgotten part of Pennsylvania's past, the canal transportation system linked the state's cities and villages with farms, mines, and factories. It was at one time the largest canal-based transportation system in the nation. It contributed to the state's material wealth, industrialization, and development.

Historians agree that the Pennsylvania canal era began in 1797 when the Conewago Canal was built. Built below York Haven on the **Susquehanna River**, the canal made it possible for boats to get around the Conewago Falls. But a canal system had been considered a hundred years earlier by **William Penn**.

From the earliest days of colonizing Pennsylvania, transport by waterways was an important part of the plans for the new territory. **William Penn** knew that waterways were necessary for encouraging trade. Penn delayed his first trip to Pennsylvania, so he could gain the colonies of present-day Delaware. He

*Although the days of canals are gone in Pennsylvania, visitors can still ride a rebuilt canal boat near Easton. Notice the wide path used by horses or mule teams to pull canal boats or barges.*

wanted control of that territory because of its water access.

Penn wanted to connect the Delaware River with the **Susquehanna River** as early as 1690. He envisioned building a canal to connect the Tulpehocken Creek from its mouth on the Schuylkill River with the Swatara to its mouth on the Susquehanna. Penn's grand canal would bind three of the state's great rivers, the Delaware, Schuylkill, and Susquehanna Rivers, into one system of waterway transportation.

The natural geography of Pennsylvania created a huge problem for transporting freight, supplies, raw materials, and manufactured goods. Along the eastern seaboard, the Appalachian Mountains created a barrier to commercial transportation. Pennsylvania had no gateway to the western part of the state, and beyond. The Juniata Valley penetrates far into the interior of the state, but stops by the huge, unbroken mass of the Alleghenies.

Pennsylvanians recognized the need for a waterway based transportation system, but it was not easy to overcome the natural Appalachian barrier. Traders drove trains of packhorses, each carrying a load as much as two hundred pounds, up and down the mountain ridges. The cost was high, and the capacity was low. Even after some Indian trails were widened to allow wagons, commerce was slow. When the Erie Canal in New York State was built between 1817 and 1825, it gave New York a clear path to the country's interior waterways. Pennsylvanians realized from this that they needed a canal system. The Erie Canal gave New Yorker's a distinct advantage over their neighbors to the south. Pennsylvania was not to be outdone.

There was a partial solution to the problem. The Delaware, Susquehanna, and Allegheny sliced through the mountains by gorges known locally as "water gaps."

*The ruin of Lock no.37 on the Union Canal, showing the remains of the lock gates, near Bernville, Berks County.*

Navigable tributaries flowed in the valleys between the mountain ranges. Canals were needed to connect the natural waterways.

Using picks, shovels, and wheelbarrows, Pennsylvanians began building a system of canals. The hard work, poor living conditions, and disease cost lives. Yet the burly men of hardy Pennsylvania stock did not give up. Their eventual water highway began the American industrial revolution, and fueled the expansion of the nation.

Pennsylvanians built hundreds of miles of canals in the Commonwealth. Hundreds of laborers, a majority of them Irish immigrants, were hired to dig canal channels and build many other structures associated with the canals. They built the lift locks, dams, aqueducts, reservoirs, feeders, waste-weirs, canal basins, towpath bridges, canal-boat weighing locks, and inclined planes. Most of the state's major canal building projects took place during the 1820s and 1830s. In 1828, the Union Canal Company adapted Penn's idea of joining the Schuylkill with the Susquehanna by a canal along the Tulpehocken and Swatara Creeks. Middletown was connected with Philadelphia by water.

The Pennsylvania Assembly of 1824 approved a public works to provide access to **Philadelphia** for the timber, mining, and manufactures of all parts of the Commonwealth, even those regions west of the Allegheny Mountains. Construction of the Pennsylvania Canal started on July 4, 1826. The canal that conquered the Allegheny Mountain by carrying canal boats, passengers, and cargo on the **Allegheny Portage Railroad** between Hollidaysburg and Johnstown was completed in 1834. In the same year, publicly owned canals connected along the Delaware from Bristol to Easton, and along the two branches of the Susquehanna to Lock Haven and Nanticoke. By 1840, the Pennsylvania "Main Line" Canal encompassed 726 miles of waterways, associated railways, and inclined plains.

*Outlet lock of the Lehigh Canal, Easton, Northampton County.*

At the same time, private projects made the Lehigh and Schuylkill Rivers accessible for trade. By 1845, the Ohio River, the Beaver Division Canal, the Erie Extension, and the Franklin Line connected the cities of **Pittsburgh**, Meadville, and **Erie**. The Youghiogheny Navigation and Monogahela Navigation companies, both private enterprises, were completed in the 1850s and connected southwestern Pennsylvania and Pittsburgh.

By 1830, the Delaware and Hudson Canal connected the coal mines of the **Lackawanna** Valley and northeastern Pennsylvania with the Hudson River and New York City. In the mid-1840s cargoes of 54 tons were shipped regularly. Pennsylvania canals connected with New Jersey canals on the east and Ohio canals on the west, furthering interstate commerce. A towpath bridge at Columbia on the Susquehanna allowed trade by linking the Pennsylvania Canal with the Susquehanna and Tidewater Canal at Wrightsville with the Chesapeake Bay and Maryland.

There were many privately owned canal systems in the state. One of those independent

*An abandoned lock on the West Branch of the Pennsylvania Canal near Lock Haven, Clinton County.*

canals was the Schuylkill Canal owned and managed by Schuylkill Navigation Company. The company completed the canal in 1825. Used chiefly to transport anthracite coal from northeastern Pennsylvania to Philadelphia, it stretched for 108 miles between Port Carbon and Philadelphia, contained 120 locks, and extended 57 miles.

The busy construction required expert engineering. A hardworking labor force dug channels along difficult riverbanks and through mountain valleys high above sea level. They built aqueducts to carry the canal across rivers and creeks. Crossing the Allegheny Mountain was difficult. Many of the country's best engineers worked on the canal projects.

Mules or horses pulled the canal boats, making transportation slow. Four miles per hour was standard for canal cargo boats and there were frequent passings through the locks. There were 18 lift-locks between Columbia and Hollidaysburg and 66 between Johnstown and Pittsburgh that overcame an elevation of 1,691 feet.

In 1852, the Pennsylvania Railroad provided a rail service from Philadelphia to Pittsburgh. It was the beginning of the end for Pennsylvania's canal systems. Canal operation ceased first in western Pennsylvania. The Pennsylvania Railroad purchased the state's Main Line Canal at a public auction for $7.5 million on June 25, 1857. In 1859, the state abolished the Board of Canal Commissioners and sold all canals owned by the Commonwealth. East of the Alleghenies, the canals in private possession were more prosperous. The Pennsylvania Railroad setup the Pennsylvania Canal Company in 1867, and freight was handled by various canal systems in the state until roughly 1875, when the business began a steady decline. By 1901, nearly all the Pennsylvania canals were shut down. The Schuylkill Navigation Company ran until 1922, and the Lehigh Coal and Navigation Company, embracing its Lehigh and Delaware Canals, continued until 1931. A few others maintained their waterways and operated until the 1940s.

In their heyday, over 4,000 miles of canals were dug throughout the new nation. In Pennsylvania, there were 1,356 miles of canals; more than in any other state. Echoes of the noise of mule teams, the calls of the canal boat driver, the sounds of boats colliding was once heard everywhere in the deep river valleys of Pennsylvania's woods. Now there is silence. Where once a brawny lock tender watched for approaching boats, only a sign exists to show the curious visitor the location of a canal from Pennsylvania's past.

## Capoose

Chief Capoose and his Indian village settled near present-day **Scranton**, following their removal from the upper Delaware valley around 1743. They were known as Munsee Indians. The town of Muncy takes its name from the Munsee tribe.

## Carbondale

The Wurts brothers founded Carbondale in 1822. The brothers were pioneers in developing the anthracite found in the region. The first underground mine was opened in June, 1831, near present-day Seventh Avenue. The state chartered Carbondale as a city in 1851.

## Carlisle

A borough in southern Pennsylvania west of **Harrisburg**, Carlisle is the seat of Cumberland County. Today it is a manufacturing center where products such as electronics, paper, wood, rubber, and food are produced. It is also a major transportation hub. Carlisle is in a central location, used as a stop off point for travel west. It was settled first by Scots-Irish immigrants in 1751 and expeditions during the **French and Indian Wars** were undertaken here. A munitions depot during the Revolution, Carlisle later served as the headquarters for **George Washington** during the **Whiskey Rebellion** of 1794.

*When the Southerners invaded Pennsylvania in June of 1863, they were well north of Carlisle. This marker along present-day Route 34 in Carlisle Springs (about five miles north of Carlisle) indicates how far north they were. They were just slightly above the center of Harrisburg.*

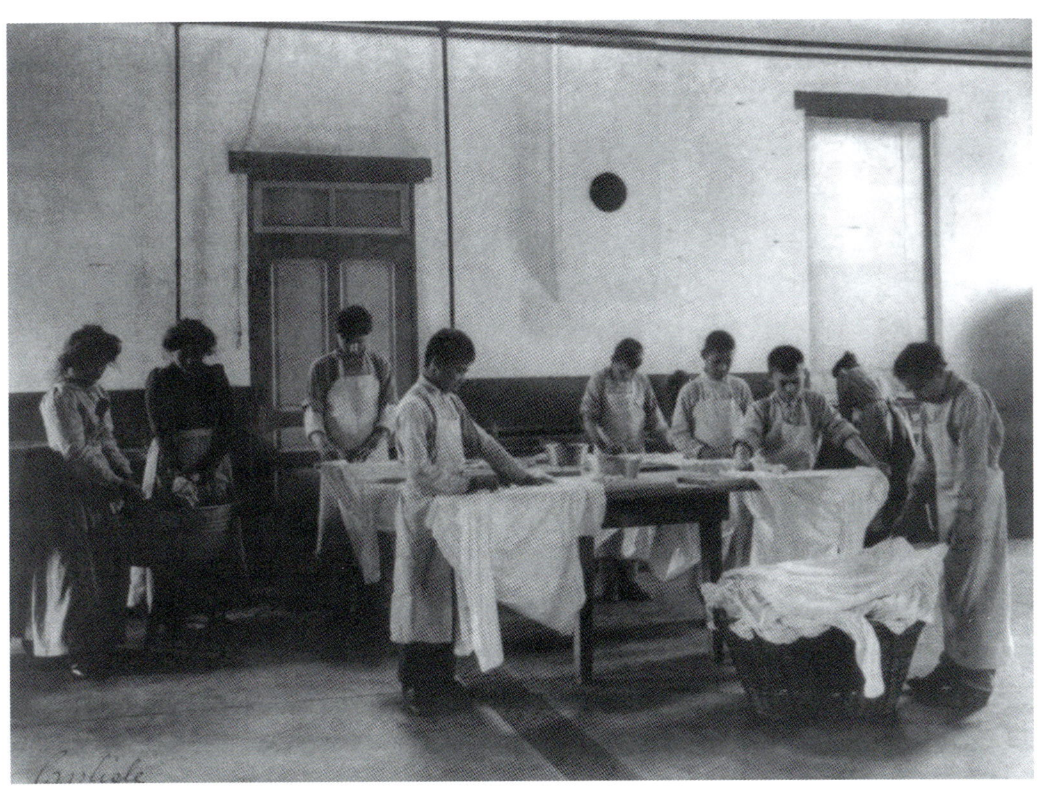

*Laundry class at the Carlisle Indian School around 1903*

*The center of Carlisle. The community was once on the western frontier of Pennsylvania. Because of its location, Carlisle still functions as a busy transportation hub today.*

In 1798, President Washington created the nation's first military school, called the Carlisle Barracks. The Carlisle Barracks are also known as the oldest Army Post in the United States. Carlisle is the home of Dickinson College, established in 1783.

In 1836, Carlisle's school system was the first in Pennsylvania to provide public education. From 1879 to 1918, the U.S. Army ran the Indian Industrial School, which was, at that time, the country's most significant effort to educate Native Americans. This school was at the Carlisle Barracks, which today is the home of the U.S. Army War College. **Jim Thorpe** attended the Indian Industrial School.

The borough was a stop on the **Underground Railroad**. Confederate General Fitzhugh Lee attacked Carlisle during the Civil War. Carlisle is the seat of the U.S. Army War College and Dickinson College. **Molly Pitcher** was buried in Carlisle.

## Carnegie, Andrew

Andrew Carnegie was born in Dunfermline, Scotland on November 25, 1835. Carnegie moved to the United States in 1848. By the age of 13, he was working full-time to help support his family. He became a railway telegrapher, and then took a position as secretary to the Pennsylvania Railroad's Pittsburgh Division Superintendent Thomas A. Scott. When he was 20, Carnegie made his first investment in an American business. Encouraged by his employer, he bought ten shares of Adams Express stock at $50 a share. By 1863, his $500 investment returned $1,500 per year in dividends.

In 1865, Carnegie entered the steel business with former blacksmith Andrew Klopman. With George M. Pullman, Carnegie became a major stockholder in the Pullman Palace Car Co. in 1867. The company built passenger cars under contract for the railway companies. Carnegie entered another partnership the same year with a scale manufacturer, Henry Phipps. Together, they founded the United Iron Mills in **Philadelphia**.

Carnegie continued his successful investments. He picked up a controlling interest in other large steel plants. By 1899, Carnegie controlled about 25 percent of American iron and steel production. In 1901, he sold his company to the United States Steel Corporation for $250 million and retired. His investments in the steel and railroad industry made him one of the richest individuals in the United States. Carnegie was also a generous philanthropist. During his lifetime, he gave more than $350 million to various educational, cultural, and peace institutions, many of which bear his name to this day. He died on August 11, 1919.

## Carpenters' Hall

The Carpenters' Company of the City and County of **Philadelphia** was a guild founded in 1724 to help its members develop architectural skills and to aid their families in times of need. In 1770, the company built Carpenter's Hall, located at 320 Chestnut Street, near 4th Street, Philadelphia.

The state's delegates for the First Continental Congress met first in Carpenter's Hall in September 1774 to air their many grievances against King George III. The Second Continental Congress transferred its sessions to the State House (now Independence Hall). Carpenters' Hall continued as a meeting place by various political groups. During the Revolutionary War, the Hall served as both a hospital and an arsenal for American forces. Today the Carpenters' Company still owns and maintains the historic building.

## Carson, Rachel

Born May 1907 in Springdale, Pennsylvania, Rachel Louise Carson became a marine biologist and author. Her writings on ecology stirred a worldwide concern for the protection and preservation of the environment. Carson was awarded the 1952 National Book Award in nonfiction for *The Sea Around Us* (1951). Her book *Silent Spring* (1962) questioned the use of chemical pesticides. She died of breast cancer in 1964.

*The first meeting place of the Continental Congress was at Carpenter's Hall, Philadelphia.*

## Catasauqua

The first long-term, commercially successful anthracite iron furnace opened in July 1840, in Catasauqua, Lehigh County. Built for the Lehigh Crane Iron Co. by David Thomas, it produced between 50 and 60 tons of pig iron each week. By 1868, the works had six furnaces. The production stopped in 1930.

## Centralia

On some maps, Centralia no longer exists. Located along state route 61, about a mile and a half from Ashland, and just inside Columbia County, what remains of the town of Centralia is still burning.

The fire in an underground mine started in 1961 as a result of burning trash in an open mine pit. A vein of coal caught fire, and continues to burn to this day. All attempts to quench the fire failed. Some predict the fire is likely to burn for the next 1,000 years.

Most of the residents received federal grants and moved to other areas. The government demolished their houses, leaving steps or sidewalks as the only signs of former habitation. Smoke and toxic gases still seep through

*Not much is left in Centralia, but the fire in an underground mine still burns. Notice the smoke rising from the ground behind this warning sign.*

from crevices in the ground. Despite the dangerous hazards of the area a few diehards still remain there.

## Chambersburg Invasion, The

Benjamin Chambers settled in the southern region of Pennsylvania near the Shenandoah Valley in the 1730s. There he laid out the town in 1764 and built a sawmill and a gristmill. Chambersburg is the seat of government for Franklin County.

While nearby **Gettysburg** receives most of the attention about Pennsylvania's role in the Civil War, Chambersburg history is also notable. The town of Chambersburg was John Brown's base of operations before his infamous raid on Harpers Ferry in 1859. Brown had posed as a prospector while collecting arms. His headquarters was on East King Street, in the heart of downtown. Following the Battle of Antietam in 1862, Chambersburg served as a major supply and hospital center for the Union Army. General Robert E. Lee and over 65,000 Confederates camped in Chambersburg in June 1863, just before the Battle of Gettysburg.

On July 30, 1864, confederate cavalry, under the command of General John McCausland, brought the misery of the Civil War to Northern soil by burning the town of Chambersburg.

Under direct orders from Confederate General Jubal Early, McCausland demanded $100,000 in gold or $500,000 in U.S. dollars from the town as repayment for the destruction of Shenandoah Valley by Union General David Hunter. The townspeople did not believe the threat, and chose not to raise the money. The Confederates destroyed the town with burning torches. The great fire destroyed more than 500 buildings, about two-thirds of the town. No civilians were killed during the massive fire.

## Children's Hospital of Philadelphia

In the middle of the 19th century, hospitals were unhygienic and full of deadly bacteria. At that time the medical profession did not know about the causes of infection. Most childhood illnesses were treated at home because they had a greater chance of survival there rather than in an adult hospital, where they usually died because of cross-infection or neglect.

After visiting the Hospital for Sick Children in London, Dr. Francis West Lewis decided to create a hospital in the United States dedicated to finding cures and treating illnesses and injuries specific to young people. The Children's Hospital of Philadelphia was established in 1855.

As the first pediatric hospital in the United States, The Children's Hospital of Philadelphia is a recognized leader in combining excellent patient care, innovative research, quality education, and extensive community service, making it one of the top-ranked children's hospitals in the world.

Today the hospital trains doctors in pediatric care while treating children. It has pioneered pediatric cancer treatment, incubator use, and works with children with speech or hearing defects. The list of pediatric care offered at the facility is extensive. It is often recognized as the best pediatric care hospital in the nation. The hospital's campus is at 34th Street and Civic Center Drive in Philadelphia.

## Chocolatetown, USA

When **Milton Hershey** enjoyed success as a chocolate maker it also provided him with a sense of moral responsibility and benevolence. Hershey dreamed of a new and different community around his factory.

Hershey built a model town for his employees that included comfortable homes, inexpensive public transportation, a quality public school, and extensive recreational and cultural opportunities. Unlike other industrialists of his time, Hershey did not want to build a faceless company town with anonymous houses. He wanted a "real hometown" complete with tree-lined streets, single- and two-family brick houses, and manicured lawns.

Hershey was also concerned about providing enough recreation and diversions. He wanted his workers to relax during their non-working time, so he built a park that opened on April 24, 1907, and expanded rapidly over the years. The park included amusement rides, a swimming pool, and a ballroom. Trolley cars and trains were bringing thousands of out-of-town visitors to the park. Many of the impressive structures in the town were built during the Great Depression, as part of Milton Hershey's "Great Building Campaign," to provide jobs. It was during this period that monumental buildings such as Hotel Hershey, the theater, community center, sports arena, and stadium were constructed, transforming the town into a major tourist attraction that still grows in popularity each year. This company town grew and was soon called Hershey.

Since his death at age 88, Milton Hershey's legacy thrives. Today, Milton Hershey School, the institution he and his wife founded, nurtures more than 1,100 boys and girls in grades Kindergarten through 12. The school benefits from the holdings of the Milton Hershey School Trust, which is supported from the profits of Hershey Foods Corporation and Hershey Entertainment & Resorts Company.

## Christiana Riots

Christiana began as a settlement in 1775 when Calvin Cooper built a mill, the first of many along the banks of the Octorara River. On September 11, 1851, Edward Gorsuch, a Maryland slave owner, accompanied by a U.S. Marshal and deputies, traveled to the small, sleepy Lancaster County village of Christiana.

*A marker in Christiana commemorates the riot and later treason trial that occurred when a slave owner from Maryland attempted to capture and return his runaway.*

C

It was just before dawn when Gorsuch and the federal officers rode into Christiana. They expected to capture and return the runaway slaves to nearby Maryland.

A violent and brutal riot erupted that alarmed the nation. It occurred one year after the U.S. Congress passed the second fugitive slave law, requiring the return of all escaped slaves to their owners in the South.

Edward Gorsuch was killed and two others were wounded during the fight with the townspeople. In the aftermath of the Christiana Riot, law enforcement officers arrested 38 men and charged them with treason under the Fugitive Slave Law. It resulted in the greatest amount of indictments ever handed down for treason in the U.S. Most of those Christiana residents were acquitted of all charges. Many went on to become assertive voices for the cause of freedom for slaves and worked for the repeal of the Fugitive Slave Act. Southerners felt that Northerners would not return runaway slaves, and that Congress could not pass laws to make Northerners return runaways. The riot at Christiana was used later on as one of the arguments for the Southern states to leave the Union and form the Confederate States of America.

## City of Brotherly Love, The

The city was born from **William Penn**'s desire to transform a religious principle into a reality. It was a "Holy Experiment" that aimed for a utopian urban dwelling without any barriers to separate people of different races. Philadelphia's motto, The City of Brotherly Love, came directly from William Penn. As an English Quaker, Penn envisioned the area as a place where anyone of any race or background could live together in peace and harmony, hence the motto. Penn chose the name Philadelphia, which translates from the Greek as "brotherly love."

## Climax Locomotives

Over 1,000 geared steam locomotives were built at the Climax plant in **Erie** County at Corry from 1888 to 1928. These specially designed locomotives were widely used on logging railroads throughout the United States and in other countries. The Climax Locomotives made new areas accessible to large-scale, lumber operations. Geared locomotives were the key to the lumber industry's growth.

## Clymer, George

Born March 16, 1739 in Philadelphia, George Clymer became an orphan at an early age. He did an apprenticeship in his uncle's counting room to prepare for a mercantile profession. He later became a patriot and leader in the disturbances in Philadelphia resulting from the Tea Act and the Stamp Act. He was a Member of the Philadelphia Council of Safety in 1773.

Clymer became a member of the Continental Congress in 1776 and served several years in such important committees as the Board of War and the Treasury Board. He played a large part, with Robert Morris, in strengthening the authority of General **Washington** and improving the provisions of the Continental Army. In 1781, he was a member of the Pennsylvania Legislature. He returned to the Congress in 1788 under the new constitution where he supported the presidency of George Washington. He was a revenue officer in Pennsylvania during the **Whiskey Rebellion**. In retirement from public life, Clymer was elected first president of Philadelphia Bank, first president of the Philadelphia Academy of Fine Arts, and vice president of the Philadelphia Agricultural Society. Clymer remained in all of these posts until his death on January 23, 1813.

## Coal

In 1806, Abijah Smith arrived in Luzerne County and settled in Plymouth. He opened a small mine in the side of the mountain near present-day Coal Street. Smith had the idea of using coal for heating houses instead of burning logs in a fireplace. Smith bought 75 acres of coal land from Calvin Wadhams. Abijah's brother, James Smith, bought another 120 acres from William Curry Jr. to start a modest partnership in the mining business.

In the beginning, the Smiths' mines were nothing more than caves in the side of a mountain. In 1807, for the first time in the nation's history, the Smiths sent their first shipment of coal from Plymouth. At the time, this was an unremarkable event, but it marked the humble beginning of the coal business in Pennsylvania.

In the same year, Abijah Smith bought a large ark for 24 dollars. He was going to use it to transport coal down the river. The barge-like ark was about 90 feet long, 16 feet wide, and had sides 4 feet high. It could carry 50 tons of coal. It took the muscles and brute strength of three big men to handle the 30 foot oar behind the pointed craft. Smith sent his first load of cargo down the **Susquehanna** to **Columbia** in Lancaster County. There he sold his black coal for ten dollars a ton.

Earning that money took a lot of work. Using a pick and shovel, Smith dug the coal from his mine, and then hauled it to the river

*A young leader and driver, Pasquale Salvo and Sandy Castina, emerge from shaft no.6 of the Pennsylvania Coal Company in Pittston, Pennsylvania.*

in wagons. Mining the coal was time consuming. Other countries were using "black stone" for heat, but in the United States, only blacksmiths were using the new fuel. In nearby **Wilkes-Barre**, Judge Jesse Fell used coal in an open indoor grate for artificial heating. It wasn't until 1808 that Judge Fell proved it was not necessary to use a forced draft (a technique employed by the blacksmith) to burn coal.

Abijah Smith and his mine produced tons of coal. In 1818, he experimented with blasting powder and eventually was able to increase coal production by blasting the coal inside the mine. Smith did not discover coal, but he did set up the first commercially successful mine in Pennsylvania, and launched the coal mining industry in the state. By 1858, Pennsylvania miners dug a million tons of coal each year.

In the early days, one out of three shipments of coal was lost because of the rapids and the changing water levels of the rivers. **Canals** were built to ship the coal, but it took years to establish the canal system in the state. By 1855, railroads replaced canals as the prinicipal method of transporting coal. The Lackawanna and Bloomsburg **Railroad** was the

*The Breaker at Chauncy Colliery. "Breaker Boys" were used in the anthracite coal mines to separate slate rock from the coal after it had been brought out of the mine. Boys of 12 and 13 would claim to be 14 to enable them to work shifts of up to 16 hours a day.*

*A disused coke works East of Lucerne, Indiana County. Coal was unloaded via the Robins car shaker (on right) before being processed.*

*Right: A typical company town, Eckley was built around the coal industry. The company houses were similar to each other, providing a coalminer with only the essentials.*

*Opposite page: The Ewen Breaker of the Pennsylvania Coal Company. The dust was often dense and filled the boys' lungs.*

*Below: Miners at the Ewen Breaker, Pennsylvania Coal Company, South Pittston, Pennsylvania, 1911.*

first to carry coal from Plymouth. The L. & B. Railroad was just one of many that further developed the state's coal industry.

In Pennsylvania, there are two types of coal: anthracite (hard coal) and bituminous (softer coal). Anthracite is found in the northeast section of the state, while the bituminous type is located in the western half.

There are many references to the early use of coal, while Pennsylvania was still a British colony. Historical records indicate that Indians brought coal to gunsmiths in exchange for repair services. Early **Conestoga Wagons** were used to transport coal to iron furnaces. Coal was used by the garrison at **Fort Augusta**. Pennsylvania coal supported the Colonial iron industry, then **Andrew Carnegie**'s steel mills in the 1800s and finally the electric power plants of more modern times.

Surface mining (sometimes referred to as strip mining) and underground mining (working in a mine) are used today to mine Pennsylvania coal. Since 1870, over 50,000

miners have lost their lives in Pennsylvania coalmines. Strict state laws have made the mines safer. Environmental concerns have brought about other rules, including reclamation requirements for surface mining. Improved safety, advanced technology, federal and state regulations, and better labor relations helped make Pennsylvania coal mines the safest and most productive in the world. However, the coal industry in Pennsylvania shrinks each year. Pennsylvania is now the fifth largest coal producer in the country. Experts say there is a 300-year supply of coal left. Despite new technology that cleans the fumes

*The coal industry provided the fuel for other expanding industries such as the furnaces of glass houses. Here two boys are going to work at 5pm at "Sheeny Joe's" Glass House in Pittsburgh January, 1913. The boy to left is 15 years old, and cannot speak English.*

*At the end of the workday and just up from the shaft of a Pennsylvania coal mine. Notice how young many of these coal miners were.*

*A once busy Pennsylvania coal mine now rusts. The booming days of the industry are gone.*

from burning coals, environmentalists fight to limit the use of coal as an energy method. Coal is used to generate electricity. About sixty percent of all railroad freight traffic is coal. About 25 percent of the nation's barge traffic is coal. Many predict the resurrection of the coal industry, but that has not yet happened for Pennsylvania. Many of the state's mines and vast coalfields are idle. Less than 1 percent of the state's economy relies on coal production.

## Coal and Iron Police, The

The coal and steel operators were influential in getting Pennsylvania State Legislature to approve what became the infamous Coal and Iron Police. In 1865, Act 228 was passed, which empowered private police forces. For one dollar each, the state sold commissions to the mine and steel mill owners, conferring police power to their own private police forces.

Through these commissions, the companies raised armies of guards, ostensibly to protect private property, but who were also used to intimidate and break up the striking mineworkers, and if necessary, evict them and their families from their homes. Often the company managers hired common gunslingers and hoodlums. In some communities, the citizens accused the coal and iron police of assault, kidnapping, even rape, and sometimes, murder. The private police continued through the **Anthracite Coal Strike** of 1902. As violence erupted in seven Pennsylvania counties, causing a nationwide coal shortage, it became clear the Coal and Iron Police commission was not workable. It was finally recognized that regularly appointed and responsible officers employed by the public should provide law enforcement. This led to the formation of the **Pennsylvania State Police** in 1905.

On June 30, 1931, Governor Pinchot revoked all coal and iron police commissions, refusing to issue any more and the Coal and Iron Police ended in Pennsylvania.

*Almost forgotten, the graves of black soldiers that served in the Civil War are within a short distance of present-day Route 30 at Columbia.*

## College of Philadelphia

In 1769, the College of Philadelphia elected Dr. Benjamin Rush professor of chemistry. Rush's addition to the college completed the various departments. The college, now fully organized, was the first medical school in America. In 1791, a university merged with the College of Philadelphia, and Dr. Rush was appointed professor of the institutes and practice of medicine, and of clinical practice, in the newly formed University of Pennsylvania.

## Columbia

Located on the western edge of **Lancaster** County, Columbia is on the eastern shore of the **Susquehanna River**. Traffic heading west from **Lancaster**, **Philadelphia**, and all points between routinely converged at Columbia. Before the Civil War, loaded **Conestoga Wagons** stopped and waited for their turn to cross the Susquehanna at first by ferry, and later by bridge. Columbia became a major connection point for **canal** traffic and the **railroad**. Columbia was the site of defensive bridge burning in June 1863 to prevent the further advance of the Confederate Army.

Columbia was once considered as a location for the federal government, but Congress opted for a location along the Potomac River to develop the district.

## Columbia-Wrightsville Bridge, Defending the

The bridge that crossed the **Susquehanna** between Columbia and Wrightsville needed to be defended at all costs during the Civil War. The Union forces of recent volunteers, who were dispatched there to guard the location, would be no match for the battle-hardened Southerners. With a force double the size of the

A lone grave of a Confederate is along the Susquehanna River. Most likely a victim of the Columbia Wrightsville Bridge Burning, his identity remains unknown.

bridge defenders, the Southerners could easily secure the bridge and move onto **Lancaster** and then **Harrisburg**. As the Confederate army approached, carpenters worked to drop a span of the bridge. After setting explosives, they were ready to collapse a section of the bridge into the river.

The Confederates, on Sunday, June 28, 1863, approached Wrightsville. They fired at the fresh Union recruits, who quickly ran back across the bridge. The Union commander ordered the section of the bridge blown, but the explosives did not work. So Federal defenders set fire to the long covered bridge, and stopped the Confederate advance into Lancaster County. The fire destroyed the bridge, and set several buildings in Wrightsville a blaze. The Confederates helped fight the fires. Confederate General Gordon and his men returned to **York** to rejoin General Early.

## Commonwealth or State

The State of Pennsylvania is actually and technically the Commonwealth of Pennsylvania. Pennsylvania is one of four states that are officially Commonwealths. The others are Kentucky, Virginia, and Massachusetts. The only difference between a state and a commonwealth is the name itself. There is no other difference in the relationship or governance of a state versus a commonwealth.

## Conestoga Indian Town

Conestoga Indian Town, located in present-day Manor Township in Lancaster County, was at one time in the early 18th century the central hub for trade between European settlers and Native Americans. Together they lived in harmony under the protection of the provincial government of Pennsylvania.

It attracted several politicians of the day to visit. **William Penn** traveled from Philadelphia to Conestoga Indian Town in 1700. There he signed a treaty, as did later Pennsylvania Governors. Quaker missionaries eventually converted the Conestoga to Christians.

## Conestoga Wagons

The Conestoga wagon was a large four-wheeled, horse-drawn vehicle, first used in 1750. Originating in **Lancaster** County, it was a primary means of transportation for hauling freight and would remain so for the next hundred years. Skilled German craftsmen perfected the unique design of the wagon. The usually massive wagon had broad wheels, a white fabric hood, and a convex wagon box. Its sets of wheels were smaller in the front and larger in the rear.

The name "Conestoga" referred to an early Indian group. Many things near their village,

*A Conestoga wagon as it would have appeared loaded and ready to haul freight down the rural roads of colonial Pennsylvania.*

which was located in Lancaster County, picked up the name. Because the wagon was developed and built in that area, people called it the Conestoga wagon. The wagons, drawn by four to six Conestoga horses, first appeared on the road connecting Lancaster with **Philadelphia** from the rich and productive farmlands of Lancaster County.

The wagon's bed, which sloped upward from the middle, had a white oak frame and poplar boards. The noticeable dip toward the center of the wagon was a deliberate part of the unusual design. It took the weight of the load off the end gates should the cargo shift as the wagon made its way up and down the hilly country. The flooring and sideboards were a half-inch thick. Some of the wagons used for carrying ore at an iron furnace had thicker boards. Often the wagon builder braced the many parts of the wagon bed with iron, and they used handmade rivets to secure the boards to the frame.

There was little uniformity in the wagon's dimensions. They varied, depending on who built the wagon. The bed of most wagons measured about sixteen feet long, four feet in width, and four feet in-depth. A chain held the end gates in position, allowing the wagon owner to drop the gate for loading and unloading. They made the axles of hickory, which is a type of hardwood. The wagon builder skillfully placed iron rims over the handcrafted wheels, which were about 4 inches wide.

*The Conestoga Wagon, built by Lancaster County craftsmen, was used to haul farm products and supplies in colonial times until the railroads were established.*

Each wagon had a series of wooden hoops, arching over the wagon bed, securely stapled to the sideboards. Stretched across the familiar white top was canvas, which had been soaked in linseed oil for waterproofing. The canvas top looked much like a bonnet. When finished, a wagon was red, white, and blue. With its Prussian-blue body, bright red running gear, and its white cover, the Conestoga wagon, hitched with its team of six horses, worked its way back and forth on the pikes, hauling needed supplies for the growing nation.

It took many skilled workers to build a classic Conestoga wagon. A wheelwright and blacksmith, as well as carpenters and helpers, took weeks of continuous labor to build one wagon. The skilled labor, the crafted metal, and the woodwork cost about $250. A Conestoga horse, now extinct, had a value of about $200. Four or six horses pulled the 3500 lb wagon. The vehicle's capacity to carry a heavy load was massive and could hold on average about seven tons of freight.

When on the road, the driver did not ride inside his Conestoga wagon. He either walked beside his team, rode the wheel horse (the rear horse on the left), or precariously perched himself on the lazy board, a heavy oak board that pulled out from beneath the wagon bed in front of the left rear wheel. The practice of driving from the left side of the wagon was another first, and is continued in the current practice of driving a car from the left.

It became a tradition for each horse of the team to wear a set of bells that made a melodious ringing to announce the approach of the Conestoga wagon. The wagon's teamsters mounted the brass bells on an arched frame. The unlucky driver of a wagon that became stuck or disabled was obligated to surrender his bells to the rescuing wagoner. The phrase, "I'll be there with bells on," seemingly originated from those days of the Conestoga wagon.

These long-distance haulers of heavy freight reached their peak of activity between

FOUNDED A. D. MDCCXCV

1820 and 1840. But the expansion of America's railroad lines rapidly brought this era to an end. By the time of the Civil War, the use of Conestoga wagons was gone. They were often left in fields to rot, or stored in the corner of an old barn.

Westward-bound immigrants used a similar version of the wagon, the prairie schooner, later on in the 19th century. Unlike the Conestoga, those wagons had a flat floor, and were often converted farm wagons.

## Congress Hall

Congress Hall was constructed in 1787–1789 as the **Philadelphia** County Court House, located at the corner of Chestnut and 6th Streets. When Congress returned to Philadelphia in 1790, the House of Representatives met on the main floor, and the Senate assembled upstairs. Some of the historic events that took place there included: the second presidential inauguration of **George Washington** and the inauguration of John Adams; the establishment of the First Bank of the United States, the **United States Mint**, and the Department of the Navy; and the ratification of Jay's Treaty with England. When Congress left Philadelphia, Federal and local courts used the building. The building, now open for tours, has been restored as much as possible to the period of time when it served as the U.S. Capitol.

## Cornplanter

Cornplanter, a Native American probably born in New York, became the Chief of the Seneca nation. His father was John Abeel, who came from a prominent Albany Dutch family.

Abeel traveled deep into the Indian country in western New York to trade with the Indians. He spent the rest of his life as a trader in the frontier. The Indians, many still hostile, welcomed Abeel there, because of his gunsmith skills. The French, Dutch, and British supplied the Indians with enough arms. The Indians needed and welcomed white men who knew how to repair them. Abeel had a temporary relationship with a Seneca woman, common then between whites and Indians, and Cornplanter was a child as a result. In the Iroquois society, the nationality of the mother determined her child's nationality. Cornplanter was reared as and remained an Indian.

During the American Revolution, Chief Cornplanter aided the British, leading raids against American forces. Cornplanter soon discovered the British, despite their promises, had neglected their Indian allies, and had abandoned them. Following the war, he became a steadfast friend of the citizens of the new nation. A powerful War Chief, Cornplanter negotiated peace with the advancing settlers.

In 1784, he signed a treaty, giving the Iroquois Confederacy all the land west of the Niagara River to the United States. He worked for President Washington, trying to negotiate peace with Indians in Michigan. He had accepted the offer of Quakers to educate his people's children. As hardy settlers continued to encroach on Indian lands and break their agreements, Cornplanter became disillusioned with Americans.

The old Indian War Chief felt remorse over his involvement in introducing his people to the culture of the white man. Cornplanter burned his military uniform, broke his sword, and destroyed his medals. He closed schools and dismissed the Quaker missionaries. He died at home on the Cornplanter Tract on February 18, 1836.

## Cornwall

Located in southern Lebanon County, Cornwall is one of the world's greatest iron mines. It was the oldest continuously worked iron mine in America. It was mined from 1742–1883. Peter Grubb originally built the

*The First Bank of the United States of America was established at Congress Hall, Philadelphia.*

charcoal iron furnace. It remains the greatest iron ore deposit east of Lake Superior.

## Counties

When **William Penn** became the proprietor of Pennsylvania, he established three counties. These were **Philadelphia**, Chester, and Bucks County. **Lancaster** County, formed from Chester County, was the fourth county Penn established. As the population spread westward and north from the southeastern corner of the state, more counties were formed.

Westmoreland County was created in 1773, and was the first county formed west of the Allegheny Mountains. The British and Indians burned the original county seat, Hannastown, on July 13, 1782.

Today there are 67 counties in Pennsylvania. Philadelphia is the largest county by population, with an estimated 1,491,812 residents (U.S. Census Bureau, 2001). Lycoming County is the largest county by size, with 1,235 square miles. In 1952, Philadelphia County and Philadelphia City, the local governments, merged into one unit.

*Route 6 meanders through the northern tier counties of Pennsylvania.*

## Covered Bridges

There are over 200 covered bridges in Pennsylvania. Found in 40 of the state's 67 counties, these wooden structures are scenic, romantic, and historic. At one point, there were over 1,500 covered bridges in Pennsylvania. More covered bridges exist in Pennsylvania than in any other state, giving it another honor as the Covered Bridge Capital of the World. Many have stood the test of time, a testament to the bridge builders' skill, ingenuity, and engineering.

Covered bridges are sometimes known as "kissing bridges," because young romantics used the privacy offered from a covered bridge to steal a kiss. Or maybe two kisses, if the covered bridge was long or the horse hitched to their buggy especially slow.

The first covered bridge, known as the "Permanent Bridge," spanned the Schuylkill River at 30th Street in Philadelphia and opened to traffic on January 1, 1805. Its builder was Timothy Palmer of Newburyport, Massachusetts. He reluctantly added the covering—the roof and sideboards —at the insistence of a prominent stockholder in the company that financed it. The investor wanted the bridge covered to protect it from the weather in an attempt to lengthen the life of the bridge. In those early days, private investors built bridges using the revenue collected from tolls charged to people crossing the bridge. It was the first covered bridge, but Palmer would go on to build many more throughout the Northern United States.

Investors and bridge builders quickly recognized the overall value of the covered bridge design. It extended the life of the wooden bridges by protecting the side supporting timbers (not necessarily the floorboards) from exposure to the weather, and thus lowered maintenance costs.

This type of design achieved its aim. Many of the bridges have survived nearly 200 years, despite floods and harsh weather. The harsh climate of the region—hot and wet in the summer and cold and icy in the winter—proved less destructive on wood if it was protected. The wooden bridges with exposed superstructures were vulnerable to rot. Covering and roofing the bridge protected them from the weather, and they lasted longer. Skilled artisans, like Palmer, knew how to build an arched support. Despite his reluctance to add it to the 30th Street Bridge, Palmer soon agreed that it was a valuable addition to the bridge.

The size of the population soon expanded beyond the streams and rivers of early settlements. To satisfy the need to cross the waterways and with an abundance of lumber, bridges made from wood were the favored method of construction.

Covered bridges were similar in design to one another, but seldom were there two that were exactly alike. For example, some included covered walkways, especially those located close to a town. The sideboards on some extended to the roof, while others were open at the roofline. In order to allow some kind of view while crossing a river or stream some had side openings or a window, which could also let in the daylight.

Many included a sign at each entrance with a warning, "Five Dollar Fine for Driving faster than a Walk," proving that speed restrictions were in force even then. The local wildlife benefited from the covered bridges too, as birds could be found nesting beneath the rafters and mice beneath the floors. Inside there were posters advertising an assortment of

*A typical covered bridge in Pennsylvania. The state has more covered bridges than any other.*

*Covered bridges were designed to be long lasting and some have survived nearly 200 years since their construction.*

products and events to catch the eye of any passing traveler, such as auctions, picnics, chewing tobacco, medicines, or axle grease.

The covered bridges that remain in Pennsylvania today are a link to this early history. Each remaining bridge is a historic part of the past, and a pleasure to visit, no matter the time of year.

## Cream Cheese

In Concord Township, Delaware County, near **Philadelphia**, early colonists settled the four villages of Concord, which were known as Concordville, Elam, Markham, and Ward.

Located at a vital transportation hub, one of these tiny communities is the birthplace of now world known cream cheese. The product, now known as Philadelphia Brand Cream Cheese, was invented at a dairy on Creamery Road in Ward. Cream cheese is one of the oldest American packaged foods. It went on sale in its protective wrapper in 1885.

## Cresap, Thomas

Between Wrightsville and Craley, along the **Susquehanna River**, Thomas Cresap settled about 1730 on lands claimed by Lord Baltimore of Maryland. He cunningly wanted to expand the borders of Maryland, at the expense of Pennsylvania and Virginia, by settling German immigrants into disputed areas and surveying the source of the Potomac River as far south as possible.

Sometimes called the "Maryland Monster," he had built a fort to protect his land claims. Agents of the Penns burned his fort and forcibly evicted him in 1736. Cresap moved on to Western Maryland, where he continued to be active in frontier affairs and died about 1790. The border dispute was settled with the establishment of the Mason-Dixon Line.

*Covered bridges were designed to prevent damage by the weather. They are still in use throughout Pennsylvania.*

## Croce, Jim

While a student at Villa Nova University, Jim Croce began his professional musical career playing in bands. The native Philadelphian found success several years later as a solo act. Croce's career abruptly ended on September 20, 1973 when his plane crashed in Natchitoches, Louisiana shortly after takeoff. He is buried in Frazer.

## Andrew Curtin

During the Civil War, Andrew Curtin served as Pennsylvania's governor. He was a staunch supporter of the Union. He had been a member of the Whig Party, but became a Republican, winning the state election in 1861. He was born in Bellefonte, Centre County on April 22, 1817. He was the first governor to raise and send troops to defend Washington, DC. He established the first and largest camp for the induction and training of Federal Troops. The camp, set up north of **Harrisburg**, was named in his honor, and was named Camp Curtin.

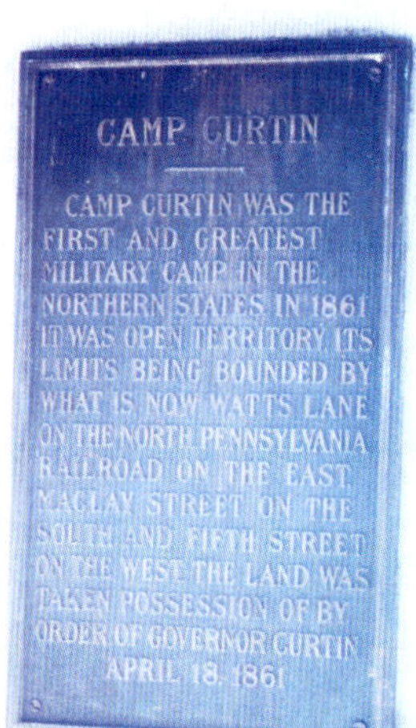


*At the site of Camp Curtin, a marker reminds visitors about the importance of the camp. It was named for Andrew Curtin, the governor of Pennsylvania during the Civil War.*

*Andrew Curtin was the governor of Pennsylvania during the Civil War. A staunch supporter of President Abraham Lincoln, Governor Curtin established the largest camp just north of Harrisburg, used for the assembly of new Federal Troops.*

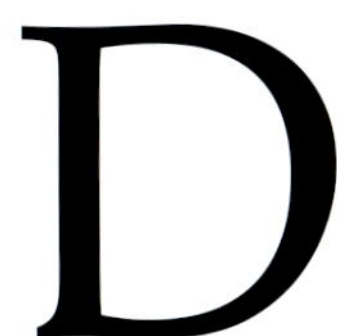

## Dairy Farms

From the beginning of colonization, Pennsylvania's farms have prospered and produced abundant foods. Pennsylvania's largest agricultural industry is dairy production. Pennsylvania is the fourth largest milk producing state in the country and the fourth in the nation in the annual production of ice cream. The top milk producing counties in Pennsylvania are **Lancaster**, Franklin, Bradford, Berks, and Lebanon. And that takes a lot of cows. Pennsylvania's dairy herd ranks sixth in the nation, with more than 1.6 million cattle.

## Davis, Phineas

*A typical Pennsylvania Amish dairy farm today. Notice that there is no electricity service. A windmill also provides mechanical power to pump water.*

Phineas Davis arrived in York as a barefoot teenage orphan, walking all the way there from New Hampshire. In 1831, he designed and built the first successful coal-burning locomotive steam engine in the United States, which he called *The York*. The locomotive reached a top speed of 30 miles per hour. He designed and built his locomotive in the foundry and machine shop he owned with partner Israel Gardner at West King and South Newberry streets in York. Davis earned a $4,000 award from the Baltimore and Ohio Steam Railway for his new locomotive. Several years before, John Elgar's *The Codorus*, America's first iron steamboat, was built in the same shop. Davis died, aged 40, on September 27, 1935 when he was riding a train that derailed.

## Declaration House, The

Located on the southwest corner at Seventh and Market Streets in **Philadelphia**, the Declaration House is where Thomas Jefferson wrote the **Declaration of Independence**. Philadelphia bricklayer Jacob Graff, Jr. originally built the house in 1775. Thomas Jefferson, as a 33-year-old delegate from Virginia to the Continental Congress, rented the two second-floor rooms after finding his lodging in the heart of the city uncomfortable. Situated on the outskirts of town, surrounded by fields and a stable across the street, Jefferson went about his task. The stable attracted large, biting horse flies, which Jefferson complained about while writing the Declaration. Although the original structure was torn down in 1883 the National Park Service rebuilt the house in 1975.

## Declaration of Independence

Everything changed after the Continental Congress first gathered in **Philadelphia** in the fall of 1774. Few would have predicted that it was to lead America into a permanent split with England.

There was a crisis brewing when delegates from 12 of the 13 original colonies gathered in Philadelphia at **Carpenter's Hall** on September 5, 1774. Georgia was the only colony that did not send delegates to consider a joint action on the situation arising from the recent laws passed by the British Parliament. Known as the Intolerable Acts, the four laws passed by the British Parliament in March 1774 were to punish the colony of Massachusetts for defying British policies. The Impartial Administration of Justice Act removed British officials from the jurisdiction of Massachusetts' courts. The Quartering Act required the colonists provide billets for British soldiers, the Boston Port Act closed the port of Boston to trade, and the Massachusetts Government Act revoked the colony's charter and banned town meetings.

Following a prolonged debate, the Continental Congress petitioned King George III, appealing to him to help restore harmony between Britain and the colonies. The Continental Congress also asked for the colonies to boycott trade with Britain. Before adjourning in October, the delegates decided to assemble in Philadelphia again on May 10, 1775.

When the Second Continental Congress convened, tension between the colonies and the King had not improved. The delegates knew they had little choice but to form committees and assume governmental duties that had previously been exercised by the King. The Congress authorized **George Washington** to organize the Continental Army.

In May 1776, the Second Continental Congress directed the colonies to form their own governments and debated a resolution in favor of independence.

On June 7, 1776, in the Pennsylvania State House (now known as **Independence Hall**), Richard Henry Lee, a Virginia delegate, rose from his wooden chair to address the Continental Congress. Lee made a motion that the colonies become free and independent states absolved from all loyalty to the British crown. Lee read his resolution beginning,

*The Declaration of Independence was signed in Pennsylvania but not as is often believed on July 4, 1776. It was approved on that date but not signed until later.*

"Resolved: That these United Colonies are, and of right ought to be, free and independent States, that they are absolved from all allegiance to the British Crown, and that all political connection between them and the State of Great Britain is, and ought to be, totally dissolved."

John Adams of Massachusetts seconded the motion, but the members of Congress deferred their vote until July 1. It was a simple motion, but a complicated, hard, and difficult decision for the delegates. They delayed the resolution for the vote until the following day. It was a momentous and complex decision.

While the members of Congress pondered if they should separate from England, a committee prepared a formal declaration document in line with Lee's resolution. Thomas Jefferson wrote the draft of the document. Jefferson worked on his draft between June 11 and June 28, 1776. He was able to write unforgettable phrases, and expressed the convictions in the minds and hearts of the American people. The political philosophy of the Declaration was not new. Other Continental philosophers had already expressed the ideals of individual liberty. What Jefferson did so well was to summarize this philosophy in "self-evident truths." He prepared a long list of grievances against the King to justify before the world the breaking of ties between the colonies and England.

John Adams, Roger Sherman, Robert Livingston, and **Benjamin Franklin** made several minor changes to Jefferson's draft before they presented it to Congress. Benjamin Franklin was sick during the draft writing process. In a letter to George Washington dated June 21, 1776, Franklin said that illness had kept him from Congress, "I know little of what has pass'd there, except that a Declaration of Independence is preparing."

Tension between British troops occupying Boston and the citizens of that city were likely

# IN CONGRESS, JULY 4, 1776.

## The unanimous Declaration of the thirteen united States of America,

When in the Course of human events, it becomes necessary for one people to dissolve the political bands which have connected them with another, and to assume among the powers of the earth, the separate and equal station to which the Laws of Nature and of Nature's God entitle them, a decent respect to the opinions of mankind requires that they should declare the causes which impel them to the separation. —— We hold these truths to be self-evident, that all men are created equal, that they are endowed by their Creator with certain unalienable Rights, that among these are Life, Liberty and the pursuit of Happiness. — That to secure these rights, Governments are instituted among Men, deriving their just powers from the consent of the governed, — That whenever any Form of Government becomes destructive of these ends, it is the Right of the People to alter or to abolish it, and to institute new Government, laying its foundation on such principles and organizing its powers in such form, as to them shall seem most likely to effect their Safety and Happiness. Prudence, indeed, will dictate that Governments long established should not be changed for light and transient causes; and accordingly all experience hath shewn, that mankind are more disposed to suffer, while evils are sufferable, than to right themselves by abolishing the forms to which they are accustomed. But when a long train of abuses and usurpations, pursuing invariably the same Object evinces a design to reduce them under absolute Despotism, it is their right, it is their duty, to throw off such Government, and to provide new Guards for their future security. — Such has been the patient sufferance of these Colonies; and such is now the necessity which constrains them to alter their former Systems of Government. The history of the present King of Great Britain is a history of repeated injuries and usurpations, all having in direct object the establishment of an absolute Tyranny over these States. To prove this, let Facts be submitted to a candid world. —— He has refused his Assent to Laws, the most wholesome and necessary for the public good. —— He has forbidden his Governors to pass Laws of immediate and pressing importance, unless suspended in their operation till his Assent should be obtained; and when so suspended, he has utterly neglected to attend to them. —— He has refused to pass other Laws for the accommodation of large districts of people, unless those people would relinquish the right of Representation in the Legislature, a right inestimable to them and formidable to tyrants only. —— He has called together legislative bodies at places unusual, uncomfortable, and distant from the depository of their Public Records, for the sole purpose of fatiguing them into compliance with his measures. —— He has dissolved Representative Houses repeatedly, for opposing with manly firmness his invasions on the rights of the people. —— He has refused for a long time, after such dissolutions, to cause others to be elected; whereby the Legislative powers, incapable of Annihilation, have returned to the People at large for their exercise; the State remaining in the mean time exposed to all the dangers of invasion from without, and convulsions within. —— He has endeavoured to prevent the population of these States; for that purpose obstructing the Laws for Naturalization of Foreigners; refusing to pass others to encourage their migrations hither, and raising the conditions of new Appropriations of Lands. —— He has obstructed the Administration of Justice, by refusing his Assent to Laws for establishing Judiciary powers. —— He has made Judges dependent on his Will alone, for the tenure of their offices, and the amount and payment of their salaries. —— He has erected a multitude of New Offices, and sent hither swarms of Officers to harrass our people, and eat out their substance. —— He has kept among us, in times of peace, Standing Armies without the Consent of our legislatures. —— He has affected to render the Military independent of and superior to the Civil power. —— He has combined with others to subject us to a jurisdiction foreign to our constitution, and unacknowledged by our laws; giving his Assent to their Acts of pretended Legislation: — For Quartering large bodies of armed troops among us: — For protecting them, by a mock Trial, from punishment for any Murders which they should commit on the Inhabitants of these States: — For cutting off our Trade with all parts of the world: — For imposing Taxes on us without our Consent: — For depriving us in many cases, of the benefits of Trial by Jury: — For transporting us beyond Seas to be tried for pretended offences: — For abolishing the free System of English Laws in a neighbouring Province, establishing therein an Arbitrary government, and enlarging its Boundaries so as to render it at once an example and fit instrument for introducing the same absolute rule into these Colonies: — For taking away our Charters, abolishing our most valuable Laws, and altering fundamentally the Forms of our Governments: — For suspending our own Legislatures, and declaring themselves invested with power to legislate for us in all cases whatsoever. — He has abdicated Government here, by declaring us out of his Protection and waging War against us. —— He has plundered our seas, ravaged our Coasts, burnt our towns, and destroyed the lives of our people. —— He is at this time transporting large Armies of foreign Mercenaries to compleat the works of death, desolation and tyranny, already begun with circumstances of Cruelty & perfidy scarcely paralleled in the most barbarous ages, and totally unworthy the Head of a civilized nation. —— He has constrained our fellow Citizens taken Captive on the high Seas to bear Arms against their Country, to become the executioners of their friends and Brethren, or to fall themselves by their Hands. —— He has excited domestic insurrections amongst us, and has endeavoured to bring on the inhabitants of our frontiers, the merciless Indian Savages, whose known rule of warfare, is an undistinguished destruction of all ages, sexes and conditions. In every stage of these Oppressions We have Petitioned for Redress in the most humble terms: Our repeated Petitions have been answered only by repeated injury. A Prince, whose character is thus marked by every act which may define a Tyrant, is unfit to be the ruler of a free people. Nor have We been wanting in attentions to our Brittish brethren. We have warned them from time to time of attempts by their legislature to extend an unwarrantable jurisdiction over us. We have reminded them of the circumstances of our emigration and settlement here. We have appealed to their native justice and magnanimity, and we have conjured them by the ties of our common kindred to disavow these usurpations, which, would inevitably interrupt our connections and correspondence. They too have been deaf to the voice of justice and of consanguinity. We must, therefore, acquiesce in the necessity, which denounces our Separation, and hold them, as we hold the rest of mankind, Enemies in War, in Peace Friends. ——

We, therefore, the Representatives of the united States of America, in General Congress, Assembled, appealing to the Supreme Judge of the world for the rectitude of our intentions, do, in the Name, and by Authority of the good People of these Colonies, solemnly publish and declare, That these United Colonies are, and of Right ought to be Free and Independent States; that they are Absolved from all Allegiance to the British Crown, and that all political connection between them and the State of Great Britain, is and ought to be totally dissolved; and that as Free and Independent States, they have full Power to levy War, conclude Peace, contract Alliances, establish Commerce, and to do all other Acts and Things which Independent States may of right do. —— And for the support of this Declaration, with a firm reliance on the protection of divine Providence, we mutually pledge to each other our Lives, our Fortunes and our sacred Honor.

John Hancock

Button Gwinnett
Lyman Hall
Geo Walton.

Wm Hooper
Joseph Hewes,
John Penn

Edward Rutledge.
Thos Heyward Junr.
Thomas Lynch Junr.
Arthur Middleton

Samuel Chase
Wm. Paca
Thos. Stone
Charles Carroll of Carrollton

George Wythe
Richard Henry Lee
Th Jefferson
Benja Harrison
Thos Nelson jr.
Francis Lightfoot Lee
Carter Braxton

Robt Morris
Benjamin Rush
Benja. Franklin
John Morton
Geo Clymer
Jas. Smith
Geo. Taylor
James Wilson
Geo. Ross
Caesar Rodney
Geo Read
Tho M:Kean

Wm Floyd
Phil. Livingston
Frans. Lewis
Lewis Morris
Richd. Stockton
Jno Witherspoon
Fras. Hopkinson
John Hart
Abra Clark

Josiah Bartlett
Wm. Whipple
Saml Adams
John Adams
Robt Treat Paine
Elbridge Gerry
Step. Hopkins
William Ellery
Roger Sherman
Samel Huntington
Wm. Williams
Oliver Wolcott
Matthew Thornton

to erupt in bloodshed, as it did a year before in the spring at Lexington and Concord. A later engagement at Bunker Hill made it difficult to remain loyal to the British crown. The king was encouraging a fight. King George III answered a final Congressional try for peace in cold language. "The lines have been drawn," he wrote. "Blows must decide."

A wildly successful pamphlet by an unknown writer, Thomas Paine, pushed Americans toward agreement on independence. *Common Sense* spoke in plain, simple English to the thousands of Americans who read it. "We have it in our power to begin the world anew," Paine wrote. By the spring of 1776, the idea of independence from England spread like a wildfire throughout the colonies. The colonists ousted the Royal governments, and colonial assemblies began drafting their own constitutions. The concept of freedom intoxicated everyone.

Still the decision to become independent was difficult for the delegates. There would be a thorny, costly war with England. The Americans would battle the strongest army in the world.

HARPER'S WEEKLY.
A JOURNAL OF CIVILIZATION
NEW YORK, SATURDAY, JULY 9, 1870.

*Harper's Weekly* published an article showing one of the first readings of the Declaration of Independence in public. George Washington is depicted on horseback in the foreground.

On July 1, 1776, Congress reconvened. The doors of the State House were locked and windows remained shut, despite the sweltering summer heat. The members of Congress debated the call of independence from England while delegates from Pennsylvania and South Carolina argued and voted against it. The members from Delaware were evenly divided, and could not decide which way to vote. New York members abstained. The debate continued throughout the day and into the night. Edward Rutledge, a delegate from South Carolina, "then requested the determination might be put off to the next day."

It was an agonizing decision for Congress. When they took another vote on July 2, South Carolina, Delaware, and Pennsylvania voted in favor of the resolution, and thus Congress passed the Lee Resolution, declaring independence from England, as the British army was landing in New York City. On July 9, the delegates from New York voted their approval, making the decision unanimous.

On July 2, the decision had been made. Congress worked on the Declaration of Independence document that recalled the years of struggle between the new nation and its former protector, and made 39 revisions to the committee's draft over the next three days. One of the most notable revisions was the deletion that denounced King George III for promoting the slave trade among the colonies.

The Continental Congress adopted the Declaration of Independence, the formal document proclaiming the independence of the 13 British colonies in America, on July 4, 1776. In language certain to inspire American patriots, and enrage the king and England, the final Declaration recounted the grievances of the colonies against the British crown, and then declared the colonies to be free and independent states. The language of the Declaration was defiant. The members of the Second Continental Congress unanimously adopted the Declaration.

*Portraits of the signatories of the Declaration of Independence.*

Congress directed the committee to supervise the printing of the adopted document. The first printed copies of the Declaration of Independence were turned out from the Philadelphia shop of John Dunlap, the official printer to the Congress. It is not known how many copies John Dunlap printed on this busy night of July 4. It was one of these Dunlap printed copies, referred to today as a Dunlap Broadside, that was sent to the king.

On July 5, John Hancock sent the first printed copies of the Declaration of Independence to the New Jersey and Delaware legislatures. On July 6, the *Pennsylvania Evening Post* was the first newspaper to publish the Declaration of Independence. On July 8, the first public reading of the Declaration took place in Philadelphia by Col. John Nixon of the Philadelphia Committee of Safety at the State House. It was also read again that evening before the militia on the Commons. Throughout the city bells were rung all day. On the same day, the Declaration was publicly read in Easton, Pennsylvania, and Trenton, New Jersey. It was these first public readings that constituted America's first celebrations of the fourth of July. In towns and cities across the new nation, after the public reading of the Declaration, there were loud shouts, cheering, firings of muskets, and the public tearing down of the British emblems. On July 9, 1776 the Declaration of Independence was read to the American army in New York by order of General George Washington.

Many think all the delegates present signed the Declaration of Independence on July 4, 1776. Congress continued its work in the summer heat. On July 19, Congress ordered the Declaration be officially inscribed and signed by its members. On August 2, the Congressional delegates began to sign the officially inscribed copy of the Declaration, including some of those members who had not voted for its adoption.

John Hancock, the President of Congress, was the first to sign the sheet of parchment measuring 24 by 29 inches. He used a bold signature centered below the text. Under prevailing custom, the other delegates began to sign at the right below the text, their signatures arranged according to the geographic location of the states they represented. New Hampshire, the northernmost state, began the list, and Georgia, the southernmost, ended it. Eventually 56 delegates signed, although all were not present in Philadelphia on August 2.

D

## Deringer, Jr., Henry

Henry Deringer, Jr. first developed his small, single-shot pistol at his gun shop located on 370 North Front Street, **Philadelphia**. Known as the Derringer (with two "r"s, even though the gunsmith only had one "r" in his name), the pistol has a large bore but is short-barreled and small enough to carry in the pocket. It was popular in the 1850s and 1860s. John Wilkes Booth famously used a Derringer pistol to assassinate President Abraham Lincoln in 1865. Deringer died in 1868.

*The Derringer pistol is small enough to be carried in a pocket.*

## Devers, Jacob

Born September 8, 1887 and raised in York, Jacob L. Devers rose to the rank of Four Star General in 1945. Devers was the U.S. Army's youngest Brigadier General. In 1940, he became commander of European operations. During World War II, General Devers had a key role in liberating France in 1944. His sixth Army Group successfully penetrated and destroyed German-held positions in central Europe. When he retired from the army, he lived in the Washington, D.C. area. He is buried at Arlington National Cemetery.

## Dickinson, John

Representing Pennsylvania to the Continental Congress, John Dickinson refused to sign the Declaration of Independence. Dickinson represented both Delaware and Pennsylvania at the founding of the new nation.

Dickinson was born into a wealthy family (his father was the first judge to the Court of Pleas in Delaware) on November 13, 1732, in Talbot County, Maryland. He received his formal education with Private tutors at the Temple of London, England, which was the most prestigious education anyone could hope for in colonial America. When he returned to America, he became a noted lawyer in Philadelphia.

Dickinson entered politics as a member of the Pennsylvania assembly in 1764, and continued with the Stamp Act Congress in 1765 where he drafted the Resolutions of the Stamp Act Congress.

It was also during this time that he wrote an important series of essays, *Letters of a Pennsylvania Farmer*, about the non-importation and non-exportation agreements against Great Britain. These essays were published in London in 1768 by **Benjamin Franklin**, and later translated to French and published in

*John Dickinson refused to sign the Declaration of Independence.*

Paris. In 1774, he attended the First Continental Congress. In 1775, and in combination with Thomas Jefferson, he wrote a "Declaration of the Causes and Necessity of Taking Up Arms."

Dickinson was opposed to a separation from England and worked to temper the language and action of the Congress, upholding the possibility of harmony. Sympathetic to colonial complaints, he nevertheless sought to avoid any violence. He abstained from voting on and signing the Declaration of Independence. When King George ordered a Royal army to New York, Dickinson considered the social contract between the King and America dissolved. Although he refused to sign the Declaration, Dickinson was among the first to put on the uniform to defend the new nation. He was elected Governor of Pennsylvania in 1782 and served until October 1785. He also served with **George Washington** at the **Battle of Brandywine**. He joined the Constitutional Convention in Philadelphia in 1787 and afterward promoted the new U.S. Constitution. With Benjamin Rush, he helped found Dickinson College, at **Carlisle**. He died on February 14, 1808.

## Donegal Church

Donegal Church in western Lancaster County (near present-day Maytown) was an early Presbyterian Church, organized in 1714. In 1777 the men of the community joined hands around the white oak at Donegal Church to pledge their allegiance, and declare their patriotism, to their new nation.

## Drake Well

In 1859, the world used whale oil, coal gas, and lard as a source of energy. Edwin L. Drake (1819–1880), an unemployed conductor and "jack-of-all-trades," was hired as the agent of the Seneca Oil Company, New Haven, Connecticut, to "find and raise large quantities of crude oil" in Titusville. The success of **Pittsburgh** refiner Samuel Kier—who demonstrated the use of simple distillation to refine kerosene from crude oil—created a demand for safer, more brilliant, and less expensive lamp fuel.

Forty-year-old Drake adapted Kier's technology for drilling from the processes used to harvest brine, where crude oil frequently contaminated the salt wells. He solved the problems of the ground caving in around the well by driving a four-inch diameter iron pipe down to bedrock and then drilling within the

*Edwin Drake at his oil well in Titusville.*

*The Drake Oil Well in northwestern Pennsylvania started the petroleum industry.*

pipe. Modern day oil well drillers still use the method that Drake perfected.

Drake employed an experienced blacksmith and salt well driller, William Smith (more commonly known as "Uncle Billy"), and in spite of skepticism from local residents, and erratic financial support from his employers, they built an engine house, erected a derrick, and purchased a steam engine for drilling. On August 27, 1859, Drake's well struck oil at a depth of 69 feet and launched the modern petroleum industry. After striking oil, his well soon produced 400 gallons per day (2,000 barrels per year) and began the first commercial exploitation of petroleum in the United States. It also brought with it a new era of kerosene lamps and stoves

In 1934, the Drake Well Museum was constructed on the actual site of Edwin Drake's successful well. In 1945, a replica of Drake's original well house was built on the grounds and a reproduction operating steam engine was added in 1986. The Drake Well Museum and Park operates all year round and attracts over 50,000 visitors annually.

## Dravo Shipyard

During World War II, the Dravo Corporation's shipyard in Allegheny County was a leader in the manufacture of Landing Ship Tanks (called

*A marker notes the achievements of Charles Duryea. While living in Reading, Duryea perfected the transmission in automobiles. He tested his designs on the twisting, climbing roads of Mount Penn.*

LSTs) for the U.S. Navy. At the time, over 16,000 Dravo workers produced 145 of the LSTs. These amphibious ships proved vital to the success of Allied landings on enemy shores during World War II. Many shipyards went on to use the techniques developed by Dravo.

## Duryea, Charles

Charles E. Duryea, along with his brother, James, built one of the first American automobiles in 1893. In the booming bicycle business, they tinkered with gas-powered vehicles. In 1900, Charles Duryea moved to Reading and there he built the first successful hill-climbing gasoline automobile in America. Duryea Drive in Reading, extending from City Park to the Pagoda, is the course Duryea used for testing his cars between 1900 and 1907. He then moved on to Philadelphia, and became a consulting engineer in the automotive industry. He died in 1938.

## Eagle Grange #1

Pennsylvania's first grange was established in Montgomery, a small village on the west branch of the **Susquehanna River** in Lycoming County. Officially organized on March 4, 1871, it opened two years before the Pennsylvania State Grange. The national grange—the order of the Patrons of Husbandry—had been established in 1867. The objectives of Eagle Grange #1, and other granges, included cooperative buying, lowering of railroad rates, and free delivery in rural areas. Granges also pioneered granting equal status to women. The grange hall in Montgomery was built in 1887.

## Eastern State Penitentiary

In 1787, the members of The Philadelphia Society for Alleviating the Miseries of Public Prisons, a group of powerful Philadelphians, assembled in the home of **Benjamin Franklin**. They expressed their growing concerns with the appalling conditions in American and European prisons. Dr. Benjamin Rush spoke about the Society's goal to have Pennsylvania set the international standard in prison design. He proposed the radical idea that Pennsylvania should build a true penitentiary, a prison designed to create genuine regret and penitence in the criminal's heart. It took the society more than thirty years to convince Pennsylvania to build the prison it suggested; a revolutionary new building on farmland outside **Philadelphia**.

Eastern State Penitentiary was radically different from the prisons of its day, abandoning corporal punishment and ill-treatment. This massive new structure, opened in 1829, became the most expensive American building so far. The Penitentiary did not simply punish, but moved the criminal toward spiritual reflection and change. The method was based on a Quaker-inspired system of isolation from other prisoners, with labor.

Life for the inmates in the early prison system was strict. To prevent any distraction, knowledge of the building, or even mild interaction with guards, inmates were always hooded whenever they were taken outside their cells. The proponents of the new prison believed strongly that criminals exposed in silence to thoughts of their behavior and the ugliness of their crimes would become penitent, which is where the word "penitentiary" came from.

When it opened, there were seven cellblocks, which allowed each prisoner to have a private cell, centrally heated, with running water, a flushed toilet, and a skylight. This was when the White House had no running water and coal-burning stoves provided heat. In the vaulted, sky lit cell, the prisoner had only the light from heaven, the word of God (the Bible), and honest work (shoemaking, weaving, and the like) to lead to penitence. A medieval facade, built to intimidate and imply that physical punishment took place behind the dark, grim walls, gave the building its identity.

Over the years, Eastern State Penitentiary expanded and more cellblocks were added. Dignitaries from around the world visited to see the penitentiary, its design, and the Pennsylvania prison system. Al Capone served a one-year prison term in Eastern State Penitentiary.

Critics of the Pennsylvania system finally prevailed, and in 1913, the state abandoned it. The state closed the facility in 1971, 142 years after it admitted Charles Williams, Prisoner Number One. Today, the prison on Fairmount Avenue is a popular tourist attraction.

## Easton's Indian Peace Councils

Provincial officials met with Native Americans in the Town Square in Easton between 1756 and 1762. Early Pennsylvania politicians used the Indiana Peace Councils to strengthen English

*The town square in Easton commemorates those that served during the Civil War. In this square, Peace Councils with Pennsylvania's Native Americans were held before the French and Indian Wars.*

friendship with the Delawares and **Six Nations**, and to bring peace with the bands of hostile Indians, drawing them away from the French.

## Eisenhower, Dwight

Gettysburg became the home of a future president in 1950. Dwight and Mamie Eisenhower, looking forward to their retirement years, bought the Allen Redding farm adjoining Gettysburg National Military Park. It was the only home the Eisenhower's owned in their lifetime. The original 189-acre farm was transformed by stages into the 230-acre country estate of the 34th President of the United States. After his election and during his Presidency, the President and Mrs. Eisenhower used their farm as a weekend retreat, a refuge in time of illness, and a comfortable meeting place for world leaders. The Eisenhowers especially enjoyed the glassed-in porch where they read, entertained their family and friends, played cards, and watched television. Eisenhower created his oil paintings on the porch. He wrote that if they ever built another home, "it would be built around such a porch."

On adjoining farms, Eisenhower raised his prizewinning herd of Angus cattle. He entertained Nikita Khrushchev, then the leader of the Soviet Union, at the farm in September 1959. From 1961 to 1969, it was Eisenhower's home during his retirement. In 1967, the President and Mrs. Eisenhower donated their farm to the United States to be administered by the National Park Service as the Eisenhower National Historic Site. It is open to the public for tours.

*A portrait of Dwight Eisenhower.*

## Emmaus

Moravians settled the "Gemein-Ort," which means congregational village, in 1761. They named their new community after the biblical

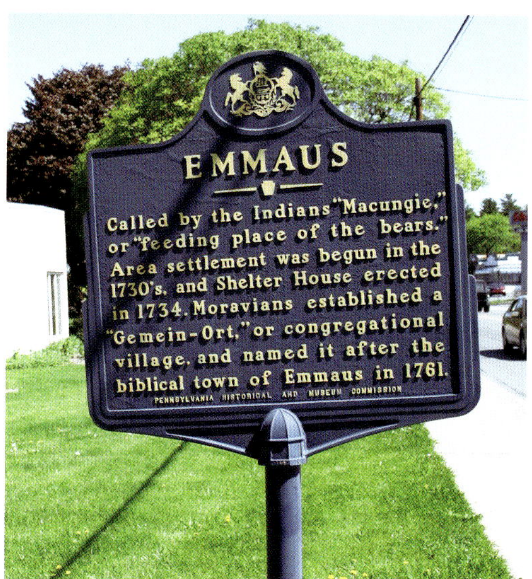

*This 1941 photograph shows a decorated German-style barn near Emmaus, Lehigh County. The hex signs on the side were painted in black and white.*

town of Emmaus. Before their arrival, the Indians called the area "Macungie" which means "feeding place of the bears."

## ENIAC—The World's First Computer

The Electronic Numerical Integrator and Computer (ENIAC), the world's first computer, started the Information Age in 1946 at the University of Pennsylvania in **Philadelphia**. Invented by Professors J. Presper Eckert and John Mauchly, its flip-flop circuitry laden with often-unreliable vacuum tubes completed previously daylong calculations within seconds. Its first application was to solve atomic energy problems for the Manhattan Project. During its first year, it calculated ballistic trajectories for the U.S. Military, as well as solving calculations for weather prediction, studying cosmic rays in astronomy and random numbers, and designing wind tunnels.

ENIAC was a monstrosity. It filled an entire room, weighed 30 tons, and consumed 200 kilowatts of power. It grew as a legend from the first time the inventors of ENIAC turned it on. A myth developed that the lights dimmed across the city of Philadelphia when the professors first switched on ENIAC.

The professors built the massive electronics in 42 panels nine feet in height, two feet wide, and one foot deep. With over 19,000 vacuum tubes, the computer also had 1,500 relays, 3,000 switches, and hundreds of thousands of resistors, inductors, and capacitors. A card reader and cardpunch provided for the input and output. It produced so much heat that its inventors placed it in one of the few rooms at the University with forced air-cooling.

The vacuum tubes were unreliable. Many electronics experts of the time predicted massive tube failures that would prevent ENIAC from ever being useful. When the professors turned ENIAC on and off daily, several tubes would burn out, making it unusable about half of the time, as predicted.

Most of these vacuum tube failures occurred during the warm-up and cool-down periods, when the tube filaments were under thermal stress. By simply deciding to never turn ENIAC off, the computer's inventors lessened the vacuum tube failures to a more acceptable rate of one tube every two days.

*Left: A Pennsylvania historical marker explains the origins of Emmaus.*

In 1954, ENIAC ran without a failure for 116 hours, the longest continuous period since its initial operation.

The ENIAC clearly established the postwar computer industry. ENIAC was the first digital computer to perform calculations at electronic speeds. Because both its arithmetic operations and data storage used electronics, the ENIAC could perform 5,000 additions per second and over 300 multiplications per second. ENIAC proved that an enormously complex electronic system could run reliably enough to solve important and complicated applications.

In 1953, the scientists increased ENIAC's memory capacity by adding a static magnetic-memory core. Built by the Burroughs Corporation and using the binary coded decimal number system, the memory core was the first of its kind. It allowed the computer to make calculations that were more complicated.

As computer technology advanced, the ENIAC soon became obsolete. Less expensive machines made it economically uncompetitive. At 11.45pm on October 2, 1955, technicians shut down ENIAC. Following its retirement from service, pieces of the machine are now on display in various museums, including the Smithsonian in Washington, D.C., and in the room at the Moore School for Electrical Engineering at the University of Pennsylvania, where Professors Eckert and Mauchly built it.

*The Ephrata Cloister, now restored, was a religious experiment in colonial Pennsylvania.*

## Ephrata Cloister

Founded in 1732, by Conrad Beissel and other German settlers seeking spiritual goals, rather than earthly rewards, the Ephrata Cloister, located in Lancaster County was one of America's earliest communal religious societies. Beissel and his followers lived calm lives of prayer and charity. Gathered in unique European-style buildings, the community consisted of three orders: a brotherhood and a sisterhood, both of which practiced celibacy, and a married order of householders who supported Cloister activities. While the householders were farmers or artisans who lived nearby, the brothers and sisters lived at the Cloister in log, stone, and half-timbered buildings reminiscent of their Rhenish homeland. The celibate orders practiced rigid self-discipline and self-denial. They farmed and worked in various industries such as papermaking and carpentry. One of the Society's outstanding contributions to its communities was the steady flow of books, broadsides, music, calligraphy, and printing. Following Beissel's death in 1768, the Society gradually declined after the American Revolution. By 1800, the celibate orders were nearly extinct, and in 1813, the remaining householders incorporated the German Seventh Day Baptist Church.

Members continued to live and worship at the Cloister until 1934. In 1941, the **Commonwealth** of Pennsylvania acquired the historic site and began a program of restoration and interpretation. Today the Ephrata Cloister is open for tours.

*The white lighthouse on Presque Isle is located on a tiny peninsula that extends into Lake Erie.*

## Erie

Pennsylvania's third largest city, Erie is the state's only lake port city. The first settlers arrived in 1795 after Pennsylvania bought the Erie Triangle from Chief Cornplanter of the Iroquois and Six Nations. The land, which comprises Pennsylvania's northwest corner, cost Pennsylvania 12 British pounds. The land purchase included over 202,000 acres.

The purchase made sense, as it would give Pennsylvania access to Lake Erie, one of America's five Great Lakes. The City of Erie and the lake was named for the Erie Indians, now a forgotten tribe. The powerful Senecas, part of the Iroquois confederacy of **Five Nations**, conquered the Eries sometime in the 1600s. The history of the Eries disappeared with their integration into the Seneca nation.

Erie's location made it a valuable and strategically important settlement. For years, control of the land spurred battles between the French and English. The French wanted a connection between their colonies in New Orleans and Canada. The English claimed land, and were not about to surrender it to the French. For years, the armies of each sought allegiance with the Indian nations, while fighting with one another. Both built forts, only to see them destroyed by the other army. Finally, the powerful British army won the battles, and controlled the area. After Pennsylvania declared and won its independence from Britain, the area's development started.

Erie played an important part in the War of 1812. Commodore Oliver Hazard Perry used Erie as his headquarters, and used ships made in the city to defeat the British in the Battle of Lake Erie in 1813.

When the Erie Canal was completed in 1825, the main growth of the community began. It further expanded with the arrival of the railroads in the 1850s.

Incorporated as a city in 1851, Erie became a commercial and manufacturing center, and served as a shipping point for petroleum, iron ore, coal, lumber, and industrial and agricultural products.

According to the U.S. Census Bureau, the population is 103,717 (2000). Major items manufactured include machinery, transportation equipment, paper, printed materials, metal, plastic and rubber products, electrical goods, and processed food.

# F

## Fallingwater

Designed by architect Frank Lloyd Wright (1867-1959), his Fallingwater house was built in 1936 as family retreat for a **Pittsburgh** businessperson, Edgar Kaufmann. Widely admired for its design, the Fayette County house is dramatically cantilevered over a waterfall. Wright's desire to link architecture with nature is obvious in this house.

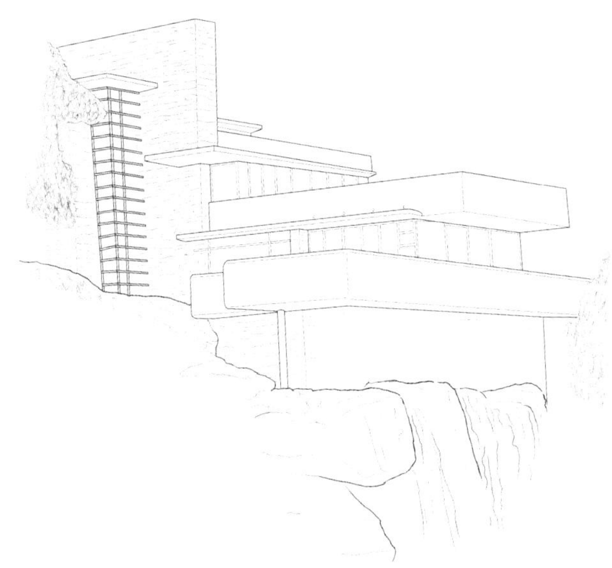

*Frank Lloyd Wright's Fallingwater, one of Pennsylvania's most notable houses.*

## Fasnacht Day

The Tuesday before Ash Wednesday is known as "Fasnacht Day" among the Pennsylvania Dutch. A fasnacht is a square doughnut, fried in fat. The tradition helped use up the fat and sugar in the kitchen, which were given up during Lent. It was the last chance before fasting to gorge on good doughnuts without reprise, before the lean days that would follow.

*The great Ferris Wheel first erected in Chicago in 1893 and subsequently moved to the World's Fair at St. Louis.*

## Ferris Wheel

George Washington Gale Ferris (1859-1896), a civil engineer, invented the Ferris Wheel. The Allegheny County resident designed and erected the world's first Ferris Wheel for the Columbian Exposition in 1892. The amusement ride has become a standard attraction at amusement parks.

## Fine, Larry

Born Louis Fienberg on October 5, 1902 on the south side of **Philadelphia**, Larry Fine was a violinist and amateur boxer when Ted Healey cast him as one of his stooges. The frizzy-haired comic became a permanent fixture of The Three Stooges. Larry remained a stooge until his death in 1975.

## First Aluminum Observatory Dome

On West View Aveune near McKnight Road in Ross Township, Allegheny County, the first astronomical observatory with an aluminum dome was erected in 1930. Designed and built by **Pittsburgh** amateur astronomers, the Valley View Observatory stood beside the Van Buren St. home of Leo Scanlon, one of the group's leaders. Following this design, over the years, many of the world's astronomical observatories were built with similar domes. Scanlon's shiny metal dome became the standard for the accepted image of modern observatory.

*Interior and exterior shots of the Shippinport nuclear power plant, which is now retired.*

## First Commercial Nuclear Power Plant

The first nuclear power plant in the world began running in Shippingport on December 2, 1957. The Duquesne Light Company of **Pittsburgh** built the Beaver County nuclear power plant. The plant was on a site the power company owned on the Ohio River. The Shippingport plant supplied electricity to the Pittsburgh area. In 1982, the Shippingport nuclear power plant went off-line and was retired. Congress assigned the decontamination and decommissioning of the reactor to the U.S. Department of Energy. It was the first decontamination and decommissioning of a nuclear reactor in the United States.

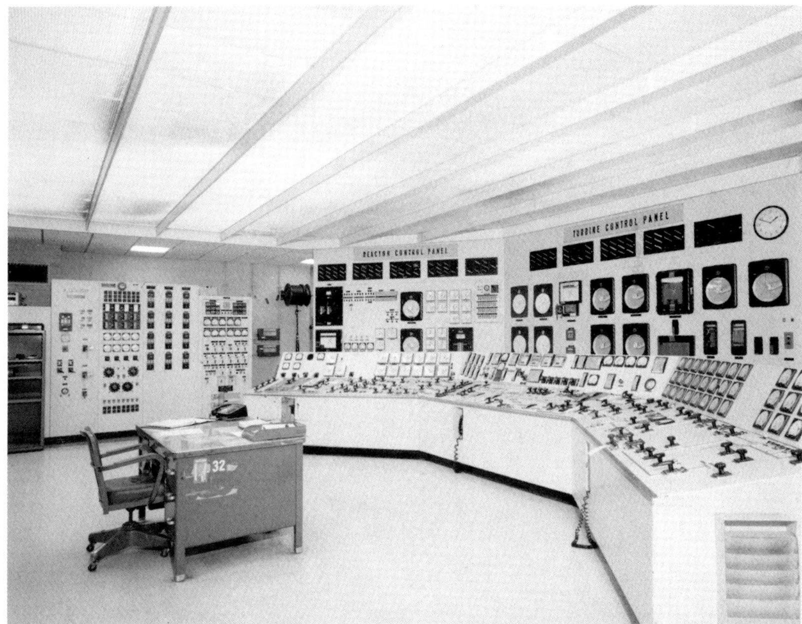


## First Commercial Use of Electricity

Thomas Edison chose Sunbury to be the basis of his operations for electrical experiments. In Northumberland County, Edison successfully used a three-wire electrical lighting system in July 1883. The City Hotel was the first commercial building wired for electricity. Sunbury became internationally famous. The hotel changed the world and was renamed "The Edison Hotel" to honor the inventor. The Edison Electric Illuminating Co. plant was at 4th and Vine Streets in Sunbury.

## First Continental Congress

Delegates from the original American colonies traveled to **Carpenter's Hall** in **Philadelphia**. On September 5, 1774, they met to consider joint action caused by the British Parliament passing the Intolerable Acts.

About 50 delegates comprised the Continental Congress. The delegates represented twelve of the thirteen colonies. Georgia was not represented. Collectively, the members of the Continental Congress decided to petition King George III, and asked him to restore harmony between Britain and the colonies. Congress also called for the colonies to boycott trade with Britain. Finally, they decided they would meet again, on May 10, 1775, in Philadelphia, to review the situation between the colonies and England.

## First Mercy Hospital

Mercy Hospital was founded in 1847 by the Sisters of Mercy as **Pittsburgh**'s first hospital. Medical internships began in 1848, and a nursing school was established in 1893. This facility in Pittsburgh was the first Mercy hospital worldwide. It cared for all patients, regardless of the capacity to pay for services.

## First Pay-TV event in America

In November 1972, Home Box Office (commonly known as HBO) broadcast a National Hockey League game from Madison Square garden to 365 Service Electric Cable TV subscribers in Wilkes-Barre. Founded in 1972 by Time, Inc. HBO was developed as a pay-movie/special service cable operation in New York. It was the first pay service for cable television in the nation.

## First Piano in America

In 1775, Johann Behrent built the first piano in **Philadelphia**. The German immigrant called it "Piano Forte." Behrent's version was square. Others built different versions of pianos in Philadelphia immediately following Behrent. It was the beginning of piano manufacturing in America. The piano was not patented in the United States until 1796.

## First Professional Football

The birthplace of professional American football is **Pittsburgh**. On November 12, 1892, at the Recreation Park, the Allegheny Athletic Association defeated the Pittsburgh Athletic

Club. The score was 4-0. William ("Pudge") Heffelfinger, who received $500 for playing, scored the winning touchdown. He was the first football player known to have been paid for playing in a game. Today, pro football traces its origin from this game.

Pennsylvania is the home to two professional football teams. The Pittsburgh Steelers and the Philadelphia Eagles provide sports fans with plenty of hard-hitting action each fall.

## First Public School

The first public school in the American Colonies opened its doors at the corner of 4th and Chestnut Streets in Philadelphia on February 12, 1698. A corporation entitled "The Overseers of the Publick Schoole founded in Philadelphia" established the school. Inoch Flower was the first Schoolmaster.

The governor and Council of this school ordered that: "All children and servants, male and female, whose parents, guardians and

*Pennsylvanians enjoy cheering their two professional football teams, the Pittsburgh Steelers and the Philadelphia Eagles.*

masters be willing to subject them to the rules and orders of the said schoole, shall from time to time, with the approval of the overseers thereof for the time being, be received or admitted, taught or instructed; the rich at reasonable rates, and the poor to be maintained and schooled for nothing."

## First Successful Twin Separation

Doctors separated Clara and Altagracia Rodriguez, conjoined twins from the Dominican Republic, in September 1974. It marked the first successful twin separation. The surgery was at The Children's Hospital in **Philadelphia**. Dr. Everett C. Koop (later the Surgeon General of the United States) was the chief surgeon.

## First Volunteer Fire Company

**Benjamin Franklin** is responsible for forming the first volunteer fire company in America. It took him several years, but his persistent goading caused a group of 30 men to come together to form the Union Fire Company on December 7, 1736. Their equipment included leather buckets, with strong bags and baskets, which they brought to every fire. These early firefighters met monthly to talk about firefighting methods and fire prevention.

## Five Nations

Indians formed confederacies such as the League of the Five Nations, which consisted of certain New York-Pennsylvania groups of Iroquoian speech. The Iroquois formed their confederacy about 1575. Known as Five Nations, it included the Mohawk, Oneida, Onondaga, Cayuga, and Seneca peoples. The leaders saw their confederation symbolically as a longhouse with an east and west door and a central fire. They were later known as **Six Nations**.

## Flag Stops

In the early days of the **Pennsylvania State Police**, patrol zones were set up and owners of telephones along the patrol zones were issued steel disks or flags to show a telephone (flag stop). The new State Police Motorcycle patrols started in 1920. Seeing a flag stop displayed, the State Police officer interrupted the patrol to telephone their station for a dispatch to an assignment. The flag stops ended in 1946 when the state police installed the first statewide radio telephone. It eliminated the need for Pennsylvania's "flag stops."

## Flight 93

The first battlefield of the War on Terrorism was in the skies over Pennsylvania. An United Airline jet smashed in a field over a reclaimed

*Thousands of mementos in honor of those that died are left by visitors at the site of where Flight 93 crashed near Shanksville on September 11, 2001.*

strip mine near Shanksville on September 11, 2001. Hijacked as part of the al-Qaeda attack on American soil, the Boeing 737 destined to San Francisco from Newark crash killed everyone on board—33 passengers, the seven members of the flight crew, and the four hijackers. "Let's roll!" was the battle cry of the passengers who fought back against the terrorists who were flying the plane to a target in Washington. Flight 93 was the fourth airline to crash that day, but the only one that did not take the lives of anyone on the ground.

## Fort Armstrong

Located on the river bank along present-day Route 66 near Kittanning, Fort Armstrong was an outpost built in June, 1779. It was named for Major General John Armstrong. It was abandoned later that year during autumn. The fort served the Brodhead expedition in its operations against the Senecas.

## Fort Augusta

Located in Northumberland County, at the confluence of the West and North Branches of the **Susquehanna River**, at present-day Sunbury, Fort Augusta was built in 1756. It was the largest and most important frontier stronghold on the upper Susquehanna, it was named for the mother of King George III. Built on land not yet obtained by agreement from the Indians, it was built on a square plan 204 feet by 204 feet, with four corner bastions and at least six buildings, a well, and an underground powder magazine. It was designed and built to accommodate 400 men. It was used through the **French and Indian War** and **Pontiac's Rebellion**. It remained in use until 1783.

## Fort Bedford

Fort Bedford, originally Raystown, was built during the summer of 1758 by the forces of Colonel Henry Bouquet. The fort (located at Bedford) was a rendezvous point for the expedition of General Forbes to advance and occupy Fort Duquesne at present-day Pittsburgh.

## Fort Duquesne

Located at the confluence of the Monongahela and **Allegheny Rivers**, it was a major strategic location and objective during the **French and Indian War**. The Virginians started building the fort in 1754. The French quickly drove them off on April 17, and completed the fort. They named it in honor of the Marquis de Duquesne, governor-general of New France. **George Washington**'s Virginia militia had failed to reach the fort before the arrival of the French. Washington returned to **Fort Necessity**. This key French position on the Ohio was used as a base for raids on the Pennsylvania frontier after 1755 during the **French and Indian War**.

On November 24, 1758, the French were heavily outnumbered. They abandoned and

*A Pennsylvania Historical Marker along the Susquehanna River in Sunbury marks the original position of Fort Augusta.*

*The point at Pittsburgh, here the confluence of the Allegheny and Monongahela Rivers empties into the Ohio River.*

burned Fort Duquesne as British General John Forbes advanced. The English rebuilt the fort and renamed it Fort Pitt, in honor of Secretary of State William Pitt. Fort Pitt was the point around which **Pittsburgh** grew.

## Fort Lafayette

Located on 9th Street near Penn Avenue in Pittsburgh, Fort Pittsburgh stood. Completed in 1792, it was built to protect Pittsburgh against Indian attacks and to serve as chief supply base for General Wayne's army in 1792 through 94. For a short time, Fort Lafayette was reactivated during the War of 1812.

## Fort Le Boeuf

As part of the French expansion from Canada into northwestern Pennsylvania, the French built a fort in present-day Waterford on U.S. 19. It was the first of three forts that was built

*Fort Le Boeuf was built three times, each for a different purpose.*

there. The French fort was erected in 1753 to guard the road into Ohio Valley. The French built Fort Le Boeuf in conjunction with **Fort Presque Isle**. The French abandoned their fort in 1759. In 1763, Indians burned the British fort, built in 1760. An American fort was built in 1794 to protect the settlers in this region of Erie County.

## Fort Ligonier

Fort Ligonier was built in present-day Westmoreland County in September 1758 as the base of British General John Forbes expedition to take **Fort Duquesne**. He was 50 miles from his objective. General Forbes ordered the building of a new road (now Route 30 or the Lincoln Highway), as well as a chain of fortifications, including this fort at the post of Loyalhanna. It was used as a supply post for a British-American army of 5,000 troops.

It served as an important link in the British supply and communication lines. During the **French and Indian War**, an attack occurred on October 12, 1758, but the post was defended and the attackers repelled. Forbes named Loyalhanna, Fort Ligonier, after his superior, British Commander in Chief Sir John Ligonier.

During the eight years of its use as a garrison, an enemy never took Fort Ligonier. It served as a post of passage to Fort Pitt. Throughout **Pontiac's Rebellion** in 1763, it was attacked but not captured. It was attacked twice prior to the decisive British victory at **Bushy Run**.

## Fort Loudon

This early fort was built in 1756 by the Pennsylvania Provincial Government. It was used as a starting point for Forbes' expedition to take Fort Duquesne at present-day **Pittsburgh** in 1758. In 1765, the colonists under James Smith forced the withdrawal of the British garrison from Fort Loudon.

## Fort Mifflin

Following Washington's defeat at the **Battle of Brandywine** in 1777, the British and Hessian troops marched into **Philadelphia**. Led by British General William Howe, his 20,000 men could have attacked the weakened Colonial Army, and probably defeated the Revolution. But Howe's own forces were running short of supplies. The supplies were on the Delaware on a fleet of British ships. General Thomas Mifflin occupied and strengthened the partially built British fort that guarded the waterways. The British attacked Mifflin's stronghold, and

*A politcal cartoon of the time taken from a London newspaper comments on the attack on Fort Mifflin, Mud Island.*

*An aerial view looking south over the fortifications at Fort Mifflin. In 1778 the fort covered over a quarter of the land that constituted the island.*

*The soldier's barracks at Fort Mifflin. The soldiers, officers, and commandant were all housed separately within the fort.*

about November 16, 1777, Fort Mifflin finally fell. The Americans had inflicted severe casualties on the British. The Colonists had carried out their mission: the British supply ships were delayed. With winter setting in, General Howe was unable to attack **Washington**'s troops. Fort Mifflin was restored in 1795, and again staffed during the War of 1812, although it saw no action. During the Civil War, the Union army used it as a prison camp. The Fort was disarmed in 1904. It is Philadelphia's only fort, found near the present-day Philadelphia International Airport.

## Fort Necessity

In the summer of 1754, the confrontation at Fort Necessity was the beginning of the war fought by England and France for control of the North American continent. The battle at Fort Necessity also was the first major event in the military career of **George Washington**. The 22-year-old colonel from Virginia surrendered to the French, the only time he ever had laid down his arms to an enemy.

Washington saw combat for the first time in the "Great Meadow," found near present-day US Route 40, east of Uniontown. When George Washington arrived in the area in May, he intended to set up a camp from which to base his operations while waiting for more militia and British regulars. After meeting the French war party, Washington returned to the Great Meadows and fortified his position by building a round stockade and earthworks around his storehouse.

On the morning of July 3, 1754, about 600 French and 100 Indians approached Fort Necessity. The French took positions in the woods. Washington withdrew his men to the entrenchments. It rained throughout the day, flooding the marshy area. Although both sides suffered casualties, the British losses were greater than French and Indian losses.

The two sides fought sporadically until about 8 p.m. Then Capt. Louis Coulon de Villiers, commander of the French force requested a truce to discuss the surrender of Washington's command. Near midnight, after several hours of haggling and negotiation, the two commanders reduced their treaty to writing. Washington signed the accord. The French allowed the British to withdraw with the honors of war, keeping their baggage and weapons, but having to surrender their swivel guns. The British troops marched from Fort Necessity to Wills Creek on the morning of July 4, and from there, they marched back to Virginia. The French burned Fort Necessity and returned to Fort Duquesne. It was the beginning of a bloody and prolonged seven-year war.

Today, the site of Fort Necessity is a national park. Its 900 acres include a visitor center, the battlefield with the rebuilt Fort Necessity, and the Mount Washington Tavern.

## Fort Presque Isle

The French considered the Ohio Valley a vital link between New France (Canada) and Louisiana. From Canada, they advanced southward and westward, from Fort Niagara on Lake Ontario, driving out English traders and claiming the Ohio River Valley for France. As part of their advance into present-day Pennsylvania, the French built Fort Presque Isle near Lake Erie in 1753, and then burned and abandoned it in 1759. The British built a fort there (now present-day **Erie**) in 1760, which Indians captured in 1763 during **Pontiac's Rebellion**. This fort supported **Fort Le Boeuf** in Waterford.

## Fort Reed

Present-day Clinton County was protected by Fort Reed, then the most western frontier defense for settlers of the Susquehanna Valley. Fort Reed served as a base of operations for the

scouting parties. William Reid's stockade house was one of the first buildings in today's town of Lock Haven.

## Fort Roberdeau

Built in present-day Blair county near **Altoona**, Fort Roberdeau was built during the American Revolutionary War. Daniel Roberdeau was a wealthy **Philadelphia** merchant, a member of Congress, and a staunch patriot in favor of independence. Philadelphia leaders elected him Brigadier General. He arrived in late April with supplies from **Carlisle** and the intentions of setting up a lead smelting operation and erecting a stockade. His "Lead Mine Fort," as it was called in the 18th century, was built during the spring and summer of 1778 to protect lead mining operations in Sinking Stream Valley. Unlike most frontier forts built of logs placed vertically, Fort Roberdeau was necessarily built of horizontal logs. The limestone strata of the valley, with scant topsoil, prevented the normal procedure of digging a trench, standing the logs in it, and then backfilling. The fort was never attacked, but it served as a safe refuge to soldiers, lead miners, and local settlers. It was designated as a storage depot for ordnance and ammunition for the Bedford County area until March, 1780, and contained four double fortified four-pounder cannons with traveling carriages. Lead produced here was shipped east.

## Fort Sullivan

Located between the Chemung and **Susquehanna Rivers** near Athens, Bradford County, General John Sullivan directed the building of a fort during August 1779. With his camp on the flats near the New York and Pennsylvania border, it was the base for the central campaign and defeat of the Tory-Indian alliance during the Revolutionary War.

## Fort Swatara

Captain Frederick Smith improved the fortifications and guarded the stockade blockhouse at present-day Lickdale, Lebanon County, in early 1756 to guard the Swatara Gap and protect the frontier settlements. Swatara Gap in the Blue Mountain, named for the Swatara Creek, was the gateway which enemy Indians used to raid the frontier settlements during the **French and Indian War**. Originally built by Peter Hedrick in 1755, Fort Swatara provided early Pennsylvania settlers with protection against Indian raids.

## Foster, Stephen

Born July 4, 1826 in Lawrenceville, Stephen Foster became America's first professional songwriter. He wrote many of his songs for minstrel shows. Foster's popular songs remain well-known classics to this day. Despite the great popularity of his music, Foster lived in poverty all his live. He died in New York City on January 13, 1864 and was buried in **Pittsburgh**.

## Foster, Thomas J.

Thomas Foster started education by mail. An editor, publisher, and veteran, Foster was born in Pottsville on January 1, 1843. He created the International Correspondence Schools in 1891. Foster was also an advocate of mine safety laws. He died in **Scranton**, October 14, 1936. The International Correspondence Schools continue today offering training and education by mail.

## Founding of Organized Labor

On November 15, 1881, in Turner Hall, a convention was held that formed the organization which became the American Federation of Labor. In a short time, it was the nation's largest labor federation. On November 14, 1938, the first convention of the Congress of

Industrial Organizations was held, representing 34 international unions. In 1955, both the American Federation of Labor and the Congress of Industrial Organizations merged into the AFL-CIO.

## Franklin, Benjamin

It is impossible to summarize the full, long, and remarkable life of Benjamin Franklin in a few words. No matter what is written, there is always something else to be written, something else to be added to his life story.

No single word describes him. Born in Boston on January 17, 1706, he was the youngest son of Josiah and Abiah (Folger) Franklin. At age 13, with little formal schooling, he was apprenticed to his brother James, a printer. While learning the printing trade, Blackbeard the Pirate was captured. Franklin wrote a ballad about it, the preview of many more of his writings to come later.

In 1720, the young Franklin left home, taking up residence in a boardinghouse. He stopped going to church on Sundays, so he had more time to study. In 1721 James started a newspaper called the New England Courant. Benjamin anonymously published articles that won wide acclaim and recognition. A few years later, Franklin became a vegetarian. In September 1723, he ran away from his apprenticeship, fleeing to New York City, and then moving on to **Philadelphia**. There he found a job as a printer, and boarded in the home of John Read. The following year, he returned to Boston and unsuccessfully tried to borrow money from his father to start a printing shop.

*The Benjamin Franklin Buildings in Philadelphia, where he lived and worked. He also established the post office and printed currency in these buildings.*

The Ben Franklin Bridge connects Philadelphia to Camden, New Jersey.

He returned to Philadelphia, and started a courtship with Deborah Read.

With the encouragement of then Provincial Governor William Keith, Franklin traveled to London to buy printing equipment. Keith's letters of credit for Franklin never appeared, so he remained stranded in London. He found work as a printer, and began attending theater. His studies flourished, as he voraciously read and published pamphlets. Back in Philadelphia, Deborah Read married John Rogers.

In July 1726, Franklin returned to Philadelphia. He worked for Thomas Denham, a merchant who had loaned him the money to return home. Franklin worked as a bookkeeper in Denham's store that sold imported clothes and hardware. Within the next few years, Franklin returned to his trade, and his fingers were again black with printer's ink. He opened a print shop in a partnership with Hugh

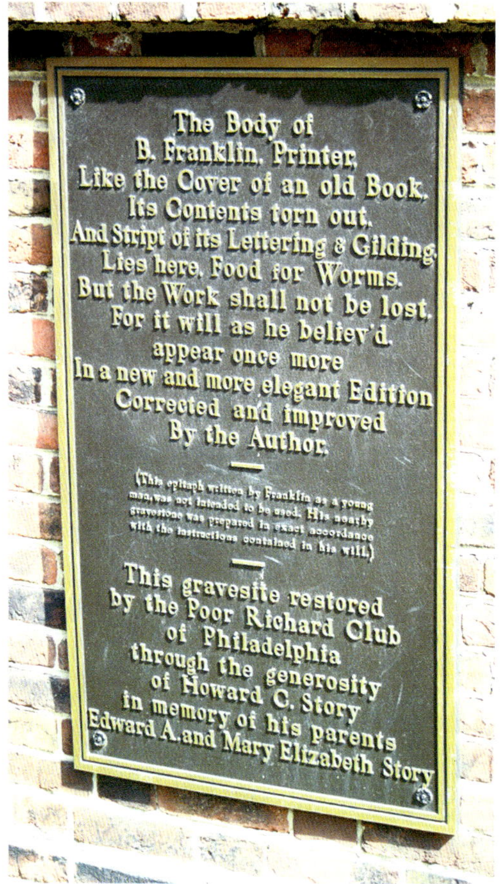


A marker on the wall at the graveyard where Benjamin Franklin is buried.

*Benjamin Franklin's grave in Philadelphia.*

*The Christ Church cemetery, in downtown Philadelphia. Five signatories of the Declaration of Independence, including Benjamin Franklin, are buried here.*

Meredith. It was in this time that an affair led to the birth of his first child, an illegitimate son named William. Later, John Rogers, Deborah Read's husband, stole a slave and fled from Philadelphia.

With his print shop set up, Franklin produced pamphlets, acquired the *Pennsylvania Gazette* and invigorated the newspaper. He became the official printer for Pennsylvania. He organized a discussion group that became the American Philosophical Society. In 1730, he married Deborah Read Rogers. In the next few years, Franklin published *Poor Richard's Alamanack*, saw the birth of his son Francis Folger, and set up the Library Company, as a private book lending organization.

In 1734, he bought his first property on Market Street in Philadelphia. Eventually, he acquired several adjoining lots, to house his print shop and for retail space. Today, this property is known as Franklin Court.

In 1736, Franklin printed currency for New Jersey, and became the Clerk for the Pennsylvania assembly. His son Francis died of smallpox. He was four years old.

The following year, Benjamin Franklin became the postmaster of Philadelphia. In 1739, he turned environmentalist and protested the slaughterhouses and tanneries that were working too close to the docks and public streets.

He went on to invent and sell the Franklin stove. He organized and publicized a project to sponsor plant-collecting trips by renowned Philadelphia botanist John Bartram.

In 1743, the year his daughter Sally was born, he developed an interest in Natural Philosophy, which included electricity. By 1746, he experimented in electricity. The following year, Franklin wrote and published *The Plain Truth*, a pamphlet arguing for better military readiness in Pennsylvania. The pamphlet included the first political cartoon published in America.

In 1748, Franklin became a soldier in the Pennsylvania militia, after turning down a commission as a Colonel, citing military inexperience. Franklin made bold proposals for changes in education, and that led to the establishment in 1751 of what today is the University of Pennsylvania.

Benjamin conducted his famous electricity experiment by flying a kite in 1752. He also wrote a plan for the union of the colonies for their common security and defense. He set up the Philadelphia Contributionship for Insuring of Houses from Loss Against Fire. He invented the lightning rod and developed an explanation that there were two kinds of electricity, positive and negative.

He went on to receive honorary degrees from Harvard and Yale. He invented the armonica, a musical instrument that used glasses to produce notes. Of all his inventions, the armonica was his favorite. Franklin had poor vision and used glasses to read, and had another pair to see distance. He tired of changing them, so he figured out a way to make his glasses let him see both near and far. He had his two pairs of spectacles cut in half and put a half of each lens in a single frame. Today, Franklin's simple invention is called bifocals. When his brother suffered from kidney stones, Franklin tried to make him feel a tad better. He developed a flexible urinary catheter that appears to have been the first one produced in America. He made eight long ocean voyages to Europe, which game him a lot of time to think. On one of those trips, his fertile mind figured out a way to make ships work better and more safely by inventing watertight bulkheads. He also invented the odometer, an invention he needed to ascertain shorter routes when he was postmaster.

It was in 1754 when he was Pennsylvania's delegate to the intercolonial congress that met at Albany to discuss the threatened French and Indian War. Franklin traveled to England, having become the Colonial Agent for Pennsylvania, Massachusetts, New Jersey, and Georgia.

After returning to Philadelphia in 1762, he again was sent to England in 1764. Franklin tried to arbitrate the conflicts between the colonies and Great Britain, but he realized the inevitability of war and sailed for America.

In 1775, back in Pennsylvania, Franklin became a member of the Second Continental Congress. He served as the chair of the

*Christchurch in Pennsylvania, one of the early churches in the colonial town.*

was elected to the position of Postmaster General of the Colonies.

Franklin presided over the Constitutional Convention of Pennsylvania in 1776. He also served on the committee of five that drafted the **Declaration of Independence**. Congress chose him to serve as a diplomat to seek support from France. Popular in French circles, Franklin secured aid and concessions that represented the turning point of the American Revolution. In 1781 Franklin, with John Adams and John Jay, were appointed by Congress to finish a peace treaty with Great Britain. The United States and Britain signed the final treaty at Versailles on September 3, 1783.

Franklin returned to Philadelphia in 1785, and then he became president of the Pennsylvania executive council. He served as a delegate in 1787 at the Birthplace of the U.S. Constitution. One of his last public acts was to sign a petition to the Congress of the United States in 1790 urging to abolish slavery.

On April 17, 1790, a beloved Benjamin Franklin died in Philadelphia at the age of 84. Over 20,000 Philadelphians mourned his death and attended his funeral at Philadelphia's Christ Church Burial Ground.

In 1728, as a young man, Franklin had composed his own mock epitaph, which read:

> The Body of B. Franklin
> Printer;
> Like the Cover of an old Book,
> Its Contents torn out,
> And stript of its Lettering and
> Gilding,
> Lies here, Food for Worms.
> But the Work shall not be lost:
> For it will, as he believ'd, appear
> once more,
> In a new and more perfect Edition,
> Corrected and improved
> By the Author.

But his gravestone simply reads:

> BENJAMIN
> and
> DEBORAH
> FRANKLIN
> 1790

Pennsylvania's most influential citizen, Benjamin Franklin cannot be described in a few words. He was a printer, writer, publisher, statesman, diplomat, environmentalist, business leader, philosopher, inventor, postal chief, political leader, revolutionary, and much more.

## French and Indian War

It started in the 1750s and lasted through the early 1760s. The British, the French, and many American Indian nations engaged in a brutal, bloody war that altered American history. There were a series of conflicts and battles, which are now collectively known as the French and Indian War.

The conflicts started over who would control the Ohio River Valley. Both the French and the British sought to dominate, govern, and rule the vast region of the American frontier. George Washington, was an early participant. The French had settlements in Canada, the Illinois Country, and New Orleans. The British settlements were east of the Allegheny Mountains, along the eastern seaboard.

The French needed to control the Ohio River Valley to connect their North American colonies. The British believed they had an indisputable claim to the entire Ohio River Valley. So did the American Indians who lived there. When the three powers—motivated by political and economic wants—wanted control over the same land, a war was unavoidable.

Eventually both France and Britain declared war on each other. War was not new to either of these two powerful European nations. They had been adversaries and enemies in many previous wars. Their bitter fighting spread from North America to Europe, the

*Early frontier forts provided a safe haven and protection for Pennsylvania's early settlers.*

*A reconstructed fort, it was used to protect early western Pennsylvania settlers from Indian attacks.*

*A young Virginian saw his first military action in Western Pennsylvania and the area of modern day Pittsburgh. George Washington, a member of the Virginia militia, recommended a fort be built at the confluence of the Allegheny and Monongahela Rivers into the Ohio River.*

Caribbean, the Philippines, and India. The American Indians fought with brutal butchery tactics for their own cause. They were influential in shaping the eventual outcome of the war.

In 1753, the French began their expansion by building a chain of forts from Lake Erie to the forks of the Ohio River. It was the beginning of their effort to protect the strategic Ohio Valley. Robert Dinwiddie, the British governor of the Virginia colony, tried unsuccessfully to warn them of their intrusion into English territory. He sent a young Virginian military officer, George Washington, with the message.

Washington traveled to present-day Waterford in northwestern Pennsylvania to meet with Legardeur de St. Pierre, the commandant of the French at **Fort Le Boeuf**. Part diplomatic mission, part a military mission to assess the French army strength, 21-year-old Major Washington was entertained cordially and politely, but was firmly told the French were not leaving the territory. Despite the **near drowning of Washington**, he returned to Virginia and delivered the French response.

The British responded by sending an armed force to expel the French. In 1754, the French defeated the British troops at the **Battle of Fort Necessity**, repelling them from Pennsylvania and sending them back to Virginia. It was the first of many clashes that would take place in Pennsylvania. Indians aligned with the French, and savagely raided settler's villages and farms. Raiders butchered and used tomahawks, clubs, and knives to hack to bits the early western Pennsylvanians. Indians kidnapped women and children as battle trophies and later slaves. There was no end to the brutality and harshness.

While British forces and colonial troops gained some small victories, the French and their Native American allies won battle after battle. When British prime minister William Pitt took office in 1757, he made victory against the French in America his top priority. Pitt launched a series of well-coordinated military campaigns and appointed able commanders to lead them. One of Pitts other accomplishments was that he began treating the Americans as allies rather than subordinates.

Settlers pushed westward in Pennsylvania, setting up homes and farms in valleys where just years before earlier pioneers were slaughtered. Despite the hardships, they continued the expansion. Frontier forts were built to provide them with protection from Indian attacks.

In 1758, a combined British and American force won several important victories and finally defeated the French main army at Québec in 1759. The fall of the French colonial city of Montreal in 1760 brought the end of fighting between the French and British on the American continent. The Treaty of Paris (1763) ended French control in Canada and all territories east of the Mississippi River. The British and French agreed Britain would control the Ohio River Valley. The French and Indian War decided that English rather than French ideas and institutions would dominate North America. The British gained more territory than it could control from across the Atlantic Ocean. Its vast new empire was difficult to govern.

The British failed to carry on their promises to the American Indians and they started new and unfavorable trade policies. The American Indians and the British continued their struggle over the land. **Pontiac's War** started in 1763. Eventually the British won, and even more settlers pushed most of the Indians westward. The British tried to raise revenue by taxing the colonies, which eventually led to the **Declaration of Independence**.

The French were desirous to avenge their defeat by the British in America, and that resulted in a French alliance with the American rebels during the Revolutionary War. The French involvement with the American Revolution eventually caused the fiscal crisis that led to the French Revolution in 1789.

The French and Indian War had a major impact on the early settlers of Pennsylvania. It cost thousands of lives, and slowed, but did not stop, the western settlement of Pennsylvania.

## Friedensstadt

Founded in 1770 by Christian Delaware Indians brought from upper Allegheny by the Reverend David Zeisberger, Friedensstadt was an Indian village near present-day Moravia, in Lawrence County. Friedensstadt was abandoned on April 13, 1773 when the Indians moved west to the Muskingum in Ohio. The

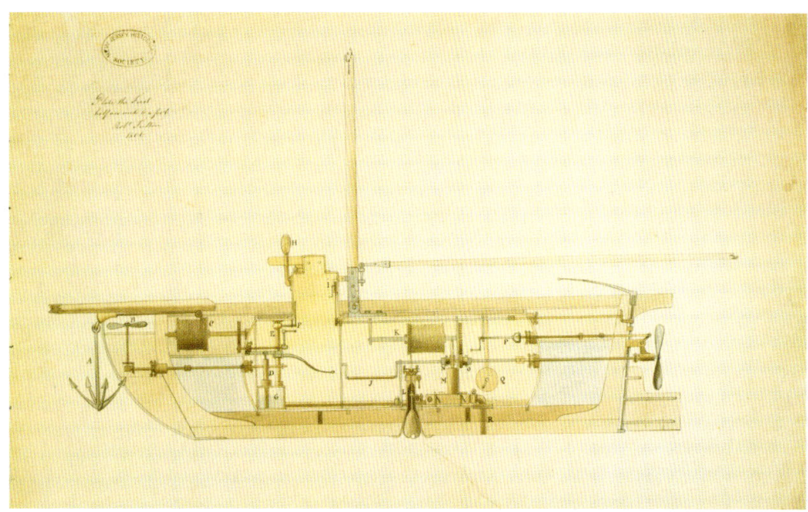

Cross-section drawing of Robert Fulton's submarine.

A portrait of Robert Fulton, the inventor of the steamboat.

Pennsylvania militia massacred some there on March 8, 1782.

## Friendship Hill

Friendship Hill was the frontier home of Albert Gallatin. Now a national historic park, it is about 12 miles southwest of Uniontown. The well-preserved country estate depicts the era immediately following the American Revolution. The grounds of the park are tranquil, with woods, meadows, trails, and a picnic area.

## Fulton, Robert

Born in 1765 in southern Lancaster County, Robert Fulton became an engineer and inventor who developed the first useful submarine and torpedo in 1800. Fulton also perfected the design of the first practical steamboat, the Clermont, in 1807. He invented many other machines before his death in 1815.

The birthplace of Robert Fulton, in Lancaster County.

## Gallatin, Albert

Although not born in Pennsylvania, Albert Gallatin was an important and well-known Pennsylvanian in his day. The Swiss born Gallatin loved the ideals of America, and contributed to setting up the financial foundation of the new nation. Surrendering his inherited fortune and social position because of "a love for independence in the freest country of the universe," Gallatin came to America and settled in the Pennsylvania frontier. During the **Whiskey Rebellion**, he played a leading role, though he was much more moderate than many, and recommended against breaking with the Federal government.

*Albert Gallatin was a Senator from Pennsylvania, Congressman, Secretary of the Treasury, U.S. Minister to France (1816–1823), and President of the National Bank of New York. He lived in western Pennsylvania.*

Gallatin served briefly as a Senator and a Representative from Pennsylvania, where he showed a great insight into the financial problems of the new nation. When the nation elected Jefferson as President, he appointed Gallatin as Secretary of the Treasury, where he served for 13 years. Gallatin proposed building the **National Road** and, as the Treasury Secretary, he arranged for the funding to buy the Louisiana Purchase and explore the new lands. When Lewis and Clark explored the western frontier, they discovered that three rivers formed the beginnings of the Missouri River. They named these rivers after the three men whom they considered to be the most important Americans alive: Jefferson, Madison, and a Pennsylvanian, Albert Gallatin.

Gallatin also served as Minister to both England and France. In 1817, he retired from public service and moved to New York. There he became the President of the National Bank of the City of New York and founded New York University.

His Pennsylvania home, known as **Friendship Hill**, in Point Marion, located on the banks of the Monongahela River, is now a National Historic Site and open for tours.

## Garard's Fort

Located in Greene County, Garard's Fort was a frontier refuge during the Revolutionary War. It was a hostile area. On May 12, 1782, Reverend John Corbly's wife and three of his children were killed while on their way to church. Two of the Baptist minister's other children were also wounded in the same Indian attack. The fort served as a station for a small number of Virginia Militia. The area had been claimed as part of Monongalia County, Virginia, before the Pennsylvania border had been established.

## Garrett, Thomas

A Quaker, Thomas Garrett, first lived at Thornfield in Delaware County before 1822, when he moved to Wilmington, Delaware. By the 1860s, he had assisted over 2,700 slaves escape to freedom on the **Underground Railroad**. He became one of the well-known abolitionists before the Civil War. His father (also named Thomas) had established Thornfield in 1800.

## Gates, Horatio

An American revolutionary soldier born in Maldon, England, Gates served as the President of the Board of War during the American Revolution. In 1777, Gates became commander of the Northern Department. He defeated the British army at the battles of Stillwater and Saratoga in New York.

While Congress was meeting in York, Gates took part in a plot to overthrow Washington as the Commander in Chief of the Continental Army. Hatched by Major General Thomas Conway, the plan was to replace Washington with Gates.

During a dinner at Gates' Home in York, a simple toast by **Marquis de Lafayette** dissolved the scheme instantly, bringing the dinner to an embarrassing end. Lafayette was the French representative to the American colonies and loyal to Washington. He threw his support—and thus the coveted support of France—behind Washington during a dinner toast. Washington remained the Commander of the Continental Army until the end of the War.

*Portrait of Horatio Gates.*

BICKERSTAFF's
BOSTON
ALMANACK,
For the Year of our REDEMPTION,
1778.
Being the Second Year of AMERICAN INDEPENDENCE.
And the Second after LEAP-YEAR.
Calculated for the Meredian of BOSTON, Lat. 42′ 25° N.
CONTAINING, beſides what is neceſſary in an Almanack, a Variety of uſeful and inſtructing Pieces.
The GLORIOUS WASHINGTON and GATES.

Calculated by BENJAMIN WEST, a Student in Aſtronomy, at *Providence*, and Author of this Almanack for twelve Years paſt, except thoſe *falſe* Editions printed by *Mycall*, of *Newbury*, for 76 and by *Boyle* and *Draper* and *Phillips*, of *Boſton*, for 77: The Author of this *genuine* Copy never had any Connexions with thoſe Printers.

DANVERS: Printed by E. RUSSELL, at his Printing-Offic

*The* Bickerstaff's Boston Almanac *in 1778 featured a dedication on its title page to Colonial Generals George Washington and Horatio Gates, leaders in the revolution against Britain.*

Gates retired and returned to his farm in the winter of 1780, but Congress recalled him and gave him command of the Army of the South. British general Charles Cornwallis defeated his forces near Camden, South Carolina.

The house that Gates lived in while in **York** has been restored, and stands beside the Golden Plough Tavern. Both places are on the National Register of Historic Places and open for tours.

## Gavin, James

Known as the "Jumping General," James Gavin was the Commanding Officer of the 82nd Airborne Division that jumped in Normandy on D-Day, 1944. Born in 1907, James Gavin was the son of an unwed Irish immigrant. After placement in a New York City orphanage as a toddler, Martin and Mary Gavin, a Pennsylvania coal-mining family living near Mt. Carmel, adopted him. His youth taught him discipline and hard work. He enlisted in the U.S. Army at age 17, and showing promise, his commanders selected him for admittance to West Point. He rose to the rank of Major General.

## Germantown

After a 75-day voyage, 13 **Mennonite** families from Krefeld, Germany, landed in **Philadelphia** on October 6, 1683. **William Penn** greeted them. The hearty Krefelders settled on a parcel of land six miles north of newly founded Philadelphia. Penn advised the new settlers not to live on scattered farms, but to use the European pattern of living together in a town.

They quickly went to work. Cellars were dug and covered, providing shelters for the first winter. Even though that Pennsylvania winter presented many hardships, the new settlers endured. The nickname for the new town, "Armentown" (town of the poor) became archaic by their hard work and skills in the trades of weaving, tailoring, carpentry, and shoemaking.

They built log homes first, and later of native stone. They raised flax, built looms, and used their spinning wheels. When they saw wild grapes, they set up vineyards. The official seal of Germantown today includes a grapevine on one leaf, flax blossoms and a weaver's spool with the inscription "Vinum, Linum et Textrinum," to show the people lived from grapes, flax, and trade. The Germantown Fair, first held in 1701 became a center of displaying and selling the products of these industrious and hardworking craftsworkers. By the end of the 1600s Germantown had a wide Main Street bordered by peach trees, and a central market. America's first paper mill, the Rittenhouse Mill was established in Germantown.

Following the **Battle of Brandywine**, the British seized Germantown. Because of its productive industries, the British recognized its strategic importance. During the **Battle of Germantown**, the British prevailed.

*The Upsala house, built in 1798, stands in the Germantown district of Philadelphia, Pennsylvania.*

## Germantown, Battle of

The Battle of Germantown occurred on October 4, 1777. A British regiment occupied Germantown, then a two-mile-long hamlet of stone houses. The British and Hessian troops (German mercenaries hired by the British) successfully defended their positions from a full assault by Washington's Continental Army. Washington launched a surprise attack and advanced into Germantown by two roads. British troops took refuge in a stone mansion owned by former Provincial Chief Justice Benjamin Chew. American soldiers, ill-trained, underfed, and poorly clothed, mistook firing near the mansion for an enemy attack and opened fire on their own troops. Attempts to take the Chew mansion by the American soldiers proved futile. Over 1,000 Americans were killed, wounded, or missing that day. Despite the bloody defeat, Americans remained

determined, and went on to endure bitter cold and starvation at **Valley Forge**. Washington's bold tactics helped to win French aid for the cause of independence.

## Gettysburg, Battle of

Just seven miles north of the **Mason-Dixon Line**, sleepy but prosperous Gettysburg was a peaceful, politically active town in Adams County. Hardly anyone had ever heard of it before July 1863. The county seat, it was a town of 3,400. It enjoyed the modern technology of the day, with a telegraph, railroad service, and three weekly newspapers.

During June 1863, Confederate General Robert E. Lee ordered his Army of Northern Virginia to invade Pennsylvania. The Confederates planned to capture **Harrisburg**, a Northern capital. It would demoralize the North, and take away their will to fight. It would cut off materials from Pennsylvania factories and farms that were supplying the Federal forces. A decisive victory in the North, the Confederate reasoned, would cause European recognition of their new government, which would force the Union also to recognize the Confederate States of America.

Following the Battle of Chancellorsville, Virginia, between May 2 and May 4, 1863, an important but costly victory for the Confederates, Lee reorganized his battle-hardened army into three corps. His corps commanders were three lieutenant generals, James Longstreet, Richard Stoddert Ewell, and Ambrose Powell Hill. Lee planned to position the federal army into a susceptible position. Lee's army had traversed the Blue Ridge Mountains, marched up the Shenandoah Valley, and, crossing Maryland, invaded the **Commonwealth** of Pennsylvania. Lee stayed in Virginia as long as possible, hoping the Union army was thinking that Washington, D.C. was their intended target.

When the Army of the Potomac realized the Southerners had invaded Pennsylvania, they set in motion a fast pursuit into

*Bullet holes are still visible in Gettysburg's houses and buildings, more than 140 years after the battle.*

Pennsylvania. Lee knew the Federals would chase his army. When he learned federal troops were north of the Potomac, Lee ordered his entire army to turn and concentrate at Gettysburg.

Lee's army was about 75,000 strong. The Army of the Potomac, under command of Union General George Gordon Meade, who had just been given his command on June 28 by **President Abraham Lincoln**, was about 85,000 strong.

*Reporting the news of the Battle of Gettysburg was important during the Civil War. Alfred R. Waud, an artist of* Harper's Weekly, *was photographed sketching on the Gettysburg battlefield.*

### Before the Battle

On June 30, troops from Confederate General Hill's corps, who were on their way to Gettysburg, faced federal troops that Meade had moved to intercept the Confederate army. The Federal troops were cavalry, under the command of Union General John Buford. He quickly recognized the Gettysburg area was an excellent place to set up a battlefield. Buford discovered the best defensive ground, and he maneuvered his troopers to engage the Confederates in such a way to delay their movements to the higher, easily defended, ground. Buford hoped to stop the advancing Confederates until the entire force from the Army of the Potomac could arrive.

### July 1

The Battle of Gettysburg began on July 1, just west of Gettysburg, with a fight between Confederate General Hill's brigades and the Union General Buford's dismounted cavalry. Federal infantry, under the command of Pennsylvania native Major General John Fulton Reynolds, relieved Buford's cavalry.

Hill faced tough resistance from the combined Union forces. The fighting continued until Confederate General Ewell arrived from the north. The Confederates pushed the federal troops from their forward positions, forcing them to fall back to Culp's Hill and Cemetery Ridge, located just southeast of Gettysburg. This was the high, good ground that Union General Buford recognized the previous day.

Both sides had fought hard that first day. The Union troops suffered more losses than the Confederates. The Confederates took more than 4,000 men prisoner, and Union **General John F. Reynolds** died of a gunshot wound in battle. The Federals captured Confederate General Archer, the first Confederate officer taken prisoner after Lee assumed command of the Confederate army. Confederate General Ewell's corps did not move in to attack the Union troops, but waited for General Longstreet to bring in his corps to reinforce the outnumbered Confederate troops. This gave the advancing Federals more time to arrive and get into position.

**July 2**

Union General Meade formed his forces in the shape of a fishhook, extending westward from Culp's Hill and southward along Cemetery Ridge to the hills of Little Round Top and Round Top. The Confederate's position was in a long, thin line, with Longstreet and Ewell on the flanks and Hill in the center.

General Lee, against the advice of Longstreet, decided to attack the Federal positions. Lee's cavalry, which was under command of Confederate General J.E.B. Stuart, had not yet arrived in Gettysburg. Not having use of his cavalry hampered Lee's strategies.

Longstreet finally advanced in late afternoon, which allowed the Federal troops to fortify their positions for the expected assault. Union General Abner Doubleday strengthened his position on Cemetery Hill.

The federals held Cemetery Ridge and Little Round Top. Longstreet moved Confederate troops along the Peach Orchard, south of Gettysburg, and drove the Federal troops under the command of Union General Daniel Sickles from their positions there. Dead and wounded lay strewn in the nearby wheat field. Ewell took part of Culp's Hill, but he could not break the federal line on the eastern part of Cemetery Ridge.

Late in the night of July 2, Meade held a council of war. After conferring with his commanders, he decided not to retreat.

**July 3**

The troops of the Army of the Potomac were now secure in their positions on the high ground and the Confederates had lost the advantage of their offensive stance. Confederate General Stuart had finally arrived, but he was too late for Lee to take advantage of the cavalry.

Despite the opposition from his other subordinate generals, General Lee ordered an attack. His offensive did not begin until the afternoon in hot, sultry summer heat. Three Confederate divisions, which included the division led by Major General George E. Pickett,

*Many buildings in and surrounding Gettysburg were turned into field hospitals during the three-day battle. Many bear historic markers.*

totaling less than 15,000 men, charged Cemetery Ridge against a punishing and contemptuous bombardment of federal artillery and musket fire. Although the Confederates broke Meade's first line of defense, they could not sustain their assault. They soon fell back. The attack, now forever known as Pickett's Charge, cost the Confederates three-fourths of their force. The Battle of Gettysburg was over but only General Lee knew it at that time.

**July 4**

The Federals waited for another attack from the Confederates. But Lee knew he could not attack again. His losses were too great. He had planned his retreat shortly after Pickett's Charge, and on July 4, his Confederate troops

*A marker designates the place where President Lincoln gave his Gettysburg Address. Visitors leave pennies to mark their visit.*

*The First Shot Marker, located about three miles west of Gettysburg (on present-day Route 30), indicates where the first shot was fired that started the three days of bloody fighting.*

*The statue of Major General John Reynolds at the Soldiers' National Cemetery in Gettysburg.*

*The gatehouse at the Evergreen Cemetery was heavily damaged during the Battle of Gettysburg.*

began the withdrawal. Lee ordered his army to return to Virginia, all the while expecting a counterattack from the Federals. Meade chose not to attack immediately, perhaps because of the heavy rains that hampered pursuit of the retreating Confederates.

**Aftermath**

During the three days of the battle, the Union Army suffered 23,000 casualties, and the Confederates had at least 25,000. Over 7,000 men were killed, and more than 20,000 were wounded. Many more were missing, or taken prisoner. The farmland of Adams County that had been turned into a battlefield was devastated. Among the destroyed crops and the dead and wounded soldiers lay tons of military equipment and over 5,000 dead horses.

Most military historians consider the Battle of Gettysburg as the turning point in the American Civil War. The battle destroyed the Confederate's offensive strategy and it stopped the Confederates' second and last major invasion of the North. The battle forced the Confederates to fight a defensive war, and their inability to make and transport goods and supplies doomed them. Once again, Pennsylvania contributed so much to the future of the nation.

## Gimbel's

Adam Gimbel and his two sons, Jacob and Isaac, opened their first department store in **Philadelphia** in 1894. Over the years, the Gimbels expanded their department store business into other major cities, including **Pittsburgh**, New York City, Chicago, Detroit, and Beverly Hills. The chain closed its last store in 1987.

## Girard, Stephen

French-born in 1750, Stephen Girard arrived in **Philadelphia** in 1776. He became an American financier and philanthropist who bought out the Bank of the United States in 1812 and helped finance the War of 1812. He became America's wealthiest citizen and contributed much to the early growth of his adopted new

G

*Groundhog, Punxsutawney Phil, the famous old seer of Gobbler's Knob makes his once-a-year weather prognostication for members of the Punxsutawney Groundhog Club, February 2, 1963.*

nation. His business interests included shipping, construction, banking, coal mining, and railroads. He died in 1831.

## Girty, Simon

There was no one more hated and feared in Colonial America than Simon Girty. Born in 1741 near present-day **Harrisburg**, what was then the western frontier of Pennsylvania, Girty became the "Great Renegade" for turning traitor during the American Revolution. From 1759 until the Revolution, Girty served as interpreter and scout at Fort Pitt. He acted as interpreter for the Continental army, but in 1778 he deserted to the British and was labeled a traitor by the Pennsylvania legislature. During the war, Girty led raiding parties of British and Native Americans along the northern and western frontiers. After the war, he settled near Detroit, which remained in British hands, and continued to lead Native American raids on outposts. The traitor was bloodthirsty, and did nothing to stop the Indians from slaughtering settlers. He died in 1818, near Butler.

## Goode, Alexander

On February 3, 1943, a torpedo hit and sank the USS *Dorchester* in the North Atlantic. Four Army chaplains lost their lives when they gave up their life jackets because the supply ran out. The chaplains helped other soldiers to board lifeboats, then prayed as they went down with the ship. One of those Chaplains was Rabbi Alexander Goode from York. Only 230 men of the 902 aboard survived the attack.

## Greenwood, Grace

Sara Jane Clarke Lippincott, born in Pompey, New York, September 23, 1823, moved with her family to New Brighton, in Beaver County, when she was a teenager. Educated at nearby schools, the pioneer woman correspondent wrote poetry and books. She also wrote many popular juvenile stories under her penname, Grace Greenwood. She was a supporter of the women's rights movement by 1850, and strong Union supporter during the Civil War. She died in New Rochelle, New York, on April 20, 1904.

## Groundhog Day

At sunrise on every February 2, the entire nation pauses for a moment. It seems that no one can predict the end of winter better than a furry prognosticator known as Punxsutawney Phil. The country waits for word from Gobbler's Knob, if the wily critter sees his shadow or not. If Phil does not, spring is just around the corner. If he does, there will be six more weeks of winter. The ritual of observing the groundhog grew from an early German settler's tradition. Pennsylvania's annual tradition became immortalized in 1993 when **Hollywood** trekked to the state to make *Groundhog Day*, starring Andie MacDowell and Bill Murray. Other groundhogs in the state are also known to offer predictions.

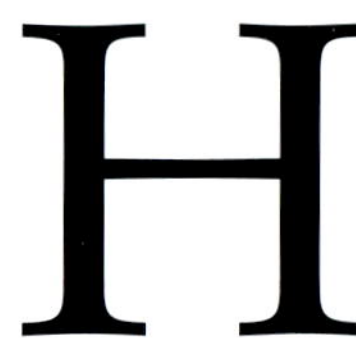

## Hancock, Winfield Scott

Born in Montgomery Square on February 14, 1824, Winfield Scott Hancock became one of the most successful and lauded Corps commanders in the Union Army during the Civil War. General Hancock organized the Union defenses on Cemetery Hill during the **Battle of Gettysburg**. On July 1, 1863 Confederate troops pushed the Union defenders back as two senior Union Generals squabbled about command. Hancock held his position on the next day of the battle, and commanded the Union center that repulsed Pickett's Charge on July 3, the last day of the battle. He was wounded that day, but would not leave the field for medical care. As the commander of the military district of Washington, D.C. in July 1865, General Hancock was the presiding officer at the execution of the **Lincoln** assassination conspirators. He was the Democratic candidate for the American presidency in 1880 against Garfield. He died February 9, 1886 and was buried in West Norristown.

## Hand, Edward

Hand accompanied the Eighteenth Royal Irish Regiment to America as a surgeon's mate in 1774, but resigned and settled in Pennsylvania. Born in Ireland in 1744, Edward Hand became the Adjutant General of the Continental Army. A notable Lancaster physician, George Washington visited him at his Rock Ford Mansion in 1791. Hand died September 3, 1802. Rock Ford, located along the Conestoga River, is open for tours.

## Hanover, Battle of

On the morning of June 30, 1863, Confederate Cavalry under General J.E.B. Stuart attacked Union Cavalry in Hanover. Both forces traded control of the town during the fighting. About 7,500 of the blue and gray horse soldiers fought that day in the town at the **Mason-Dixon Line** in southern **York** county. When the battle was over, more than 200 Yankees and 100 Southerners were casualties. Union General Judson Gilpatrick occupied the town and the high ground north and northwest, which blocked the Confederate Cavalry from meeting with Jubal Early's Southerners returning to Gettysburg. Stuart finally rejoined Lee in the afternoon on the second day fighting at the **Battle of Gettysburg**. The Battle of Hanover delayed Stuart's advance, and kept Lee from having use of his cavalry. In the Civil War period, a cavalry was an army's "eyes and ears" and General Lee may have made different decisions if Stuart's men were providing updated information to him.

## Hanover Junction

On November 17, 1863 at 5pm, **President Abraham Lincoln** arrived in Hanover by way of the Northern Central Railroad. His staff was small, and he traveled in a regular coach car with the other passengers. Hundreds gathered at Hanover Junction to get a look at their president. When Lincoln changed cars, he emerged from his passenger car and the crowd applauded. He shook a few hands and made a brief impromptu speech."Well, you have seen me, and, according to general experience, you have seen less than you expected to see," President Lincoln quipped, much to the amusement of the crowd.

His stop was a brief one. It lasted eight minutes. The smoky steam engine chugged away from Hanover Junction to Gettysburg, with the President of the United States sitting comfortably on board. The next day, President Lincoln delivered the Gettysburg Address.

## Harriet

What appears like weird string art in human form is all that remains of Harriet Cole. She is on display at the Hahnemann Medical College Library in **Philadelphia**. Harriet was an African-American scrubwoman at the medical school who died in 1888. She willed her body to the school, where Dr. Rufus B. Weaver turned her into a display for students to learn anatomy. Weaver took five months—working eight to ten hours a day—painstakingly removing every bit of Harriet's bone and flesh, leaving only her nervous system and eyes. During the difficult dissection, Dr. Weaver wrapped each strand in gauze and preserved it with white lead-based paint and shellac. He then mounted the exposed nervous system on a board with hundreds of tiny pins.

## Harrisburg

Present-day Harrisburg, the city on the eastern shore of the **Susquehanna River** and the capital

*Lady Commonwealth, the statue that sits atop the state Capitol Dome in Harrisburg, is also featured on the Pennsylvania state quarter. In this picture, the statue had been removed from the dome for cleaning and maintenance.*

*A view of Hanover Junction, located in southern York County. The railroad from Gettysburg connected here, and Abraham Lincoln changed trains here.*

of Pennsylvania, is located about 100 miles west of **Philadelphia**, and 200 miles east of **Pittsburgh**. Its population is 48,950 (2001). From its humble beginning as nothing more than Indian trails, Harrisburg has grown into a vast community of highways, rail, and air routes.

When John Harris, a native of Yorkshire, England, arrived in Philadelphia he was one of the state's earliest immigrants, enticed by the promises of **William Penn**. About 1719, Harris moved west with his wife Esther from Chester County. They eventually built a log cabin on the banks of the Susquehanna, near the present intersection of Paxton and Front streets. From his new home, Harris built a ferry and trading post.

The ferry was the first to cross the Susquehanna. It became popular and the Harris settlement was no longer called by its Indian name of Peixtan, but instead Harris' Ferry. Harris developed a large trade with the nearby Indians in fur and skins and set up several trading posts. He farmed on a small-scale and introduced the first plow to the vicinity. Other settlers came to the area at this time to set up their homesteads. On December 17, 1733, the proprietors of Pennsylvania granted Harris 300 acres, which included the present site downtown Harrisburg.

John Harris, Sr. died in 1748. Following his request, his family buried him beneath the shade of a mulberry tree along the Susquehanna River. Hostile Indians tied him to this very tree and would have burned him to death, had he not been rescued in time.

John Harris, Jr., who was born in about 1727, operated the ferry started by his father. He also argued successfully against the inconvenience of traveling to **Lancaster** to conduct legal business and attend court sessions. His appeal to the General Assembly, in 1782, to carve out a separate county around Harris' Ferry sparked a lively debate over whether the county seat should be in Harris Ferry or Middletown. Harris won, and by an act of the General Assembly, on March 4, 1785, Dauphin County was established, providing that its seat of government and justice should be "near Harris's Ferry."

The new county was named "Dauphin," to honor the eldest son of the King of France, who aided the colonies during the American Revolution. Harris granted two lots on Market Street and two on Walnut Street for use by the county. He also gave the southern part of current Capitol Park for the use of Pennsylvania, should the seat of state government be chosen for this centrally located area. In 1791, the growing community of Harris Ferry was renamed "Harrisburg," following a brief time as "Louisbourg" in honor of the French King Louis.

The first county courthouse was a small log cabin on South Front Street, owned by John Harris. An unpretentious two-story red brick building on the side of the old Lancaster Road was the next courthouse. Its construction was financed largely from the earnings of the operation of the Harris Ferry. That courthouse became the temporary Capitol of Pennsylvania in the fall of 1812, when the state government was moved to Harrisburg from Lancaster. In January 1822, the first State House was completed on Capitol Hill, and the courthouse used as the Capitol was returned to the county for its courts and business.

Harrisburg was the site of the first national Whig Party convention in 1839. The chief employer is the state government, but the city is also an important commercial, manufacturing, and transportation center. Products include electronic equipment, clothing, office machines, building materials, steel, and processed food. Insurance is also an important industry. The west shore area, which consists of many smaller municipalities, as well as

*Harrisburg is the state capital, and the Capitol Building is impressive with its notable green dome. It is the center of the Capitol complex in downtown Harrisburg.*

many other communities on the eastern shore of the Susquehanna near the city, contribute to today's greater Harrisburg metropolitan area.

## Heinz, Henry John

Born October 11, 1844, Henry Heinz began peddling surplus homegrown vegetables to his neighbors when he was eight years old. By the time he was 16, Heinz made three wagon deliveries of his vegetables a week to grocers throughout **Pittsburgh**. In 1869, Heinz formed his first partnership selling grated horseradish, but by 1875 they went bankrupt. The following year, Heinz started the F. & J. Heinz Company with his brother and cousin as partners. The new company produced prepared pickles and condiments. The company introduced its tomato ketchup in 1876, still a best-seller today. When Henry Heinz died in 1916, his company had grown to employ thousands of employees at 25 separate factories, processing the harvest from over 100,000 acres.

## Henderson, Richard

Born into slavery in Maryland in 1801, Richard Henderson escaped when he was a boy. Around 1824, he traveled to and settled in Meadville. A barber by trade, he was active in the **Underground Railroad**. His Arch Street house in Meadville, Crawford County was estimated to have provided a safe haven to over 500 runaway slaves prior to the Civil War. The Henderson house no longer exists, having been torn down long ago.

## Hershey, Milton

His last name is known everywhere around the world. The familiar brown wrapper with silverish ink identifies "the great American chocolate bar." Milton Hershey was a man that repeatedly failed, refused to give up, and became wildly successful, all from chocolate.

On September 13, 1857, Milton Hershey

*An interior shot of the Capitol Building's dome in Harrisburg.*

*Milton Hershey and his wife left their fortune to the Hershey School, a nonprofit ophanage for boys.*

was born on a farm near Derry Church, a small Pennsylvania community. The only surviving child of Fannie and Henry Hershey, Milton's mother raised him in the strict discipline of the **Mennonite** faith. There were frequent family moves that constantly interrupted his schooling. He only completed the fourth grade, and with no formal education, Hershey became an apprentice to a confectioner in **Lancaster** for four years. He set up his first candy making shop in **Philadelphia**. It failed, as did his next two tries in Chicago and New York.

Hershey returned to Lancaster in 1883, and launched the Lancaster Caramel Company. Hershey's fascination with German chocolate-making machinery, displayed at the 1893

*The world's largest chocolate factory is at Hershey's.*

World's Columbian Exposition, resulted in him buying the equipment for his Lancaster plant. He began producing various chocolate creations. He sold the caramel business in 1900 for $1 million, which gave him the funds he needed to focus on chocolate. He needed a large supply of fresh milk, the vital ingredient for producing and perfecting fine milk chocolate. Excited by the possibilities of milk chocolate, which at that time was mainly a Swiss luxury product, Milton Hershey developed his own formula. Through trial and error, he created his own unique recipe. In 1903, he started to build a new factory in the middle of dairy farms. It was a triumphant return to rural Derry Church.

The Hershey Chocolate Company became the world's largest chocolate manufacturing plant. The facility, which was completed in 1905, manufactured chocolate using the latest mass production techniques. Hershey produced a five-cent chocolate bar that became popular, nearly synonymous with American chocolate. But Hershey was more than a simple chocolatier. His efforts to attract and keep talented workers led him to create a "company town," complete with stores, schools, and its own amusement park. In 1909, unable to have children of their own, he and his wife Catherine set up a trade school for orphan boys.

Milton Hershey's business success allowed him to practice an extensive philanthropy. In

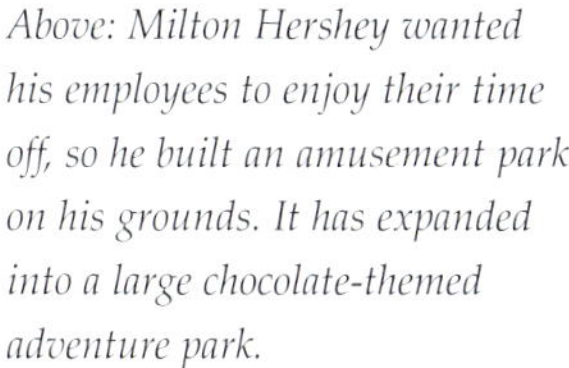

*Above: Milton Hershey wanted his employees to enjoy their time off, so he built an amusement park on his grounds. It has expanded into a large chocolate-themed adventure park.*

*Above, left: The streetlights in Hershey are unique, taking the shape of the chocolate company's famous "Kiss."*

*Left: This is just one of the signature rides in the park.*

1918, three years after Catherine's premature death, Milton Hershey endowed the school with his entire fortune of Hershey Chocolate Company stock. For the rest of his life, he placed the quality of his product and the well-being of his workers ahead of profits. He died October 13, 1945, leaving his fortune to the school.

## Hex Signs

When groups of peasant farmers from Rhineland in Germany immigrated to Pennsylvania, they brought their old world language, art, dress, food, and traditions to their new home. Attracted by the religious freedom offered to them by **William Penn**, they brought many quaint customs with them. One such oddity was their use of hex signs.

These painted round signs incorporated different designs, such as stylized stars, rosettes, birds (called distelfinks), or wheels, all thought to be magical. These signs, painted on barns by the Pennsylvania Dutch, were to ward off misfortune or evil spells.

Six-pointed star designs were popular. The German word for six, "sechs," sounded more like hex to their English-speaking neighbors. In time, everyone called these "hex" patterns hex signs.

## Hickory Grove Cemetery

Established in 1807 in Waverly, then known as Abington Center, the Hickory Grove Cemetery in **Lackawanna County** is one of the oldest known cemeteries associated with African Americans in northeastern Pennsylvania. The cemetery is the burial ground for many runaway slaves who came to the area via the **Underground Railroad** in the mid-19th century. By the end of the 19th century, there were 75 former slaves living in Waverly.

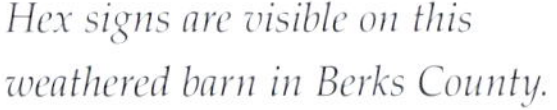

*Hex signs are visible on this weathered barn in Berks County.*

## Hoffman, Bob

Born in Tifton, Georgia on November 9, 1898, Bob Hoffman's family moved to Pennsylvania when he was five years old. In World War I, he was a decorated soldier for outstanding service in Europe. When he returned from the war, he was manufacturing oil burners. In 1929, he began lifting weights and making barbells in his oil-burner factory in **York**.

Hoffman became universally known as "the Father of World Weight Lifting." He sold his interest in the oil-burner company and started York Barbell Corp on Broad Street in 1932.

He became an Olympic weight lifting coach, 1948–64, and actively promoted the sports of power lifting and bodybuilding. He published magazines and books, and developed various products for the sports. Hoffman served as an official adviser on youth physical fitness for Presidents **Eisenhower**, Kennedy, and Nixon. He died July 18, 1985 from heart disease. The York Barbell Corp continues business today, and is the home of the Weight Lifting Hall of Fame.

## Hollingsworth, Anthony

On June 26, 1845, 12-year-old Anthony Hollingsworth, a runaway slave from Virginia, was in Indiana, Pennsylvania. Chased by southern slave hunters hired by his ex-master, Garrett Van Meter, they captured Anthony and held him in the Indiana House Hotel. Word quickly spread among the town's residents about the plight of the fugitive slave. Armed residents of Indiana surrounded the hotel, demanding his release in clear defiance of federal law. Judge Thomas White made it official, freeing Anthony in the town's old courthouse, from which he fled to Canada.

During raids at a nearby farm, the slave hunters captured two other slaves, Charles Brown and Jared Harris, who had traveled with Anthony. The slave hunters shackled and returned Brown and Harris to slavery.

## Hollywood Comes to Pennsylvania

Over the past several decades, many popular movies have been partially filmed in Pennsylvania. Some of the familiar films are *Witness*, *Lucky Numbers*, *Philadelphia*, *Girl Interrupted*, *The Mollie Maguires*, *The Deer Hunter*, *The Wonder Boys*, *Slapshot*, and the *Rocky* movies. Hollywood has been coming to Pennsylvania regularly, partly due to several offices designed to encourage movie making in the state.

## Homestead Strike

On the summer morning of July 6, 1892, on orders of the Carnegie Steel Company, 300 Pinkerton agents in boats tried to land. Striking steelworkers, joined by local citizens, repulsed the Pinkertons. Seven workers and three Pinkertons were killed during the attempted landing. A force of over 12,000 state militia arrived on July 12. By November, the strike—which was really a lockout—was broken. The striking workers went back to work without a union contract. Henry C. Frick, a frank and brutal union-hater, was the company's superintendent.

## Honesdale

The Wayne County town of Honesdale, strategically situated along the Lackawaxen River, boasts a unique history as the birthplace of the American Railroad. On August 8, 1829, Horatio Allen experimented with the *Stourbridge Lion*, a steam engine imported from England. It was the first steam locomotive to run on commercial tracks in the United States. Honesdale was involved in transporting coal by gravity railroad from Carbondale to the towpaths of the Delaware and Hudson Canal—before it finally

reached New York City. It is renowned in the U.S. for its early use of the steam engine.

## Horseshoe Curve, The

Located about four miles west of **Altoona**, the Horseshoe Curve is, at first appearance, nondescript. Standing beside it, it seems little more than a few train tracks. All that changes, however, when the first freight train passes. Suddenly the size of the marvel become obvious. From a distance, the train rumbles and it takes time for it circle the canyon. As it gets louder, clearly it is descending the gradual grade. The 220 degree arc that forms Horseshoe Curve has a radius of more than 600 feet. Several hundred Irish laborers used not much more than their own sweat, gunpowder, and pack animals to carve out the track's bed on the slopes of the Allegheny Mountains. The laborers toiled as they cut away the front of the mountain to form a ledge for the tracks. During World War II, Hitler had dispatched saboteurs to destroy the curve, but the FBI captured them before they had a chance to destroy it. Over 500 trains still use the Horseshoe Curve each week. It is now a tourist destination, attracting several thousands of visitors each week.

## Hosanna Meeting House

Established by the many free Blacks who had settled in the southern portion of Chester County close to the **Mason-Dixon Line**, the Hosanna Meeting House was first known as the "African Meeting House." Located on the old Baltimore Pike (at present-day Lincoln University campus), locals formally organized the House in 1843 as an African Union Methodist Protestant church. The building became a station stop on the **Underground Railroad**. Runaway slaves enjoyed their freedom when they finally arrived at the Hosanna Meeting House. During its use, some of its many visitors included Sojourner Truth and Frederick Douglass.

## Hughes, Daniel

Daniel Hughes was a lumber raftsman on the **Susquehanna River**. He lived in Lycoming County from 1854 to 1880. He ferried runaway slaves to Lycoming County from Maryland, protecting them before they continued north via the **Underground Railroad**. Hughes donated part of his land for a cemetery, and among those that are buried are nine African-American veterans of the Civil War. The cemetery he created is The Freedom Road Cemetery.

# I

## Independence Hall

Located on Chestnut Street between 5th and 6th Streets, the State House of the Province of Pennsylvania was constructed between 1732 and 1756. Scholars consider it a fine example of Georgian architecture.

From 1775 to 1783 (except for the winter of 1777–1778 when **Philadelphia** was occupied by the British Army), this building was the meeting place for the Second Continental Congress. In the Assembly Room of the building, Congress appointed George Washington commander in chief of the Continental Army in 1775 and adopted the **Declaration of Independence** on July 4, 1776. In the same room, Congress agreed to the design of the American flag in 1777, adopted the **Articles of Confederation** in 1781, and drafted the **U.S. Constitution** in 1787.

*Known first as the Pennsylvania State House, the building fell into disrepair until Philadelphians later realized how important and significant it was to the nation's history. Independence Hall is open daily to visitors.*

Independence Square
Philadelphia 1861

The Pennsylvania State government moved to **Lancaster** in 1799. At the time, there was no immediate use for the building, nor was there any thought of preserving it. The visit of the **Marquis de Lafayette**—Washington's old comrade-in-arms—in 1824 finally stirred the first feelings of public veneration for the old structure. Lafayette's visit spurred the preservation of the State House.

Now known as Independence Hall, the building, inside and out, was restored wherever possible to its original late-18th century appearance. Most of the furnishings are period pieces. The "rising sun" chair used by George Washington as he presided over the Constitutional Convention is original. Independence Hall is open all year. The U.S. Park Service offers free tours, though hours vary by season.

## Indian Jasper Quarry

Lehigh County is the location of the most famous of Pennsylvania's Indian quarries. The Indians made items from the jasper they quarried. The Indians carried the quartz-like crystals as far away as New England.

## Indians of Pennsylvania

The Susquehannocks were at one time a powerful Iroquoian-speaking tribe who lived along the **Susquehanna River** in both Pennsylvania and Maryland. An energetic people living in Algonkian-speaking tribes' territory, they engaged in many wars with other Indians. They died from new diseases brought by European settlers, and from the attacks by the Iroquois, which destroyed them as a nation by 1675. A few of their descendants were known as the **Conestoga** Indians who were massacred in 1763 in **Lancaster** County.

The Delawares, who called themselves Leni-Lenape or "real men," originally occupied the area around the Delaware River basin. An important tribe of the several that spoke an Algonkian language, the Delawares were first to feel the pressure of white European settlements. Soon they roamed westward to the Wyoming Valley, then onto the Allegheny region and into eastern Ohio. Many of the Delawares aligned with the French side in the French and Indian War. They joined in **Pontiac**'s War, and then fought on the British side in the Revolutionary War. Later, some migrated to Ontario and the rest wandered further west. Remaining descendants of the Delaware now live on reservations in Oklahoma and Ontario. The Munsees, a division of the Delawares, lived on the upper Delaware River, north of the Lehigh River.

The Shawnees also spoke Algonkian. They came to Pennsylvania from the west in the 1690s. Some groups of the Shawnees settled in the lower Susquehanna region, while others lived with the Munsees near Easton. They too migrated to the Wyoming Valley, and then to the Ohio Valley, where they joined other Shawnees that had gone there previously.

The Shawnees, like the Delawares, became allies of the French in the **French-Indian War** and of the British in the Revolution. After General **Anthony Wayne**'s victory over the Shawnees at Fallen Timbers, Ohio, in 1794, they settled near the Delawares in Indiana and their descendants also now live in Oklahoma. They remained almost constantly at war with the settlers for 40 years preceding the Treaty of Greenville in 1795.

The Iroquois Confederacy of Iroquoian-speaking tribes, at first known as the **Five Nations**, included the tribes of Mohawks, Oneidas, Onondagas, Cayugas, and Senecas. After 1723, when the Tuscaroras from the South were admitted to the Five Nations confederacy, its name changed to the **Six Nations**.

The five original tribes, when first encountered by the newly arriving Europeans,

*Independence Square in Philadelphia, 1861.*

*Indiantown in northern Lebanon County has given its name to the National Guard fort.*

controlled much of New York State, from the Genesee River to Lake Champlain.

From their position, they gradually extended their power and their influence. They acted as go-betweens with the western Indians in the fur trade, and as intermediaries experienced with dealing with the European whites. This largest single group of Indians in northeastern America gained influence over other tribes from Illinois and Lake Michigan to the eastern seaboard. The Senecas, the tribe farther west, set up their villages on the upper Allegheny in the 1730s. Small groups of Iroquois later scattered westward into Ohio. They became known as Mingoes.

During the colonial wars, both the French and the British eagerly sought the Six Nations alliance or their neutrality. During the American Revolution, most of the Six Nations aligned with the British side, but the Oneidas and scores of Tuscaroras were pro-American. American General Daniel Brodhead's expedition up the Allegheny River and General John Sullivan's expedition up the Susquehanna River destroyed their villages and cornfields in 1779, and disorganized their established society.

Many from the Six Nations who had fought for the British moved into Canada after the American Revolution, while the rest worked out peaceful relations with the United States under the leadership of such chiefs as **Cornplanter**. In 1791, Pennsylvania's General Assembly recognized this noted chief of the Seneca Nation by granting him a tract of land near present-day Route 59 in Warren County, east of Warren, near the Kinzua Dam. The last Seneca left the tract of land in 1964.

There were other tribes in Pennsylvania, but they cannot be identified. They occupied western Pennsylvania before the Europeans arrived, but were eliminated by wars with other tribes, and diseases in the 17th century, long before the Delawares, Shawnees, and Senecas started migrating there. The Eries, another great Iroquoian-speaking tribe, lived along the south shore of **Lake Erie**, but the Iroquois wiped them out around 1654. The Mahicans, an Algonkian-speaking tribe related to the Mohegans of Connecticut, lived in the upper Hudson Valley of New York. The Iroquois and the white settlers drove them out, some joining the Delawares in the Wyoming

Valley about 1730. Others settled at Stockbridge, Massachusetts.

The Saponis, a Siouan-speaking tribe from Virginia and North Carolina, moved north to seek Iroquois protection. They were eventually absorbed into the Cayugas. Two Algonkian-speaking tribes, the Conoys and the Nanticokes, moved northward from Maryland early in the 18th century. Settling along the Susquehanna, while others moved on to settle in southern New York, they eventually moved west with the Delawares, with whom they merged. There were also temporary villages of Wyandots, Chippewas, Missisaugas, and Ottawas in western Pennsylvania during the late 1700s, as they migrated to new areas.

## Indiantown Gap

Located in northern Lebanon County, Indiantown was a native village of the Delawares. A creek, gap, and nearby military reservation can trace their names from the village. Fort Indiantown Gap is an army training base created in 1932.

*Throughout Pennsylvania, historic markers denote the location of Indian villages and major Indian paths.*

# J

## Jamison, Mary

For years, local residents of Adams County told stories about the capture of Mary Jamison. She was born on a ship sailing to America, as her parents fled Ireland for America.

In the late 1750s Buchanan Valley was attacked by gunfire. Four Frenchmen and six Indians shot a man and horse, and burst into the Jamison cabin, which was located west of present-day Gettysburg. The raiding party was part of the French effort to drive settlers off their land during the **French-Indian War**. They took everyone there as prisoners, and searched the log house for meat, meal, and bread. Taking their ten prisoners with them, they traveled rapidly west. Not even stopping for food, the men would beat the children if they did not keep up.

Around noon the next day they passed a fort, which is now Chambersburg. Fearing a pursuit if they continued to travel with their prisoners, the Indians and Frenchmen butchered eight of the ten settlers. The Pennsylvania settlers were then scalped and their naked bodies were discarded and thrown into a swamp. The search party in pursuit of the raiders later found the mangled, battered bodies.

The Indians, however, took Mary down the Ohio River to a small Seneca Indian town. She was raised among the Senecas. Many years later, the **Six Nations** gave Mary a large tract of land in an act of compensation.

## Jim Thorpe

First called Coalville, the name of the town on the Lehigh River changed to Mauch Chunk, which means "Bear Mountain" in the Lenni Lenape language. Mauch Chunk prospered from the heavy deposits of anthracite. It became the seat of Carbon County.

Now along Route 903, on the east side of the town, stands a large granite mausoleum of Jim Thorpe, one of the greatest athletes of the twentieth century. The Native American Hero of the 1912 Olympics in Stockholm was buried there in 1953 when the towns of Mauch Chunk and East

*Asa Packer House looks over Jim Thorpe. If it looks haunted, it might be because the Walt Disney Company used it as a model for their Haunted Mansion attraction.*

*The gravesite of Jim Thorpe in the town named in his honor.*

Mauch Chunk merged and changed their names to honor his memory—even though Thorpe had no direct connection to the area.

The town of Jim Thorpe, once a gritty coal community, is historic and picturesque. The town is nestled in a valley between three mountains and the Lehigh River flows through its center. It likes to call itself the "Little Switzerland of America."

During the early 1800s the Switchback Gravity Railroad and the Delaware and Lehigh Canal were used to send over 30,000 tons of anthracite from Jim Thorpe to Philadelphia yearly.

Jim Thorpe also became the home of Asa Packer. His mansion, located in the center of town, is open for public tours. At the **Old Jail**, the strange handprint of convicted murder accomplice Alexander Campbell, one of the **Molly Maguires**, remains on the wall of cell number 17.

White-water rafting, hiking, camping, cycling, and other outdoor activities surround Jim Thorpe. With the decline of the anthracite business, the small town remains vibrant as a tourist destination with its nearby outdoor adventures, attractions, specialty shops, unique restaurants, and Victorian bed and breakfasts.

## Johnson House, The

Built in 1768 for John Johnson, Johnson House is at 6306 Germantown Avenue, **Philadelphia**. It was home to three generations of this Quaker family who worked to abolish slavery for African Americans. In the 1850s, the Johnson House was a station on the **Underground Railroad**. Runaway slaves used the House and other buildings on the property as shelter before they moved on to the next stop.

## Johnstown Flood, The

The **Commonwealth** of Pennsylvania built a large dam for a reservoir for the canal basin in Johnstown. But along came the Pennsylvania Railroad, making the canal system throughout Pennsylvania obsolete.

The Pennsylvania Railroad eventually bought the Pennsylvania Mainline Canal and managed many sections of it for years. While

*The Johnstown Flood completely destroyed buildings such as this one in 1889.*

under the railroad's ownership, the dam broke in 1862. At the time, the lake was only half-full. It was a dry summer.

John Reilly of **Altoona**, a member of Congress bought the particular property from the railroad. Reilly planned to sell the land to a group of investors interested in starting a resort. Reilly's land speculation fizzled. There were no interested buyers, so he sold his investment property to a local sportsmen's club at a loss.

After their purchase of the property, the

*The total devastation from the Johnstown Flood was indescribable in the spring of 1889. This picture shows the damage from the flood to the Cambria Iron Company's office and storerooms looking from Pennsylvania Railroad depot.*

South Fork Fishing and Hunting Club began repairs to the dam in 1879, and completed the maintenance in 1881. The club named the lake created by the dam Lake Conemaugh and they stocked the lake with hundreds of black bass and it became well known as a place for recreation, north of Johnstown, in south central Pennsylvania. Consequently, it attracted wealthy families who built their homes in the area.

The city of Johnstown, founded in 1800, is located in a deep, narrow valley at the confluence of the Conemaugh River and Stonycreek. The Allegheny Mountains tower over the town, which grew to a population of 30,000 by 1889. It was a working-class town, with foundries and coal mining as the major sources of employment. Recent immigration brought thousands of new Americans to the growing town.

In late spring of 1889, heavy storms pelted the area with massive rains. During the heavy rains, men worked endlessly on the South Fork dam. Their work was a crude attempt to keep the dam from breaking.

Elias Unger, then the president of the South Fork Fishing and Hunting Club, was hoping that the people in Johnstown would heed the telegraph warnings he'd sent. He told them the dam might break. At 3:10pm, May 31, 1889, it finally happened. The earthen dam collapsed. The wall, which stood 90 feet high, was 14 miles away, northeast of Johnstown in the mountains

The dam's distance did nothing to protect the city. A devastating 35-foot high wall of water rushed down the Conemaugh River, hitting Johnstown with a mighty, destructive force. The torrent of water roared into the city at 50 miles an hour, and its force tossed a 48-ton locomotive one mile. On that tragic Friday, over 2,200 people died, and thousands more were injured. It was one of the worst disasters in our Nation's history. It took years for the area to recover. The water washed some of the victims away, and no one ever found them.

*This old photograph shows the damage to Johnstown caused by the flood of 1889. This view shows Wood, Morrell & Co.'s store and office from Prospect Hill.*

The city's moniker became "The Flood City," following two more floods in 1936 and 1977. The two later floods, while costing lives and causing extensive property damage, were far less costly than the flood of 1889.

## Johnsville Naval Air Development Center

Located at Warrington in Bucks County, the U.S. Navy acquired this site during World War II from the Brewster Aircraft Corporation. The Johnsville Naval Air Development Center served as a strategic location for weapons development and the testing of modern aircraft. The center was also an important training facility for America's Mercury, Gemini, and Apollo space programs.

# K

## Kaufman, Daniel

Daniel Kaufman helped run the **Underground Railroad** from 1835 to 1847 at Boiling Springs, Cumberland County. Runaway slaves that made it to Kaufman's were hidden in his barn, in a densely wooded area on his property, and on Island Grove, located at the south side of the Yellow Breeches Creek. Kaufman provided food and transportation to fugitive slaves passing through this area. In a high profile case, a Maryland slave owner successfully sued Kaufman, and he received a $4,000 fine in 1852.

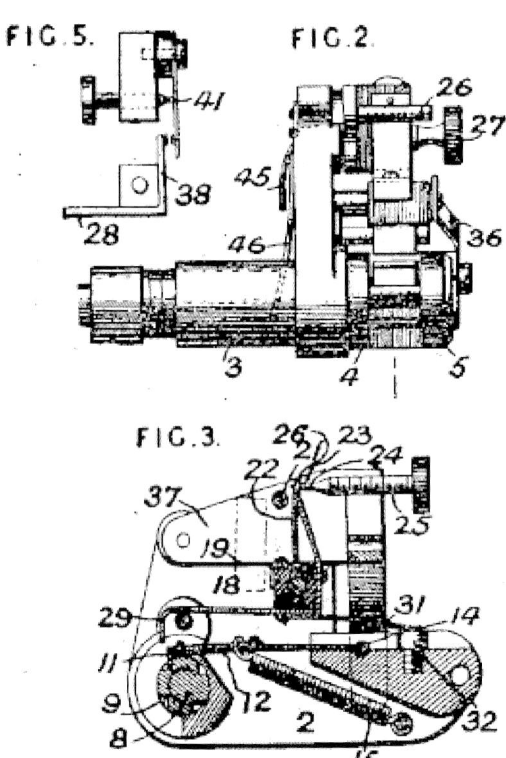


*The illustration for a patent titled "Improvement in Electric Contact Devices (1907)" by Atwater Kent.*

## Kennett Square

Located in southern Chester County near the Delaware Border, tiny Kennett Square is known for two things: mushrooms and **Longwood Gardens**. Each year, the mushroom growers in and around Kennett Square produce tons of mushrooms, giving the town the honorary title of mushroom capital of the world. Nearby is Longwood Gardens, the world's premier horticultural display garden. Created by industrialist Pierre S. du Pont in the early 1900s, the massive garden attracts thousands of visitors each week.

## Kent, Atwater

After dropping out from Worcester Technical Institute in Massachusetts, Atwater Kent moved to **Philadelphia** and set up his manufacturing business. He developed an ignition sparking system that was adopted by all car manufacturers. He is also known for manufacturing radios. By 1925, the Atwater Kent Manufacturing Company became the largest maker of radios in the nation.

In 1929, the company reached its peak performance with over 12,000 employees manufacturing nearly one million radio sets. When Kent died in 1949, he held over 93 patents.

## Kentucky Rifle, The

Early frontier settlers, such as Davy Crockett and Daniel Boone, would have carried this long barreled rifle into the deep woods of America. Developed in **Lancaster**, circa 1725, its name, Kentucky Rifle, is something of a misnomer. German handiworkers refined and perfected the design and it became known as a standard gun.

A typical Pennsylvania-made rifle was .50 caliber, made of curly maple, had a full stock, and sported a 42–46 inch barrel. A crescent-shaped buttplate, patchbox, and cheekpiece were also common. Although Lancaster was the center for the rifle's manufacture, it got its name from its use in the untamed wilderness of Kentucky.

## Keyser Creek

At present-day Taylor, the first white settlement in **Lackawanna County** was set up in 1769. Early settlers included Timothy Keys, Andrew Hickman, and Solomon Hocksey. In July 1778, Indians killed Keys and the others. The Keyser Creek is named for Keys.

## Keystone State

Pennsylvania's nickname is the Keystone State. The word keystone comes from an architectural term and refers to the central,

*Keystone State: Pennsylania's nickname was coined at Thomas Jefferson's Republican rally in 1802.*

wedge-shaped stone in an arch, which holds all the other stones in place. Pennsylvania's nickname is based on a 13-stone arch where there are six rocks on one side and six rocks on the other. The 13th rock in the middle, the keystone, holds the other rocks in the archway in place. Of the original 13 states, six are northeast of Pennsylvania and six southeast.

Exactly when Pennsylvania was first called the "Keystone State" cannot be traced to any single source. Its use as the state's nickname started soon after 1800. At a Jefferson Republican victory rally in October 1802, everyone present toasted Pennsylvania as "the keystone in the federal union." The following year a newspaper referred to the state as "the keystone in the democratic arch." Because of Pennsylvania's vast contributions to the nation, the nickname seems most fitting.

## Kinzua Railroad Bridge

Situated deep in the Allegheny National Forest in McKean County, the Kinzua Railroad Bridge near Mount Jewett was acclaimed "the highest and longest railroad viaduct in the entire world." At the time it was built in 1882, the engineering marvel rose 301 feet from the valley floor at its center and was 2,100 feet in length.

The Kinzua Viaduct, built from 1,552 tons of iron, was completed in 94 days. When it was finished, some hailed it as the Eighth Wonder of the World. But since the last freight train crossed it in 1959, the bridge has fallen into disrepair. It became a tourist attraction and part of a state park, open only to foot traffic. But the structure weakened over time. In July 2003, severe thunderstorms with winds up to 80mph caused the middle section of the Kinzua Viaduct to collapse, sending most of it crashing into the Kinzua Creek gorge below.

*Kinzua Railroad Bridge was an engineering marvel when it was built in 1882.*

## Kittanning

The site of present-day Kittanning in Armstrong County was the location of the most notable Delaware Indian village west of the Alleghenies. Kittanning means "great river," referring to the Ohio-Allegheny. Armstrong's expedition in 1756 destroyed the Delaware village.

## Knox Mine Disaster

On January 22, 1959, 12 miners died in an accident at the River Slope Mine near Port Griffith, Luzerne County. The Knox Coal Company had been illegally excavating a mine beneath the **Susquehanna River**. When the force of the ice-laden Susquehanna River broke through the rock, over ten billion gallons of water gushed through the mine. This disaster ended deep mining in the Wyoming Valley.

## Kresge, S.S.

Sebastian Spering Kresge was born July 31, 1867, in Bald Mount, near Scranton. After he had completed a business degree, Kresge sold tinware from 1890–97 before opening his first discount retail store. All merchandise sold for a dime or less. Kresge started the business with one of his customers, J. G. McCrory, who owned a chain of stores in the northeast. Together, they expanded and opened more of the "five-and-dime" stores before Kresge bought out McCrory and named the company S. S. Kresge in 1912 with 85 stores. Kresge upheld a position in the market as a discount retailer and eventually became Kmart Corporation. This Pennsylvanian died on October 18, 1966.

## Kulp, Nancy

Nancy Kulp was born in **Harrisburg** on August 28, 1921. She graduated from Florida State University and then joined the Naval Reserve, and became a WAVE in 1943. She went on to star in several movies and television shows. Kulp became typecast for playing Miss Jane Hathaway on the 1960s television comedy series, "The Beverly Hillbillies." In 1984, Kulp ran as Democrat for the Ninth Congressional District in Pennsylvania. Despite her popularity as a TV star, she lost the election after a hard-fought campaign that turned ugly when her former "Hillbillies" co-star, Buddy Ebsen, recorded a thirty-second radio commercial endorsing her Republican opponent. Kulp died February 3, 1991.

## Kuskuskies Towns

Located in Lawrence County, Kuskuskies Towns were a group of Indian towns near present-day New Castle. They were first inhabited by the Senecas, but after 1756 the towns were settled by Delawares from eastern Pennsylvania. Kuskuskies Towns were abandoned during the Revolutionary War.

In 1785, General William Irvine toured the Kuskuskies Towns before their division into tracts given to Revolutionary soldiers in payment of their service. The area became known as Donation Lands.

## Lackawanna Anthracite Mine Disaster

During the morning of April 7, 1911, the Pancoast mine in Throop was the scene of a disastrous fire. Seventy-two miners died by suffocation. A rescue worker was also killed. This tragic fire soon led to state legislature passing a law that required all interior buildings at coalmines to be constructed of fireproof materials.

## Lackawanna County

Lackawanna is an Indian word meaning "stream that forks." Formed August 13, 1878 from Luzerne County, Lackawanna County is Pennsylvania's 67th and the last county created. **Scranton** is the county seat. The area is the center of Pennsylvania's anthracite coal mining region.

## Lake Erie, Battle of

A naval conflict, the Battle of Lake Erie, was fought in September 1813 as part of the War of 1812. The American fleet, led by Commander Oliver Hazard Perry, engaged the British forces under the command of Commodore Robert H. Barclay. Six vessels in Perry's Fleet, including the **Brig *Niagara*** were constructed in **Erie**. That in itself was a remarkable feat. The village had only 500 residents. Shipbuilders and supplies were brought to Erie to construct the American naval fleet.

The fighting occurred at close quarters, with all units of both fleets engaged. Eventually, Barclay's flagship, the HMS ***Detroit***, surrendered with three other British vessels. The two remaining British vessels tried to escape but were overtaken and captured. It was during the Battle of Lake Erie that Commander Perry wrote his famous report to General William Henry Harrison: "We have met the enemy and they are ours."

The Battle of Lake Erie culminated the moves by the United States designed to challenge British supremacy in the Great Lakes region. The British gained control of the area after occupying Detroit in August 1812. Within three weeks following the Battle of Lake Erie, the British were forced to evacuate Detroit.

## LaFayette, Marquis de

The Marquis de LaFayette joined the Continental Army just before the **Battle at Brandywine**, and it is where the young French volunteer saw his first military action in America. The young Frenchman showed such courage and energy, continuing to fight even when wounded, that he became a permanent favorite of General **Washington** and many of the Continental soldiers. On the

eve of the battle, he stayed in the house of Gideon Gilpin, a Quaker farmer. After the battle, British soldiers plundered and foraged Gilpin's property. The claim for losses filed by Gilpin proves how prosperous this Quaker farm was in September 1777. Included among Gilpin's losses were: "10 milch cows, 1 yoke of oxen, 48 sheep, 28 swine, 12 tons of hay, 230 bushels of wheat, 50 pounds of bacon, 1 history book, and 1 gun."

## Lancaster

The oldest inland city in the United States, Lancaster was laid out in 1730. It was named for Lancaster in England. The county seat, it is located on the Conestoga River, in the heart of the **Pennsylvania Dutch** Country. Chartered as a borough in 1742, it served as the Pennsylvania State Capital from 1799 to 1812. For one day, the **Continental Congress** met in the courthouse in the center of Lancaster, making it the nation's capital. Following the Congressional session on September 27, 1777, the members moved to nearby **York**.

Lancaster is as rich in historic sites as in trade and industry. Formed on May 10, 1729 out of Chester County, Lancaster County is known for its rich farmland and ethnic mixture. Both **Mennonites** and **Amish** add to its diversity. Lancaster remains a center for manufacturing and is situated in the most productive agricultural region in the United States.

Government activities, tourism, and financial institutions contribute to the city's economy.

Lancaster is the home of Franklin and Marshall College (1787), Lancaster Theological Seminary (1825), and the Lancaster Bible College (1933). President **James Buchanan** lived and died in Lancaster. The city's population is 56,348 (U.S. Census, 2001.)

## Langhorne

The Bucks County town of present-day Langhorne was the site of hospitals used during the Revolutionary War. American soldiers who died of wounds suffered in the two Battles of Trenton, December 1776 and January 1777, and from disease incurred during the harsh winter are buried in the town's cemetery. Following the battles with the British forces, General Washington's troops occupied four hospital buildings in the village, then known as Four Lanes End. Over 160 soldiers died and were buried there.

## Largest Cities

Pennsylvania's ten largest cities, according to the U.S. Census Bureau's population lists of 2001 are:

| | |
|---|---|
| Philadelphia | 1,491,812 |
| Pittsburgh | 334,563 |
| Erie | 103,717 |
| Allentown | 106,632 |
| Reading | 81,207 |

*The Millersville State Normal School has since become Millersville University. It is located southwest of Lancaster, and close to Conestoga Indian Town. This picture shows the college buildings around 1920.*

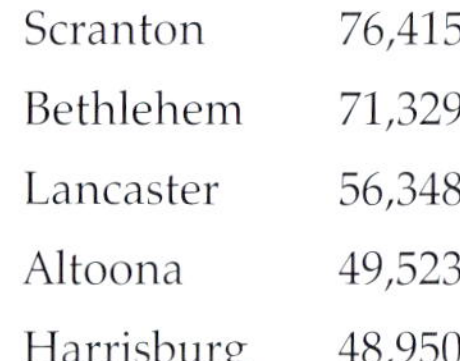

| | |
|---|---|
| Scranton | 76,415 |
| Bethlehem | 71,329 |
| Lancaster | 56,348 |
| Altoona | 49,523 |
| Harrisburg | 48,950 |

## Lattimer Massacre

On September 10, 1897, nearly 400 striking, immigrant coal miners were met and fired on by sheriff's deputies, near Hazleton at Harwood. Unarmed, the striking miners were marching from Harwood to Lattimer. They were seeking higher wages and better working conditions. The deputies of Sheriff James Martin, Luzerne County, killed 19 of the marchers and wounded 38. Some of the strikers were shot in the back as they tried to run away. The Lattimer Massacre was one of the worst acts of violence in American labor history. None of the deputies were convicted of the murder of the strikers, who were Polish, Slovak, and Lithuanian.

## Lead Pencils and Pennsylvania

One of the most popular tools for nonpermanent writing is the pencil. Many inaccurately call them lead pencils. These handy writing tools contain no lead, but most include a Pennsylvania contribution. A mixture of finely ground graphite and clay powders, and water becomes the "lead." This mixture solidifies in the grooves of a cedar plank. Another plank is glued on top, then a saw cuts the assembly into individual pencils, which are painted.

Most pencils include an attached eraser, a handy invention by a Pennsylvanian. Hymen L. Lipman of Philadelphia patented the pencil with an attached eraser on March 30, 1858. The metal ring that crimps the eraser in place is known as a ferrule. The U.S. Supreme Court later rejected his patent. Lipman owned a book and stationery store located at 139 Chestnut Street in Philadelphia.

## Lehigh University

Asa Packer, one of the country's early industrialists and philanthropists, founded Lehigh University in Bethlehem in 1865. He gave $500,000 and 60 acres to establish the school. Packer saw a need for a technical school, which would produce professionals that could help the development of the Lehigh Valley.

Pennsylvania chartered Lehigh University in 1866. Its main building, Packer Hall, was completed in 1869. Packer erected a library building in 1877.

Lehigh University soon became a leading school in combining the study of liberal arts with a technical and scientific education.

## Leiper Tramway, The

In 1809, Thomas Leiper hitched his team of horses to a wagon to pull rock from a quarry at Crum Creek to a nearby boat landing on Ridley Creek in Delaware County. It was the first time rails were utilized for freight transportation. This first rail line in Pennsylvania later became part of the Baltimore and Ohio Railroad.

## Liberty Bell

No one can see liberty, but nothing symbolizes the ideal of liberty more than the Liberty Bell.

The inscription on the Liberty Bell reads, "Proclaim liberty throughout all the land unto all the inhabitants thereof—Lev. XXV, v. x. By order of the Assembly of the Province of Pensylvania [sic] for the State House in Philada." Those words have come to mean different things to different people, but the bell is the symbol of liberty to all Americans and an international icon of freedom.

When **William Penn** first created the government for Pennsylvania, he allowed citizens to take part in making laws and gave them the right to choose their own religion. The Pennsylvania colonists were proud and loved the freedom that Penn granted them.

*Visitors can see the Liberty Bell in Philadelphia. It is now on display in a new pavilion near Independence Hall.*

In 1751, the Pennsylvania Assembly ordered a new bell for the State House. On that bell, the assembly included a Bible verse: "Proclaim LIBERTY throughout all the Land unto all the inhabitants thereof" (Leviticus 25:10). The original bell for the Pennsylvania State House, cast in London, cracked soon after it arrived in **Philadelphia**. Local artisans John Pass and John Stow cast a new bell in 1753, using metal from the English bell. Their names appear on the front of the bell, with the city and the date.

As the official bell of the Pennsylvania State House (today known as **Independence Hall**), it rang many times, mostly for public announcements. On July 8, 1776, it rang to announce the first public reading of the **Declaration of Independence**.

A group trying to outlaw slavery in the 1830s first called the old State House bell the "Liberty Bell." These abolitionists remembered those words inscribed on the bell and adopted it as a symbol of their cause. A small crack began to affect the sound of the bell. Workers repaired the bell in 1846 and rang it for a **George Washington** birthday celebration. The bell cracked a second time and to prevent further damage, it has not rung since. It is a mystery about why the bell cracked.

In an attempt to heal the divisions caused by the Civil War, in the late 1800s the Liberty Bell was taken around the country to expositions and fairs. The symbol of liberty reminded Americans of their earlier days when they worked and fought together for their independence. In 1915, the bell made its final trip out of Pennsylvania, and came home to Philadelphia, where it remains silent.

The Liberty Bell weighs about 2000lbs. It is made of 70% copper, 25% tin, and small amounts of zinc, arsenic, lead, gold, and silver. It hangs from what is believed to be its original yoke, made from American elm, which is sometimes also known as slippery elm.

The Liberty Bell is on display at the Independence National Historic Park. The entrance to the Liberty Bell Center is on Market Street between 5th and 6th Streets. The building is open year-round, though the hours vary by season. The Liberty Bell itself is on display in a magnificent glass chamber with Independence Hall in the background.

## Liberty Bell, Return of the

Just north of **Philadelphia**, near present-day Kulpsville, the Allentown Road in Towamencin Township was the scene of an unusual and significant colonial parade. It was in June of 1778 when a 700-wagon caravan escorted the new nation's Liberty Bell on its return to Philadelphia from Allentown.

As British troops invaded the city in September 1777, the colonists feared its destruction. They rushed their precious symbol of their new freedom to Allentown, hiding it from the red coats. On its celebratory and triumphant return to Philadelphia, the Liberty Bell attracted the attraction of the farmers living along the rural road.

## Library Company

On July 1, 1731, 25-year old **Benjamin Franklin** and many of the members of a discussion group drew up the Articles of Agreement to found a library. As a group, when they foundered on a point of fact, they needed a printed authority to settle their divergence of opinion. In early colonial Pennsylvania, there were few books. Standard English reference works were expensive and rare. Alone they could not afford many imported books. By pooling their resources, they could. Fifty subscribers invested 40 shillings each and promised to pay ten shillings each year to buy books and preserve a shareholder's library. It was the beginning of the Library Company of **Philadelphia**. Still in operation today at 1314 Locust Street, the library served as the Library of Congress when Philadelphia was the nation's capital. Its holdings today include half a million rare books, 75,000 graphics, and 160,000 manuscripts. It is now the only major intact colonial library in America.

## Lightning Guider Sleds

Located at 722 Market Street, Duncannon, in Perry County, the Standard Novelty Works factory started manufacturing Lightning Guider Sleds in 1904. In 1920, the factory marked the production of more children's sleds than any other factory. Then it was producing 1600 to 1800 a day. Standard Novelty Works factory also made children's wagons, porch swings, porch gates, and furniture products. William Wills and P. F. Duncan set up the company in 1904. The factory closed in 1990.

## Lincoln in Gettysburg

At 6pm on November 18, 1863, a train carrying President Abraham Lincoln rolled to a stop in Gettysburg. A large crowd cheered the president as he stepped out. Bands played patriotic music, entertaining the large crowd as Lincoln was escorted to David Wills' home, the largest house on the town square.

After dinner, a large crowd gathered outside, calling for the president. Lincoln finally appeared, but did not say anything. He retired to the guest bedroom in the Wills house, where he would finish and review his speech that he would give the next day. The President traveled to Gettysburg to attend the dedication of the Soldiers' National Cemetery.

On Thursday morning, November 19, 1863, the weather was bright and clear. At 10am, cannons on Cemetery Hill south of town boomed. Shortly before noon, Lincoln arrived in the cemetery and took his position on the platform. Bands played patriotic music. The crowd was over 10,000.

*The procession in Gettysburg when President Lincoln gave his address at the dedication of the Soldiers' National Cemetery.*

*The only known photograph of President Lincoln at the dedication of the Soldiers' National Cemetery in Gettysburg. Lincoln is barely visible, but discernable.*

*Blurry, but discernable, this is the only known photograph of President Abraham Lincoln at the dedication of the Soldiers' National Cemetery.*

*Longwood Gardens, near Kennett Square in southeastern Chester County, lures thousands of visitors each week to its expansive gardens and displays.*

Edward Everitt, a noted orator of the day, was introduced. He looked over the hushed crowd, and he began speaking. His voice thundered and was filled with passion and emotion. He spoke for over two hours, and neared exhaustion. He closed his presentation with a strong appeal for once again raising the flag of the United States over the southern capitols.

There was a brief musical interlude, and then the president rose from his seat and faced the crowd. He took two pieces of folded paper from his coat pocket. He spoke for just two minutes, and then returned to his chair. There was polite applause for the president. Many were stunned that his speech was so short. On returning to his seat Lincoln reportedly remarked, "That speech won't scour. It is a flat failure."

When the cemetery dedication was finished, the Marine Band and other members of the military escorted Lincoln back to the center of Gettysburg. Following a dinner at the Wills' house, President Lincoln greeted guests in an informal reception. Lincoln then went to the Gettysburg train station, and traveled to Washington.

His speech had been brief, yet to the point. Its purpose was clear: unification of the northern people to support the Union cause and see the war through to the end. Some newspapers later ridiculed the president's short speech. Others mostly hailed his Gettysburg Address for its simplicity. The greatest compliment came from the day's orator, Edward Everett, who wrote the president the next day. He said, "I should be glad if I could flatter myself that I came as near to the central idea of the occasion in two hours, as you did in two minutes."

Although Lincoln himself was not impressed with his speech, and thought its delivery a failure, his simple words were destined to become immortal. His address is forever known as the Gettysburg Address.

## Lincoln Homestead

Mordecai Lincoln, the great-great-grandfather of Abraham Lincoln, bought 1,000 acres near present-day Birdsboro in Berks County. On it he built a stone house in 1733, which today is known as the "Lincoln Homestead." President Abraham Lincoln once wrote, "My ancestors were Quakers from Berks County, Pennsylvania." The house where his ancestors settled is privately owned and still standing.

## Linden Hall

Linden Hall is the oldest girls' resident school in the United States. Founded in 1746 by the Moravian Church in Lititz, Lancaster County, it was originally a day school. Since 1794, it has attracted boarding students from a wide area.

## Little League

Carl Stotz was the founder of Little League Baseball. He developed the idea of a Little League in 1938. In the next year, three teams played 24 games. Over the years, the number of teams spread to thousands with millions of players in many nations. Each year, the Little League World Series is played at Williamsport. Stotz served as the league Commissioner through 1955. The Peter J. McGovern Little League Museum is nearby.

*The entrance to Longwood Gardens, near Kennett Square, Chester County.*

## Longwood Gardens

Located near Kennett Square in southern Chester County, the massive plantation-like garden was created by Pierre S. du Pont. Over 1,050 acres, Longwood Gardens features 20 outdoor gardens, 20 indoor gardens within four acres of heated greenhouses, 11,000 different types of plants, and spectacular fountains. The exquisite grounds often hosts concerts and elaborate shows and displays. Started in the early 1900s, Longwood Gardens is open daily and attracts nearly one million visitors yearly.

*Longwood Gardens has four acres of heated greenhouses.*

## Loyalist Raid of 1778

On February 19, 1778, while British troops occupied **Philadelphia**, about 40 armed Loyalists raided the tavern located at present-day State & Mercer Streets, Newtown. The fighting in Bucks County left American soldiers dead, wounded, or captured. Tailors were working at the tavern, making uniforms for use at nearby **Valley Forge**. Over 2,000 yards of cloth were lost during the raid by those loyal to the British Crown.

## McCrory, John G.

John Graham McCrory opened his first discount department store in Scottdale, Westmoreland County, in around 1880. The single store grew into a chain that topped 1,300 units, doing business under such names as McCrory's, McLellan, H.L. Green, T.G.&Y., J.J. Newberry, and G.C. Murphy. McCrory was a business partner of **S.S. Kresge**.

## McDonald's Big Mac

McDonald's Big Mac debuted in Uniontown, Fayette County, in 1967. It was the brainchild of Jim Delligatti, one of McDonald's earliest owner/operators. Struggling with sub-par volume, Delligatti was convinced the best way to broaden his customer base was to broaden the menu. He tested the large burger, which he called the Big Mac. Test results showed a twelve percent sales increase. McDonald's then tested the burger in other markets, and it scored ten percent or better sales gains in every test. From its humble start in Pennsylvania, McDonald's today serves its signature burger by the tens of thousands every day, worldwide.

## Molly Maguires

The Molly Maguires was a secret society, comprised mainly of immigrant Irish Catholic coal miners in Pennsylvania. Its members started one of the first labor movements in the country. At the time, the Irish were not well regarded by many facets of American society. Many employers offering employment had signs posted that read, "Irish Need Not Apply."

One of the only jobs the Irish immigrant could get was working in the Pennsylvania coalmines. The job of coal miner was slave labor, at best. It was a hard life. Working for pennies in exchange for their long hours of hard work, they endured poor working conditions and the lack of safety equipment. Child labor was common. The Pennsylvania coal miners had continual health problems, high death rates, and were totally powerless against the harsh conditions created by the mine

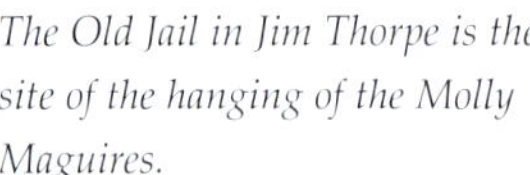
*The Old Jail in Jim Thorpe is the site of the hanging of the Molly Maguires.*

owners. These Irish immigrants were forced to buy all their own work equipment from the mine bosses. They had to pay rent to the coal mine owners who owned their houses. They could only shop at the coal bosses' town store, and were forced to pay high costs for groceries and provisions.

With no improvement, they formed the Molly Maguires. From the mid-1860s to the late 1870s, they organized a secret campaign of violence against those they considered their oppressors, including the mine owners, their superintendents, and the police, who were controlled by the mine owners.

The mine owners retaliated, ruthlessly pursuing anyone they suspected of being a Molly Maguire. In 1869, Frank B. Gowen, a lawyer, took control of the **Reading Railroad** Company. Gowen led the railroad into the coal mining business with a policy of scaring the mine operators and destroying the unions. Gowen had the money, the political power, and the police in his control. He hired the Pinkerton agency to infiltrate the Molly Maguires.

The activities of the Molly Maguires ended after a private detective joined the society, conducted espionage, and presented questionable evidence in court in 1876 and 1877. The Molly Maguires were found guilty of murdering coal management and vandalizing the mines and mining equipment. Seven were hanged in present-day **Jim Thorpe**. Management effectively snuffed out the Molly Maguires by using the state's power to execute men that tried to organize labor.

## Malaria Outbreak in Philadelphia

In 1793, **Philadelphia** was hit with a malaria outbreak. By August, with the heat of summer and an active mosquito population, Yellow Fever started to take its toll on the city. The symptoms were a severe fever and nausea, followed by black vomit, deep drowsiness, a rapid, feeble pulse, incontinence, and yellow coloring of the skin. Philadelphians reacted in varying ways to the out-of-control epidemic. Some stayed to care for the sick, while others fled in fear. Businesses and, most importantly, the federal, state, and city governments had to shut down. At the time, Philadelphia was the new nation's capital. As the situation worsened, even President Washington left the city. Finally, as Fall arrived, the weather cooled and the disease subsided as the mosquitoes died. The yellow fever epidemic devastated Philadelphia by killing over 5,000 citizens, which was ten percent of the population at the time.

## Mansfield, Jayne

Born Vera Jayne Palmer in Bryn Mawr near **Philadelphia** on April 19, 1933, Jayne Mansfield became a blonde bombshell in Hollywood. Following a pictorial layout as a Playmate in *Playboy*, she made many appearances in films as a scantily clad actress. After a string of bad marriages, Mansfield died in a tragic auto accident on June 29, 1967 in Louisiana. She was buried in her native Pennsylvania in Pen Argyl, Monroe County.

## Mason-Dixon Line

Although it is often associated with the issue of slavery and dividing North and South, the history of the Mason and Dixon Line predates the Civil War. But the Line's origin has nothing to do with the issue of slavery. The famous Line, which now decides Pennsylvania's southern border was in fact the result of a bloody and endless land dispute between the proprietors of Pennsylvania and Maryland, when America was still just a collection of British colonies.

In 1632, King Charles I of England granted the first Lord Baltimore, George Calvert, the colony of Maryland. Fifty years later, in 1682, King Charles II gave **William Penn** the territory

*One of the original markers for the Mason-Dixon Line.*

to the north of Lord Baltimore's colony, which became Pennsylvania. A year later, Penn received more land on the Delmarva Peninsula (the peninsula that today includes the eastern portion of Maryland and the entire state of Delaware).

A problem soon developed. The description of the boundaries in the land grants to Penn and Calvert did not match. There was much confusion over where the boundary lay. Maryland claimed its border, from its charter, was at the 40-degree north parallel. That would have put **Philadelphia** in Maryland.

In 1750, England's chief justice declared the boundary between Pennsylvania and Maryland should lay 15 miles south of Philadelphia. This line infringed on the Delaware territory. The court's solution was to draw a 12-mile radius from the then capital of Delaware, Newcastle, creating the rare circular boundary. A decade later, the two families agreed on the compromise and set out to have the new complicated boundary surveyed. It was a difficult job for a colonial surveyor, so the families hired two experts from England, Charles Mason and Jeremiah Dixon, British astronomers, surveyors, and mathematicians. They arrived in Philadelphia in November 1763. After finding out the exact location of Philadelphia, they then worked on fixing the arched border that formed the top of Delaware. Next, they determined the Delmarva border between Maryland and Delaware. Finally, they worked on the border that marked the line between Pennsylvania and Maryland. At times, the survey team employed up to 115 men as axmen, chainmen, cooks, and wagon drivers.

Traveling and surveying in the frontier was difficult and time-consuming. The surveyors used the most advanced astronomical and surveying equipment available. At some points along the line, they were off one inch, while other places they were off as far as 800 feet. As they worked, they marked the line with stones. Huge blocks of limestone—measuring between three and five feet long and weighing 300 to 600 pounds—were quarried in southern Great Britain and shipped to America. Carried by wagon to their final resting place on the line, the surveyors positioned the stones at one-mile intervals. Mile markers included vertical fluting, with a "P" on the north face and an "M" on the southern face. Every fifth mile along the line the stones were engraved with the Penn coat of arms on the Pennsylvania side and the Calvert coat of arms on the other. Many of the markers still exist today, although some are being lost due to vehicle damage, vandalism, or neglect.

The duo used Native American guides, although once they reached a point 36 miles east of the end point of the boundary, their guides told them not to travel any farther. Hostile area residents kept the survey from reaching its end goal. Thus, on October 9, 1767, almost four years after they began their surveying, the 233 mile-long Mason-Dixon had almost been surveyed.

On completion of the survey, both Mason and Dixon returned to England to continue their contributions to the advancement of science. In 1786, Charles Mason returned to America. He soon became ill and died a short time later. He was buried in the Christ Church burial ground in Philadelphia, PA.

## Mead, Margaret

The world-renowned anthropologist and writer was born in **Philadelphia**. She lived in Doylestown and graduated in 1918 from the Doylestown High School. Among her most famous works are *Coming of Age in Samoa* (1928) and *Male and Female* (1949). She also analyzed many problems in modern American society, and particularly those that affected youths. She died in 1978.

## Mennonites

The Mennonites were one of Pennsylvania's earliest religious groups. Accepting **William Penn**'s invitation to come to his new colony, where religious freedom was promised, the Protestant evangelical Mennonites settled in Pennsylvania. They had originated in Switzerland at the time of the Protestant Reformation.

Today's Mennonites are divided into many separate bodies. Some are more conservative and withdrawn from modern society than others. All Mennonites, however, hold in common the ideal of a religious community based on New Testament models. The rite of baptism is administered only on the profession of faith, while infant baptism is rejected. The Lord's Supper is celebrated, and the rite of foot washing is sometimes observed with it. Many Mennonites refuse to bear arms, to take judicial oaths, or to hold public office. Their plain living lifestyle and simplicity of dress distinguish the more conservative Mennonite groups. Mennonites are traditionally rural farmers.

The Mennonites emerged in the 1520s as radical Protestants. Since they rejected a state church and refused to accept military service, they were regarded as subversive and were persecuted. The Hutterites were a similar group from southern Germany and Austria. Menno Simons in the Netherlands led one of the groups. It is from him where the name Mennonite derives. Persecuted in the Rhineland, they immigrated to Pennsylvania. Their first settlement in Pennsylvania was in **Germantown**. The Mennonites soon found they had much in common with the Quakers, and thrived in their new homeland. Both groups opposed taking an oath by swearing, and were granted the right of affirmation.

The parent church of the **Amish** is the Mennonites. The Mennonite belief in adult baptism, the most important of their doctrines, attracts no attention today from the rest of the world. But their often plain dress does. Unlike the Amish, many Mennonites reject bright colored clothing, preferring grey or black. The men are usually clean-shaven. They wear coats with stand-up collars, without lapels, and flat broad-brim hats. The women wear small black bonnets with house caps of fine white linen under them. Their dresses feature tight bodices

*Mennonite woman arranging baked goods at the farmers' market near Lititz in 1942—the traditional dress has not changed over the years.*

*Mennonite children in prayer at their church near Hinkletown in the early 1940s.*

*A Mennonite church.*

and full skirts with high necks and long tight sleeves. A kerchief of the same material as the dress comes to a point at the waist in front and in back and at both shoulders. Often the women wear aprons and prefer shawls instead of coats. Their distinctive dress earned them the name "plain people."

There are many contrasting differences between the Amish and the Mennonites. Today's Mennonites consist of many diverse groups. Some still appear much like the Amish, using horse-drawn buggies for transportation. Others are modern in appearance and lifestyle, looking no different from any other American. The range of people practicing the Mennonite religion is equally diverse.

## Millersburg Ferry

About 20 miles north of **Harrisburg**, along the eastern shore of the **Susquehanna River**, is the little historic town of Millersburg. Sometime in the early 1800s, a ferryboat started running from Millersburg to the western shore of the Susquehanna, about two miles south of Liverpool. Today, mostly a tourist attraction, the ferry still runs, from May through October. It is the only ferryboat still running on the Susquehanna.

## Mills Brothers, The

William Mills, a barber in Bellefonte, Centre County, was also a local Jubilee Singer. His barbershop operated from 1871 to 1931. His son, John, grew up around William's singing, and later moved to Ohio. There, William's grandsons formed the first vocal group to overcome racial barriers, gaining mass audience. The group started in 1925 and lasted until 1981.

## Mingo, White

On Sunday, January 10, 1768, Frederick Stump murdered White Mingo and five other Indians. Six Indians, White Mingo, Cornelius, John Campbell, Jones, and two women, came to Stump's house, near the mouth of Middle Creek, in present-day Snyder County.

Being drunk and disorderly, he endeavored to get them to leave, which they would not do. Fearing injury to himself, he killed them, dragged them to the creek, and chopped a hole in the ice. He threw in their bodies.

Worried that the news might be carried to the other Indians, Stump traveled the next day to two cabins, fourteen miles farther up the creek, where he found one woman and two girls, with one child. He killed them, placed their bodies into the cabin, and burned it. These killings were on the run that enters the creek at Middleburg. Stump and his companion, known as Iron-Cutter, were arrested and taken to **Carlisle** jail. They were forcibly rescued on the 29th, sheltered at **Fort Augusta** for a few days, and then fled the country. According to tradition, Stump died in Virginia many years later.

William Blythe gave this account of the murder of White Mingo at **Philadelphia**, having heard much of the story directly from Frederick Stump. He also explored and found evidence of the crimes. Blythe received two tracts of land (which were surveyed on applications in the names of his daughters, Margaret and Elizabeth), containing, together, 640 acres, immediately south of White Deer Creek. Blythe was one of the first settlers of Buffalo Valley, an Indian trader at Shippensburg in 1748, and served as a lieutenant in the French and Indian War.

## Mister Rogers' Neighborhood

In 1928, Fred McFeely Rogers was born in Latrobe, about 40 miles east of **Pittsburgh**. He studied music in college and, in the 1950s, he worked as a puppeteer for "The Children's Corner." Both were learning opportunities for Rogers. He would later use his music knowledge to write songs for his TV show where many of his character puppets would appear. In 1963, he was ordained a Presbyterian minister and continued his work with children and families through television. With his trademark gentle voice and manner, Fred Rogers created a children's show called *Mister Rogers' Neighborhood*. A PBS show that originated from WQED in Pittsburgh, Rogers' show became the longest running show on public television. He filmed the last original show in 2001. With nurturing warmth, it showcased Rogers' humble and real-life demeanor. On the wall of his office, Mr. Rogers kept a simple sign: "Life is for Service." *Mister Rogers' Neighborhood* won dozens of awards, including four Emmys. His cardigan sweater hangs in the Smithsonian. In 2002, President George W. Bush presented Rogers with the Presidential Medal of Freedom, the nation's highest civilian honor, recognizing his contribution to the well-being of children and a career in public television. On February 27, 2003, Fred Rogers died after a brief battle with cancer.

## Mix, Tom

Born January 6, 1880, in Driftwood, Cameron County, the famous cowboy star of cinema was a soldier during the Spanish-American War. He became popular and successful for his "wild west" roles in hundreds of silent and sound motion pictures between 1910 and 1935. Remembered for his scenes with his trusty steed, "Tony, the Wonder Horse," Tom Mix died on October 12, 1940 in an auto accident in Arizona.

## Morewood Massacre

In April 1891, at the Morewood Mines of the Frick Coke Co., sheriff deputies shot and killed seven strikers. They were among thousands of immigrant workers striking for higher wages in Pennsylvania's coke region. Ten thousand mourners attended the strikers' funeral. The families of the strikers opted for their burial in a mass grave in St. John's Cemetery, Scottsdale. By late May, the strike collapsed, and the union organizing of coke workers failed.

## Morris, Robert

Robert Morris was born in Lancashire, England, in January 1733. At the age of 13, he moved to America with his father, a tobacco agent from Liverpool, England. Settling, at first, in Maryland, Morris was later sent to **Philadelphia** to serve an apprenticeship in the counting house of Charles Willing, one of Philadelphia's first successful merchants. Morris flourished in his position and went on to become a full partner in Willing and Morris, a firm that went on to establish transatlantic connections. In his 39-year partnership with Willing, Morris made large-scale investments in ships and land, and as his success grew in the importing business he soon began to amass his own legendary fortune. His grand Philadelphia town house, which became a popular venue for important social gatherings, was presided over by his wife, Mary White, whom he married in 1769.

When the British Stamp Act hurt his enterprises Morris chose independence from England. Elected to the **Continental Congress** in 1775, he served on many of the committees involved in raising capital and supplies for the Continental Army. Representing Pennsylvania, Morris was one of the signers of the **Declaration of Independence**. Late in 1776, the Continental Army was in severe deprivation because of a shortage of capital and the failure of several of the colonies in paying for the war. Morris loaned $10,000 of his own money to the new government.

By 1781, Morris had developed a plan for a National Bank, which he presented to Congress. Following congressional approval, the newly established Bank of North America brought stability to the colonial economy, eased continued finance of the War effort, and set up the credit of the United States with the nations of Europe. Congress appointed Morris Financial Agent (Secretary of Treasury) of the United States to direct the operation of the new bank. Morris declined the Secretary of the Treasury when President Washington offered it to him, and suggested Alexander Hamilton as an alternative.

Morris retired from public life in 1795, but his opponents continued to criticise his unsuccessful attempt to settle wartime accounts with the government. The following year Morris gave bonds for $93,312 to clear his ledger of

*Above: An 18th-century cartoon comparing the U.S. Constitution to a ship going on a journey via Philadelphia. Morris is depicted at the helm of the ship, saying "I will venture all for Philadelphia."*

*Right: Portrait of Robert Morris.*

these debts. At this time he was generally considered to be the richest man in America, but behind the public facade of his immense land holdings lay an ever-decreasing supply of cash.

Morris went on to join James Greenleaf and John Nicholson in a grand scheme to develop the newly designated capital of Washington, where he invested in over 7,000 lots. But after a London bank failure Morris lost £124,000—a loss that he was never able to recover. What little was left of his fortune was soon lost to land speculation in the western part of New York. Faced with bankruptcy and hounded by debt collectors, Morris retreated to his country home. In February 1798 he was taken to debtors' prison in Philadelphia, with an estimated debt of $3 million. Released from jail in August 1801, Morris lived the rest of his life a humble man, relying heavily on the charity of friends. Morris died in poverty on May 8, 1806 at the age of 73.

## Morton, John

John Morton was born in Ridley Park, Delaware County, in 1724. His stepfather, a well-educated surveyor from England, provided Morton with a sound education in surveying. In 1756, Morton was elected to the Provincial Assembly, and was elected president of the Assembly in 1775. Morton held numerous civil offices in Pennsylvania, including Justice of the Peace, High Sheriff, Presiding Judge of the General Court and the Court of Common Pleas. In 1774, he was appointed Associate Judge of the Supreme Court of Pennsylvania. That year he was elected to the **Continental Congress**. Representing Pennsylvania, Morton was one of the signers of the **Declaration of Independence**. Morton served on several committees and was the chairman of the committee which prepared and presented the **Articles of Confederation**. Morton died at the age of 53 in 1777.

*Left: Session of the first Congress, September, 1774. John Morton was elected to the Continental Congress as Pennsylvania's representative.*

*Far left: The statue of Robert Morris in Philadelphia.*

# M

*Portrait of Anna Jarvis, who championed Mother's Day in America.*

## Mother's Day

Anna Jarvis (1864–1948) from the small town of Grafton, West Virginia, wrote thousands of letters to influential people in her effort to gain recognition for the traditional female role of motherhood. Jarvis had moved from her native West Virginia to Pennsylvania in 1904 to take a position as a literary editor for a **Philadelphia** publisher. Her efforts worked. Pennsylvania declared Mother's Day a state observance in 1913. The state was the first in the nation to recognize Mother's Day. Congress followed Pennsylvania's lead a year later, proclaiming the second Sunday of May as Mother's Day.

## Mount Davis

Located within Forbes State Forest, Mount Davis is the highest point in Pennsylvania, at 3,213 feet above sea level. The Mount Davis Natural Area comprises 581 acres in Elk Lick Township, in Somerset County, surrounding the rock known as Mount Davis on the summit of Negro Mountain. Picnic areas are available and, from there, many people hike to the top of Mount Davis.

## Mummers

Mummery is a tradition in **Philadelphia**, and the annual famous Mummers Parade dates from pre-Colonial times. It resulted from a blend of Swedish, Finnish, Irish, English, German, African-American, and other European heritages. When the Mummers go into full swing, the New Year's holiday is celebrated in Philadelphia as it is nowhere else in the world. The term "mummer" comes from the Old French momer, which means to wear a mask. The dictionary tells us that it means a masked or costumed merrymaker, especially at a festival. That is what the Philadelphia Mummers do: they turn New Year's Day into a festival. Despite harsh, cold winter weather, the Mummers strut, dance, and play music in a

*Just one of the Mummers that appear in the Philadelphia New Year's Day Parade.*

daylong parade. The annual parades include juried competitions. The revelry is as intense as the rivalry between the many mummer groups of Philadelphia, assuring the hearty spectators a great show.

## Mütter Museum

Set up by Thomas Dent Mütter in 1856, this **Philadelphia** museum was intended to display medical rarities. Today, it is one of Pennsylvania's most unusual museums. Its collections contain some 20,000 human specimens and medical instruments from the 19th century to the present. From displays of skeletons to a collection of human skulls, from dried-out organs to an exhumed body of an obese woman, the Mütter Museum does not display reasonable facsimiles, but, rather, the real thing. Even the Secret Tumor of Grover Cleveland, which is no longer a secret, is on display at the museum located at 22nd Street, just south of Market, in Philadelphia.

# N O

## National Road

In the southwestern corner of Pennsylvania, there are 90 miles of a roadway that helped to build the nation. The first federally funded road in the United States, the portion in Pennsylvania is currently known as Route 40.

As settlers moved west, a means of linking the people and cities along the Eastern seaboard to those on the frontiers west of the Allegheny Mountains became important. Easterners were unable to take advantage of the plentiful produce and goods from the western frontier. Settlers moving west lacked a well-defined roadway. Construction began in 1811, and by 1818, the road stretched from Cumberland, Maryland, through Pennsylvania, to what is now Wheeling, West Virginia. When finished, it eventually ran 600 miles to Vandalia, Illinois.

*Wilson Bridge spans Conococheague Creek on the old Route 40.*

## Nescopeck

The small town of Nescopeck was named for the Shawnee-Delaware Indian village that was located along the **Susquehanna River** at the present-day Luzerne and Columbia County border. It was a meeting place for Indians fighting the English during the **French and Indian War** until the British built **Fort Augusta** in 1756. Nescopeck is an Indian word meaning "black, deep, and still water."

## Nixon, John

The first public reading of the **Declaration of Independence** was on Monday, July 8, 1776. Colonel John Dixon, of the **Philadelphia** Committee of Safety at the State House read aloud the text of the document in Philadelphia. Throughout the city, bells were rung all day.

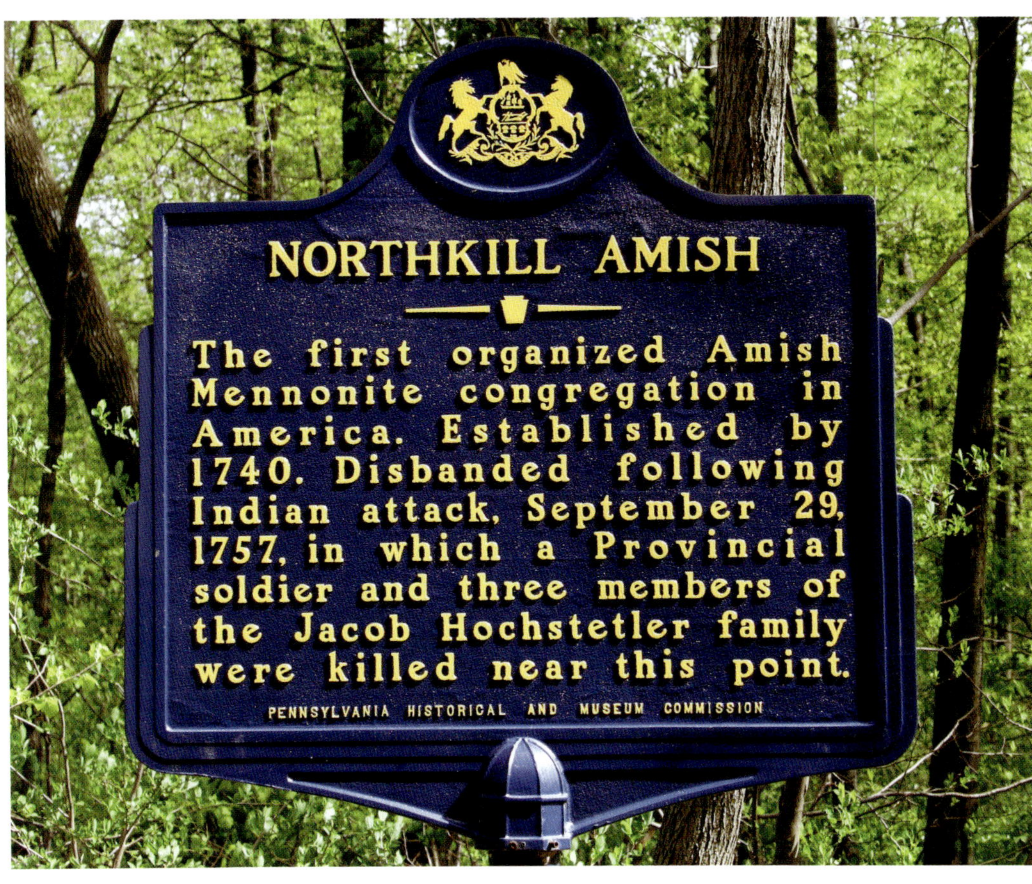


*Only this historic marker remains of the first Amish settlement in the early Pennsylvania frontier.*

## Northkill Amish

Early settlers established the first organized **Amish Mennonite** congregation in America in 1740, west of Hamburg, in Berks County. The area was, at the time, deep in Pennsylvania's frontier. The congregation disbanded following an Indian attack on September 29, 1757. A provincial soldier and three members of the Jacob Hochstetler family were killed during the Indian raid.

## Old Jail

Located in Jim Thorpe, the Old Jail at 128 West Broad Street, was opened in 1871. Alexander Campbell, accused of being a leader of the **Molly Maguires**, was convicted of being an accessory to murder in 1877, but proclaimed his innocence to the end. When Campbell was led to the gallows from cell 17, he slapped his grimy handprint on the wall. Campbell declared the handprint would remain for all-time a reminder of the injustice that took his life. Over the years, despite the best efforts of superstitious sheriffs of Carbon County, Campbell's handprint has survived being cleaned, painted over, concreted over and having a new wall applied. The cursed handprint always reappeared. Recent scientific examination by forensic experts cannot explain this phenomenon.

# P

## Packer, Asa

Born in Mystic, Connecticut on December 20, 1805, Packer started his long, prosperous career as an apprentice carpenter. He moved to Mauch Chunk, and owned and operated canal boats, which moved coal to **Philadelphia**. He eventually established the Lehigh Valley Railroad, which ran rail lines to major cities in Pennsylvania. He also donated money and land to found **Lehigh University**.

Packer entered politics, and became a member of Pennsylvania state house of representatives, 1842–43; a state court judge in Pennsylvania, 1843–48; and a U.S. Representative to Congress, 13th District, 1853–57. He was a candidate for Democratic nomination for President in 1868 and then a candidate for Governor of Pennsylvania in 1869. He died in Philadelphia on May 17, 1879. Some believe he held the largest fortune in Pennsylvania at the time of his death.

*The Asa Packer mansion is open for public tours in Jim Thorpe.*

## Paoli Massacre

In 1777, the British Army camped at Tredyffrin in preparation for crossing the Schuylkill River and entering **Philadelphia**. Lord Howe received word that General "Mad" **Anthony Wayne** lurked nearby, waiting to ambush the red coats. Howe changed his battle plans. He instead would ambush Wayne at his camp in Paoli. Just after midnight on September 21, 1777, the British struck Wayne's unprepared American camp. The British commander, Lord Grey, had ordered his men to remove the flints from their rifles before their attack. Razor-sharp bayonets—a weapon Americans considered barbaric—were their weapons of choice. The British killed 53 Americans and wounded over 100 in Grey's lightning raid. The use of the bayonet, coupled with the belief that the British stabbed the Americans who tried to surrender, made martyrs of those Americans maimed and killed at what became known as the Paoli Massacre.

## Paxton Boys, The

The Paxton Boys lived in Paxton (Paxtang) Township near **Harrisburg**, which was then the western frontier of colonial Pennsylvania. They protested the colonial government's unwillingness to aid the western settlers against the Indians. Therefore, they simply took matters into their own hands. With a force numbering in the hundreds and armed mostly with hand weapons, the Paxton Boys stayed outside the English law and common decency for several years. Fed by a frenzy of reports of what the warriors loyal to Chief Pontiac were doing in western Pennsylvania, the Paxton Boys vowed revenge. This group of organized thugs, self-appointed militia, and protectors of the settlers found the Conestoga an easy target. In 1763, the mounted Paxton Boys galloped into **Conestoga Indian Town**, and quickly slaughtered the six people they found in the village. True to their word, they brutally killed any Indian they saw.

The provincial council of **Lancaster** County ordered the remaining Conestoga to be taken into protective custody. However, the government's plan failed. Authorities transported 14

Conestoga—men, women, and children—to the jail, and locked them in for their own protection. The Paxton Boys rode back into town, and like bloodhounds, found the Conestoga. They broke into the jail. There they did their dirty work, slaughtering all 14 Conestoga, beating them to a bloody pulp. The blood-splattered Paxton Boys did not stop until all the Conestoga were dead. Not a single person challenged any of the Paxton Boys. Authorities never charged anyone with a crime. Although most colonists were appalled when they heard the news of what had happened, no one answered for the vicious attack that had occurred in Lancaster. There were never any legal consequences for anyone that participated in the massacre of the Conestoga.

Only two Conestoga, a husband and wife, known as Michael and Mary, who happened to be working at another farm that day, survived the attack. Pennsylvania Governor John Penn eventually issued papers of protection, which remained in effect until their death. When Michael and Mary died, it was the end of the Conestoga, the first inhabitants of Lancaster County.

## Penn, William

Although William Penn founded Pennsylvania, he only spent about three years of his life in the state. Dying at the age of 73 at Ruscombe in Berkshire from the complications of a stroke, William Penn was buried at Old Jordan's Cemetery, Jordan, England. Under a simple headstone, William Penn forever rests, thousands of miles away from the British colony he founded, all because of his religious beliefs.

William Penn was born October 24, 1644 somewhere close to the Tower of London, the fortress prison where he would later spend nine months in solitary confinement. His father was a famed English admiral, Sir William Penn. Young William grew up during a stormy time of revolution and reaction in England. He was educated at the University of Oxford. For a short time, he was a soldier, and successful enough that he thought of making a career in the British army. But while at the University, he converted to Quakerism, which was also known as the Society of Friends. Seeing violence and persecution, Penn dreamed of a society where war had no place, and anyone could worship according to his own conscience. Quakers, who were pacifists, fought political battles for freedom of religion, assembly, and the right of trial by jury.

In 1666, his father had sent him to Ireland to oversee his estates, but his newfound religious convictions conflicted with the authorities, and they threw him in prison. When he returned to England, Penn wrote a religious tract, *The Sandy Foundation Shaken*, that he published without a license. Again, Penn landed in jail, and while imprisoned in the Tower of London in 1669, he wrote *No Cross, No Crown* and *Innocency with Her Open Eyes*.

He was imprisoned again in 1671, and while in custody, he wrote *The Great Cause of Liberty of Conscience*, a defense of the doctrine

*Historic late 18th-century print of the harbor frontage at Philadelphia by engraver Balthasar Leizelt.*

of toleration. In 1672 he married Gulielma Maria Springett. It was also the year that he wrote the "Concessions and Agreements" charter for Quaker colonists who were settling in the newly acquired New Jersey. Among its provisions were the right to trial by jury, the freedom from arbitrary imprisonment for debt, and an edict against capital punishment. Penn strongly argued for religious freedom, writing "no Men . . . hath Power or authority to rule over Men's Consciences in Religious matters."

In 1681, in payment for a debt owed to his father, William Penn got a land grant from King Charles II. Out of "regard to the memorie and meritts of his late father," the King gave the younger Penn a huge tract of land in North America and named it, in honor of the Admiral, "Pennsylvania," or Penn's Woods.

Now he could set up a land that would tolerate religious freedom. Penn's plan included making money by selling tracts of land. Although he was able to attract investors, he never realized the profit he imagined. Penn saw this venture as more than a moneymaking exercise. It was a "holy experiment." He confidently predicted that this experiment would become, "the seed of a nation."

Penn imagined a "free, sober, and industrious people" living by their own laws. In 1682 he drafted these laws in the First Frame of government, which included many of the terms he wrote for the New Jersey settlement. With several friends, he sailed for America in September 1682, and in October he met with the Native American tribes. He planned and named the city of Philadelphia, which meant the city of brotherly love. He advertised for settlers, and, for two years, he governed the new colony wisely.

He was only able to stay two years. It was toward the end of the reign of Charles II of England, and Penn returned to England to aid persecuted Quakers there. Penn was twice accused of treason, but he was acquitted. Under suspicion of treason, Penn lost control of his colony from 1692 to 1694. His wife died in 1694, though he married Hannah Callowhill a year and a half later.

In 1699, Penn made a second visit to Pennsylvania, where his presence was required to restore peace and order after the arbitrary actions of his appointed deputy. Penn stayed at the Slate Roof House, a **Philadelphia** home owned by Samuel Carpenter. It was in this house that his son John Penn was born on January 29, 1700. The only one of Penn's children born in Pennsylvania, John would always carry the nickname of "the American." Penn spent little time at his estate, Pennsbury Manor.

Penn's accomplishments during this visit included suppressing piracy, granting a charter to Philadelphia, and the issuance of the Charter of Privileges, a guarantee of religious freedom.

Although Penn planned to stay in the New World, living at his Pennsbury Manor, further political troubles in England forced him to return. He left for England late in 1701, leaving the management of his affairs to an agent whose manipulations ruined him. Then in 1712, Penn suffered a disabling attack of apoplexy. His wife Hannah managed his affairs until Penn died in Buckinghamshire on July 30, 1718. After her death in 1727, the ownership of Pennsylvania passed to their sons, John, Thomas, and Richard.

## Pennsbury Manor

Penn's cousin and deputy governor, William Markham, chose the site of Pennsbury months before **William Penn**'s arrival in America. A three-storied, brick manor house, rebuilt on the original foundations, stands on the point of land formed by the Delaware River between Morrisville and Bristol, north of **Philadelphia**. The land deed of July 15, 1682 was the first

*The country estate of William Penn. The proprietor and governor of Pennsylvania only stayed a short time at Pennsbury, located in present day Bucks County. Pressing matters in England forced Penn to return there. He spent less than a year at his estate.*

executed between Penn and the Indian Sache. Pennsbury became Penn's home in the New World. When he returned to Pennsylvania the second time in 1699, he and his second wife Hannah stayed at the home, despite being difficult to reach. The existing roads were nearly impassable except on horseback. The only comfortable means of travel was by water. Penn left Pennsylvania in 1701, never to return to his beloved Pennsbury Manor.

## Pennsylvania—The Nation's Capital

Three different Pennsylvania cities served as the nation's capital before Congress established Washington, D.C. Those cities were **Philadelphia**, **Lancaster**, and **York**. The First Continental Congress met in **Carpenter's Hall** in Philadelphia, from September 5, 1774 to October 24, 1774. The Second Continental Congress met in the State House, now known as **Independence Hall**, from May 10, 1775 to December 12, 1776. Congress then moved to Baltimore.

Congress reconvened in Philadelphia at the State House from March 4, 1777 to September 18, 1777. As the British advanced toward Philadelphia, Congress fled to the safety of Lancaster, meeting there just one day, September 27, 1777, in the Court House. Congress decided it was safer to move west of the Susquehanna River.

From September 30, 1777 to June 27, 1778, Congress met in the Court House in York. Then known as Yorktowne, it is here that Congress passed the **Articles of Confederation** and first proclaimed a day for Thanksgiving. In York, it was the first time the new country and former

P

colonies of Britain referred to themselves as the United States of America.

Congress returned to Philadelphia on July 2, 1778. On March 1, 1781 the Articles of Confederation went into effect. Congress remained in Philadelphia until June 21, 1783, when they moved to Princeton, then Annapolis, Maryland; Trenton, New Jersey; and then into New York City.

Congress remained in New York until adjourning on August 12, 1790. Congress returned to Philadelphia on December 6, 1790 and remained there until May 14, 1800. While in Philadelphia, Congress met at the Philadelphia County Building. When Congress left Philadelphia, it reconvened in Washington, D.C. on November 17, 1800.

## Pennsylvania Dutch

The Pennsylvania Dutch are not from Holland. German Protestants came to Penn's Woods in search of religious freedom. Those Germans, moved further inland from **Philadelphia**. They became known as Pennsylvania Dutch, derived from the word Deutsch, a German word meaning Germans.

**Lancaster** County became the center of these "Dutchmen" but they also settled further north in the Lebanon Valley and Lehigh Valley, as well as west of the **Susquehanna** in **York** and Adams County. They spoke their native language of German, not Dutch, until they learned English.

## Pennsylvania Grapes

Few people associate grape growing with Pennsylvania. From its early colonization, grapes have been successfully grown throughout the state. In recent years, Pennsylvania wineries have sprung up throughout the state, fermenting locally grown grapes into different wines.

In Erie County, located in the Grape Coast region of Pennsylvania, the city of North East has four thriving wineries. It is also the home to the largest Welch's grape processing plant in the country. The Concord, Massachusetts-based company is the world's leading producer of juice, jam, and jelly products made from Concord and Niagara grapes.

## Pennsylvania Hospital

Colonial America's first hospital was in **Philadelphia**. **Benjamin Franklin**'s legendary challenge to the Colonial government stated that he could raise the same amount of money from the community as he and the hospital's cofounder, Dr. Thomas Bond. The Pennsylvania Assembly granted the charter establishing Pennsylvania Hospital on May 11, 1751.

The hospital includes America's first surgical amphitheatre, constructed in 1804, and is on the top floor, where it had access to the best natural light. Doctor Benjamin Rush, a signatory of the **Declaration of Independence**, taught and practiced at the facility. Soldiers of every American war, starting with the Revolutionary, have been treated at this hospital. Located at 800 Spruce Street near 8th Street, the hospital today offers tours that focus on surgical artifacts, the nation's first medical library, and exhibits depicting early-American medical procedures. The grounds feature the preserved Pine Building, which includes an apothecary, and a winding three-story staircase that leads to the 13,000-volume library featuring a preserved seven-pound tumor and a variety of surgical instruments.

## Pennsylvania Lottery

The Pennsylvania Lottery was established on August 26, 1971 by the state legislature. The Pennsylvania Lottery is the only state lottery that targets all of its proceeds to benefit older citizens. Since its introduction, program benefits have expanded to include rent rebates, free and reduced-fare transit, reduced car registration fees, a co-pay prescription drug program, and funding for Area Agencies on Aging services. Since inception and through June 2003, the Pennsylvania Lottery provided more than $13.8 billion to programs benefiting older Pennsylvanians. The Lottery has also paid more than $17.68 billion in the form of prizes to individual players.

*Pennsylvania's Lottery is the only state lottery that benefits older residents of the state. A senior citizen witnesses the daily drawings.*

## Pennsylvania Signers

Nine Pennsylvanians signed the **Declaration of Independence**. In **Philadelphia**, they signed the document that started the new nation. Each affixed their signatures to the document that ended, "And for the support of this Declaration, with a firm reliance on the protection of divine Providence, we mutually pledge to each other our Lives, our Fortunes and our sacred Honor." Signing for Pennsylvania was Robert Morris, Benjamin Rush, **Benjamin Franklin**, John Morton, George Clymer, James Smith, George Taylor, James Wilson, and George Ross.

## Pennsylvania State Police

At the beginning of the 20th century, Pennsylvania's **coal**, iron mills, **railroads**, and timber forests had played a role in the Industrial Revolution. Pennsylvania had changed from a largely agricultural state into a complex industrial center.

By 1900, bitter labor disputes between the managers and the workers they employed were becoming more frequent in the area. Violence became common in the new communities that sprang up around the coalfields, iron mills, textile factories, and railroad yards. It was obvious the town constables, sheriffs, and similar local officials, who had been enough to keep the peace in more stable times, were becoming unable to cope with the new populations and the violent labor disputes that were prevalent at the time.

The Pennsylvania State Police was created as an executive department of state government by legislation (Senate Bill 278), signed into law by Governor Samuel W. Pennypacker on May 2, 1905. It was the first uniformed police organization of its kind in the United States and served as a model for other state police agencies throughout the nation.

In the beginning, opposition to creating the State Police was strong, vocal, and persistent. Organized labor feared the State Police would be used as a private army. To allay those fears, the law limited the original complement to only 228 men. The State Police were to patrol Pennsylvania's entire 45,000 square miles. The new police force was divided into four Troops, which were positioned in Reading, Wilkes-Barre, Greensburg, and Punxsutawney.

As the new officers began law enforcement in Pennsylvania, they proved their worth. They tracked down criminals, handled mob control, and patrolled the rural agricultural areas. They dealt fairly and impartially with the public. Training became important, and the first State Police training facility in the nation was established, first in Newville, then in Hershey. As automobiles came into use, the State Police patrolled with motorcycles, and used a **flag stop** for calls.

A separate State Highway Patrol department emerged in 1923, to handle the growing number of highways. The Highway Patrol merged with the State Police on June 29, 1937.

The new department became the Pennsylvania Motor Police. In 1943, the state legislature changed the name again to the Pennsylvania State Police. Today, the approved complement of the Pennsylvania State Police is over 4,500 sworn members. In addition, there are over 1,600 civilians serving in various roles throughout the Department.

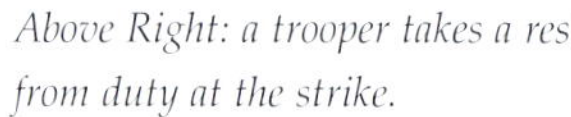

*Above Right: a trooper takes a rest from duty at the strike.*

*Right: The Pennsylvania Motor Police were on duty at King Farm near Morrisville during the strike when workers protested against the low wage of seventeen cents and twenty cents an hour.*

## Pennsylvania Turnpike

The Allegheny Mountains that divide Pennsylvania have always posed a barrier to transportation. Both William Vanderbilt and **Andrew Carnegie** found that out. The two tried to build a railroad from **Harrisburg** west to **Pittsburgh** to compete with a more northerly route provided by the booming Pennsylvania Railroad. Over one-half of the roadbed was constructed and seven tunnels partially excavated before Vanderbilt ran out of money in 1885.

By 1910, proposals to convert the abandoned railway route into a motorway surfaced. Each year, the idea of a turnpike to cross the Alleghenies circulated and the trucking industry as well as the motoring public supported it. A feasibility study began in 1934 with surveyors collecting information and engineers selecting routes and preparing plans. In 1937, the state legislature created the Pennsylvania Turnpike Commission during a period when the nation was still recovering from the Depression. President Franklin Roosevelt supported the construction on the turnpike to lower unemployment through his WPA (Works Progress Administration) program.

Officials displayed a model of this new superhighway at the 1939 New York City World's Fair. The new turnpike was similar to Germany's 100-mph autobahns, built to serve the needs of the users, rather than the terrain into which it was built.

The Pennsylvania Turnpike project was from Middlesex, located west of Harrisburg, 160 miles to Irwin, east of Pittsburgh. For the project to be constructed and completed on schedule in a mere 20 months, 1,100 engineers were employed. At first, the turnpike's engineers considered building a tunnel near Everett, but later it was decided to remove 1.1 million cubic yards of rock and earth to create the largest open cut of its time. The engineers chose a standard sight distance of 600 feet. Engineers designed straight sections to suit speeds up to 100 mph and the spiral curves were designed to allow speeds up to 70 mph. The road builders carved easy grades through valleys, ravines, and mountains. Almost 70 percent of the original turnpike was straight, and the longest, a 40-mile stretch west of **Carlisle**, was relieved by one curve to break the monotony.

Whenever possible, the turnpike designers laid out a route with southern exposures to allow the sun to heat the ice and snow on the roads. Tollbooths off the turnpike were located on downhill grades to allow drivers time to react instead of suddenly coming upon them unexpectedly. Besides the roadway, there were over 300 bridges and culverts, nine interchanges, ten service plazas, and 11 tollbooths to design.

After the engineers completed the final plans in October 1938, 155 construction companies and 15,000 workers from 18 states were under contract with the Turnpike Commission. Six of the seven original railway tunnels, ranging from 3,500 to 6,800 feet, needed to be completed, or widened, to allow two lanes of vehicles. Work began at a slow pace because of difficulties getting right of way, but a year later 50 crews were building a superhighway at a rate of three and a half miles a day.

On October 1, 1940, the Pennsylvania Turnpike officially opened. The new road displayed the newest ideas of superhighway design and proved that revenue bonds could finance toll roads. Planners predicted that 1.3 million vehicles would use the turnpike each year, but early use was 2.4 million vehicles. There were times when as many as 10,000 vehicles per day used the turnpike.

The turnpike lessened travel time between Pittsburgh and Harrisburg by three hours. It also created an economic boom to areas along its path. Following the success of the Pennsylvania Turnpike, other states began plans to build their own toll roads after the war, including Ohio, Indiana, Illinois, New York, and New Jersey. The Pennsylvania Turnpike Commission expanded the 160-mile route to 514 miles. Today, the Pennsylvania Turnpike, part of Interstate 76 and carrying 156.2 million vehicles a year, is still recognized as the first of a new breed of American tollways in the interstate highway system.

## Pennsylvania's Animal Life

Pennsylvania has an abundance of animal wildlife. Many are protected by the state's game laws, and their habitats are protected by state forest natural areas, sanctuaries, or state game lands.

The white-tailed deer is the most common large animal in the state. Black bears, at one time nearly extinct in Pennsylvania, are now plentiful and found throughout the state. Among the various small animals in Pennsylvania are woodchucks, squirrels, and rabbits. Other fur-bearing animals include the muskrat, coyote, opossum, beaver, raccoon, gray and red fox, skunk, ermine, and weasel.

Salamanders, amphibians, reptiles, and fish are found throughout Pennsylvania. Although most snakes in the state are harmless, poisonous rattlesnakes and copperheads live in some mountain and forest areas. Trout, pickerel, bass, pike, perch, and catfish are abundant in the state's lakes and streams.

Game birds include wild turkeys, partridge, ruffed grouse, and geese. The songbirds in the state include the mockingbird, oriole, cardinal, song sparrow, mourning dove, robin, and bobolink.

## Pennsylvania's Biggest Pothole

Archbald Pothole State Park is a 150-acre park in northeastern Pennsylvania, and includes the state's biggest pothole. The park gets its name from Archbald Pothole, a geologic feature that formed around 15,000 years ago during the Wisconsin Glacial Period.

The pothole has an elliptical shape and is 38 feet deep. The diameter of the pothole decreases downward. The largest diameter is 42 feet by 24 feet. At the bottom of the natural pothole, it is 17 feet by 14 feet. The pothole has a volume of about 18,600 cubic feet, so it could hold about 140,000 gallons. Archbald Pothole State Park is located in Lackawanna County, nine miles north of **Scranton**.

## Pennsylvania's First Railroad Tunnel

In 1833, the Staple Bend Tunnel east of Johnstown was the first railroad tunnel built in the Western Hemisphere. The **Allegheny Portage Railroad** used the tunnel during its operation.

## Philadelphia

Philadelphia, the largest city in Pennsylvania, was founded by **William Penn** in 1682. Located in the southeast corner of the state on the western shore of the Delaware River at the confluence of the Schuylkill River, it is about 100 miles inland from the Atlantic Ocean. Philadelphia is strategically located about halfway between Washington, D.C. and New York City.

Philadelphia's nickname may be the best known of any in the United States. Often referred to as the City of Brotherly Love, the nickname traces from the Greek meaning of the word Philadelphia. Penn chose the name to coincide with his master plan of opening the city to people of diverse religious and ethnic backgrounds. Penn welcomed anyone, which added a rich diversity to the new establishment. That diversity is still prevalent today.

Philadelphia is also known as the **Birthplace** of the Nation because of its role in the struggle for independence from the British. Both the **Declaration of Independence** and the **U.S. Constitution** were drafted and adopted in Philadelphia.

William Penn's original street plan was a grid of established blocks. Penn's grid set up rectangular blocks, and included public squares. Numbered streets ran north and south, and streets named for trees ran east and west. Today, those streets still exist, and include names such as Pine, Chestnut, Spruce, Walnut, and Locust. Penn offered large lots to those willing to invest and settle in Philadelphia. His plan eliminated the overcrowding that was prevalent in other 17th-century cities.

Early settlers dug cellars, and spent their first winter in them. As better weather arrived in the spring, their industrious labor produced permanent structures. Along Penn's streets in his beloved Philadelphia, row houses of two and three stories were built. His city grew into a population center spurred by commerce and industry. Original lot owners divided their land, added alleys, and courts. They built

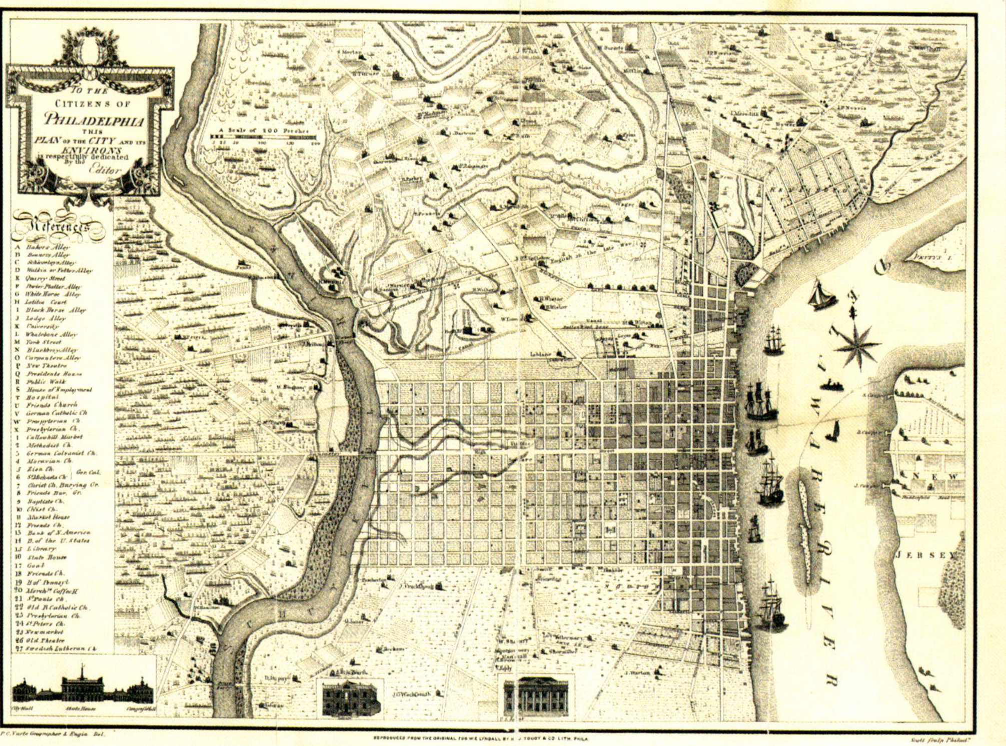


*Map of Philadelphia from 1875.*

rental units. Tenements offered affordable housing for thousands of Jewish, Irish, and black immigrants.

Center Square, today known as Penn Square, marked the center of William Penn's original plan. It is where two main thoroughfares, Broad and Market Streets, intersect. In 1871, the City of Philadelphia started constructing a massive city hall building. Thirty years later, it was completed. When finished, it was the largest municipal building in the country. A prominent statue of William Penn stands on top of the structure. For years, no building exceeded the height of the Penn statue, keeping it a focal point in the city.

Philadelphia contributed much to the growth of Pennsylvania and the nation. As a center of commerce, the city was the home to many of the founders. Most notable is **Benjamin Franklin**. The historic district of Philadelphia, which includes some of the nations most distinguished symbols, is known as Center City. The Independence National Historic Park protects many of the buildings, such as **Independence Hall**, **Carpenter's Hall**, the **Betsy Ross House**, and other important artifacts, such as the **Liberty Bell**.

Philadelphia is home to several important universities, including the University of Pennsylvania, Jefferson Medical College, Drexel

*Modern day Philadelphia skyline at dusk. The city mixes modern architecture with its historic buildings.*

P

*Right: Philadelphia City Hall in the evening; notice Ben Franklin atop the steeple. For years, no building was permitted to be taller than Ben Franklin's hat. The ordinance has since changed, and Philadelphia now has it share of modern skyscrapers.*

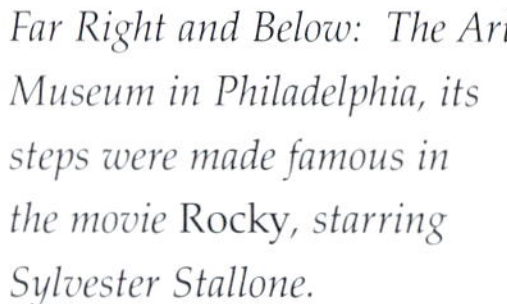

*Far Right and Below: The Art Museum in Philadelphia, its steps were made famous in the movie* Rocky, *starring Sylvester Stallone.*

*The tomb of the Unknown Soldier in Washington Square, Philadelphia.*

University, La Salle University, and Temple University. There are a dozen more schools of exceptional prominence in Philadelphia.

Philadelphia is a cultural center for the arts. The Philadelphia Museum of Art (immortalized by Hollywood when Sylvester Stallone's character Rocky ran up its steps) is just one example of an important cultural center. Performing arts, symphonies, and even the Mummers add to the city's diverse culture.

The Phillies, Eagles, Flyers, and 76ers are the major sports teams that call Philadelphia home. Hometown hero Wilt Chamberlain (1936–1999), a 7-foot tall center for the 76ers, was one of the NBA top scorers. In 1967, he led his hometown team to win the national championship.

Philadelphia's economy today is based on various industries, including food processing, manufacturing, and service industries. Tough

*First known as the Pennsylvania State House, the building is now called Independence Hall.*

*A view of Center City over Lemon Hill.*

cop Frank Rizzo, a straight-talking law-and-order politician, served as the city's mayor in the 1970s. In May 1985, Wilson Goode, the city's first black mayor, approved a plan to oust a radical group known as MOVE. The police dropped a bomb on their house from a helicopter. The result was a massive fire that killed 11 and destroyed 60 homes. Despite the incident, Goode was re-elected, and the city began to heal from racial and ethnic divides.

Still noticeable on city street maps are the old neighborhoods that isolated its residents into specific groups. While the city is a popular tourist destination—because of its historic sites, shopping malls, hotels, and restaurants—neighborhoods in the cities north and south sides have deteriorated. High unemployment, poverty, and failing schools challenge the city's future.

## Pinchot, Gifford

Born to wealth on August 11, 1865, at his family's summer home in Connecticut, Gifford Pinchot became a forestry expert, conservationist, and a two-term governor of Pennsylvania. From 1898 to 1910, he served as chief of the Division of Forestry in the U.S. Department of Agriculture. Pinchot advocated that American forests and other natural resources should be protected by government regulation of commercial land use. Under President Theodore Roosevelt, Pinchot's policy became a national policy.

His first term (1931–1935) as Pennsylvania governor brought about major governmental reorganization. During his second term, he pushed for the paving of rural roads throughout the state to provide unemployment relief and "get the farmer out of the mud."

His ancestral home is at Gray Towers, Milford. On October 4, 1946, he died aged 81 of leukemia.

## Pine Creek Gorge

Before the glaciers, the Pine Creek flowed in a northeasterly direction. Then the glaciers covered the area with ice. As the glacier melted, it created a natural dam of gravel, sand, and clay that blocked the flow of the Pine Creek. This natural dam forced Pine Creek to reverse its flow to the south, forming what is now the Grand Canyon of Pennsylvania.

Covering approximately 160,000 acres in the Tioga State Forest, the Grand Canyon of Pennsylvania is south of Ansonia along U.S. Route 6 and continues for approximately 47

*Pennsylvania's Pine Creek Gorge is located near Wellsboro. It offers spectacular views.*

miles. Exposed rock formations are over 350 million years old. The maximum depth of the canyon is 1,450 feet at Waterville, near its southern end. At both the Leonard Harrison and Colton Point State Parks, the depth of the canyon is more than 800 feet. The distance from rim to rim is approximately 4,000 feet.

Overlooks at the Grand Canyon of Pennsylvania offer some of the most magnificent views in the state. This area received national recognition in 1968 when the National Park Service designated a 12-mile section of Pine Creek Gorge a National Natural Landmark.

## Pioneer Explosion, The

Following John Elgar's successful launch of America's first iron steamboat, the *Codorus*, two other steamboats tried upriver navigation in 1826. The *Pioneer* traveled to Williamsport and returned successfully. The *Susquehanna* traveled from York Haven to Northumberland and returned without incident. Officials from Maryland, hoping to capitalize on two-way river navigation, backed the steamboat's later exploration of the river's branches. The *Susquehanna* exploded near present-day Berwick, killing several passengers that included a Maryland state legislator. Only Pennsylvania's canals allowed commerce in both directions on the **Susquehanna River**.

## Pitcher, Molly

Mary "Ludwig" Hays McCauley, better known as "Molly Pitcher," was the heroine at the Battle of Monmouth in June 1778. There she carried water to the parched soldiers and took over her husband's gun when he fell. As bullets zipped around her, she took the rammer and worked the gun. Her bravery earned her a non-commissioned officer designation in the Continental Army, issued by General **George Washington**. Her grave is in the Old Graveyard in **Carlisle**.

## Pittsburgh

The second largest city in Pennsylvania, Pittsburgh is the nation's largest inland port,

*The grave of Molly Pitcher is marked by an impressive statue of the hero.*

providing access to an extensive 9,000-mile U.S. inland waterway. Today, over 50 million tons of cargo worth $8 billion in goods moves through Pittsburgh's rivers each year.

Pittsburgh is at the point where the Allegheny and Monongahela Rivers converge to form the vast Ohio River. The flowing water is the foundation of Pittsburgh's history. No one knows for certain when the first Europeans discovered the natural intersection of the three rivers, but by the 1750s, both the British and French recognized its geographic importance. France knew that they needed to control the land at the confluence of the Allegheny and Monongahela. Defending that point would link their two North American colonies in Canada and in New Orleans. With the Ohio River flowing into the Mississippi River, the French needed to control this important point.

The British, always experiencing a prickly relationship with the French, also recognized the significant importance of this location. In 1753, Major **George Washington** traveled to this area as an emissary to warn the French to evacuate the region. In his report, Washington urged the British to erect a fort at the Forks of the Ohio. Washington was not only asserting the British claim to the area, but also the claim of Virginians who held a charter of 500,000 acres in the Ohio Valley.

Washington met with a French officer in command of **Fort Le Boeuf**, on French Creek to the north of the river intersection. Despite a pleasant, polite, and cordial meal offered to the 21-year-old British major, the French commander made it clear that the French were in Pennsylvania and intended to stay.

Over the next few years, the British and French traded control over the strategic location, each building a fort only to see it later destroyed. The British finally took control of the land in 1758, and founded Pittsburgh. The English named the town after British Secretary of War William Pitt. The struggles for control of the area were only preludes of the bloody and ferocious fighting to come during the **French and Indian Wars**.

*The point at Pittsburgh, here the confluence of the Allegheny and Monongahela Rivers flow into the Ohio River.*

P

*Pittsburgh has changed its image from a rusty, dying iron, steel, and coal town to a modern, robust city. Pittsburgh continues its growth today.*

With a population of 334,563 (2001 U.S. Census Bureau), Pittsburgh is a major financial and transportation center. It is served by several railroads, inland-water carriers, and major highways, as well as the nearby Greater Pittsburgh International Airport. After the domestic steel industry collapsed, Pittsburgh's economy was successfully transformed from one tightly connected to manufacturing to one balanced among high technology, health, and business services.

Around 1792, George Anshutz built a blast furnace, which was the first step in developing the city's great iron and steel industry. In 1834, opening the Pennsylvania Canal and the Portage Railroad brought increased commerce to Pittsburgh. A fire destroyed much of the city in 1845 and its main growth came after 1850.

In the late 1800s, industrial manufacturers built massive steel and iron empires in Pittsburgh. A flood in 1936 caused severe damage and smoke from the factories spread pollution throughout the city. In the 1940s, Pittsburgh created an anti-pollution program and since the 1950s, Pittsburgh launched a

*Pittsburgh's skyline. It is easy to see the Allegheny and Monongahela Rivers flowing into the Ohio River.*

*Pleasure cruises offer tourists a different perspective of Pittsburgh.*

*The Pittsburgh skyline shows its new prosperity as a business center.*

*Typical row homes in present-day Pittsburgh. This type of housing is prevalent in working-class neighborhoods throughout the state.*

large-scale redevelopment and started programs that addressed flood prevention and sewage disposal.

Pittsburgh, which contains more than 700 bridges, calls itself the City of Bridges. The city is positioned on an upland plateau dissected by the merging rivers. Pittsburgh's main business area occupies the level peninsula formed at the confluence of the Allegheny and Monongahela. The manufacturing industries are concentrated in areas bordering the riverfronts, while the residential neighborhoods are located on the highlands. Two cable car lines climb from the river into the hills.

## Pittsburgh Grease Plant

The Pittsburgh Grease Plant, located at 33rd and Smallman Street, was a major producer of lubricating grease for industry, transportation, and the military. It was founded in 1885 by Grant McCargo. During World War II, it produced over 5,000,000 pounds of grease, a vital item in the mechanized army and navy. It closed in 1999.

*The Andy Warhol Museum is located in Pittsburgh.*

P

*Andrew Carnegie established many institutions. One benefactor is Pittsburgh's Carnegie Museum of Art.*

## Pittsburgh Plate Works

The first glass factory in **Pittsburgh** was established by James O'Hara and Isaac Craig in 1797. The factory manufactured bottles and window glass until the 1880s. It was the beginning of Pittsburgh's dominance as the nation's largest glass producer.

## Poe, Edgar Allan

While living in **Philadelphia**, American writer Edgar Allan Poe (1809–1849), his wife Virginia, and his mother-in-law Maria rented several homes. He lived in the city for six years, from 1838 to 1844, and it was his most prolific period in his short life. Known today for his macabre stories and poems, Poe's emotion ranged from the high of being a popular lecturer to the despair of learning that Virginia was ill with tuberculosis.

Poe was an editor and critic for two major magazines *Burton's Gentlemen's Magazine* and *Graham's*, and he published about 50 works (among them are his classics *The Fall of the House of Usher*, *The Pit and the Pendulum*, *The Murders in the Rue Morgue*, and *The Masque of the Red Death*). Only the last house where the Poe family resided has survived. That Spring Garden home, located at 532 N. Seventh Street, is where the author lived in 1843–44. It is today preserved by the National Park Service as a memorial to one of America's most fascinating authors.

## Pontiac's Rebellion

The chief of the Ottawa people and leader of a confederation of tribes against the British from 1763 to 1765, Pontiac organized a confederacy that embraced virtually all the tribes of the Ohio Valley and Great Lakes region. Unhappy with the British, following their victories with the French, Pontiac pontificated for a return to traditional ways and for the rejection of contact

*Poe House, Philadelphia.*

with the English. Pontiac's Rebellion occurred toward the end of the **French and Indian War**.

During a war council in April 1763, Pontiac directed each tribe to attack a nearby British garrison. While Pontiac led the assault at Detroit, other tribes attacked Pennsylvania forts. Fort Pitt was also the target of the allied Indians. British relief forces under Colonel Henry Bouquet were en route to the besieged fort when they encountered a large Indian force. The resulting **Battle of Bushy Run** on August 5th and 6th, 1763 was costly to the British, but they defended Fort Pitt successfully. The Indian confederacy was highly successful during much of 1763. Eight British forts fell, including **Fort Presque Isle**.

Pontiac's Rebellion provided the **Paxton Boys** with the excuse they needed to attack and murder the **Conestoga Indians** in Lancaster. In 1769, a member of the Illinois tribe murdered Pontiac.

## President's First House, The

While the White House in Washington, D.C. is recognized as the President's House, there was first a Presidential home in **Philadelphia**. For years, the exact location of the building, long demolished, was in question. Many books included the wrong address. In the 1930s, a team of historians and architects completed an exhaustive study of the President's House. The President's Mansion was located at present-day 526–30 Market Street. At the time, the number would have been 190 High Street. The property was on Market Street, between 5th and 6th Streets, on the south side. Both Washington and Adams lived in the property.

## Priestly, Joseph

Northumberland was the home of Joseph Priestly, a British chemist, born in Yorkshire, who is considered one of the founders of modern chemistry. Born in 1733 and educated as a

P

minister, he was ordained in 1762 and served in a number of places in England.

First working with electricity, Priestly became interested in gases, and went on to discover oxygen. He determined oxygen's importance in combustion and respiration and worked in France with other scientists as he developed his theories.

Following his open support of the French Revolution, a mob burnt Priestley's house and possessions in 1791. In 1794, he emigrated to the United States, where he pursued writing for the remainder of his life. Priestly lived in Northumberland until his death in 1804.

Today, the Priestly House, built in 1794, is open for guided tours. The house is furnished with authentic period objects, and features Priestly's lab and other exhibits.

## Purvis, Robert

An abolitionist, Robert Purvis fought for human rights and equality through his lecturing, writing, and activity in several anti-slavery societies. As an agent for the **Underground Railroad**, he built a secret area at his house, on Mt. Vernon Street in **Philadelphia**, to hide runaway slaves. He provided transportation for slaves by giving them rides in his carriages.

## Queen Esther

An Indian known as Queen Esther is remembered as "the most infamous of all monsters." During the night of July 3, 1778, following the **Battle of Wyoming**, she positioned 16 American soldiers around a huge stone, since known as Bloody Rock. Held in place by the Indians of her tribe, Queen Esther smashed their skulls, one after the other, with her tomahawk and a club. The Bloody Rock is in present-day Luzerne County.

## Railroads in Pennsylvania

Before the railroads, horse-drawn tramways, such as the one owned by Thomas Leiber, would haul quarried rock to boat docks. **John Stevens** was promoting the virtues of railroading as early as the 1820s. The first steam engine to run on commercial railroad tracks in the United States was the Stourbridge Lion, imported from England by Horatio Allen. The Delaware & Hudson Canal Company's railroad at **Honesdale** started on August 8, 1829. What was to follow was a large web of track that stretched across Pennsylvania. It was the beginning of a new age for the state. From a colony of farmers and their agricultural economy to an industrialized and manufacturing-based economy, Pennsylvania's railroads would fuel the growth of the nation.

Stevens tried to convince the state to build a railroad, arguing against a canal system to move freight and supplies because of its restricted use in adverse weather.. He reasoned that a railroad would "insure the farmer a fair price for what he brings to market." The state legislature opted to build a canal system, but in 1823, "on the memorial and representation of John Stevens," it enacted a charter setting up the "President, Directors, and Company of the Pennsylvania Railroad Company." The line was to extend from **Philadelphia** to the eastern shore of the **Susquehanna** at **Columbia**, Lancaster County. The charter directed the railroad to be erected "under the superintendence and direction of John Stevens."

Stevens was unable to convince financiers to support the construction of his proposed railroad, even through he successfully proved by demonstration that a locomotive could climb the hills where canals could not. Stevens was thinking beyond his first proposed route that would link Philadelphia and Columbia. He talked about connecting a railroad to **Pittsburgh**, and then into Ohio and the Great Lakes. He also intended to cross New Jersey, connecting Philadelphia to New York City. Philadelphia would become the center of this commerce.

In what probably seemed like a foolhardy plan at the time, Stevens' ideas would later become reality. The Pennsylvania Railroad, under a new charter in 1846, became a giant among the

*The Railroad Museum of Pennsylvania, based in Strasburg, offers visitors a large display of locomotives.*

Q R

American railroads, extending from its Philadelphia headquarters to New York, Washington, D.C., St. Louis, and Chicago. The Pennsylvania Railroad's main line followed the original route surveyed by Stevens.

In the 1830s, railroads grew rapidly, not only in Pennsylvania, but the nation. A massive maze of track was laid for mainlines and short lines in Pennsylvania. The Baldwin Works in Philadelphia produced the steam engines that pulled the cars.

Pennsylvania railroads were used during the Civil War to transport supplies, troops, and equipment to the battlefront. Following the **Battle of Gettysburg**, the railroad transported supplies, prisoners, the wounded, and the dead. Less than six months later, President Abraham Lincoln traveled to Gettysburg by train to deliver his address at the dedication of the Soldiers' National Cemetery.

Being true to its nickname, dozens of railroads crisscrossed the **Keystone State** because of its key location. The Pennsylvania Railroad grew and consolidated other smaller railroads. The Baltimore and Ohio, the Reading Company (a major hauler of anthracite), the Bessemer and Lake Erie (serving the steel industry), the Lehigh Valley, the Norfolk and Western, and the New York Central hauled freight and passengers into Pennsylvania.

Many short line railroads connected remote villages and isolated towns. They served factories, mines, and the lumber industry. Some trains rolled through Pennsylvania with passengers or freight. Others stopped at each hamlet and siding to pick up passengers, milk, raw materials, mail, and finished products. Settlements developed along the railroads, each with its own depot, which became the bustling center of news, commerce, and information. Several Pennsylvania cities, including **Erie**, Philadelphia, **Reading**, Pittsburgh, **Scranton**, and **Harrisburg**, became hubs for major railroads.

The railroads during their heyday employed thousands of Pennsylvanians. Railroad towns such as **Altoona** expanded into major manufacturing and repair centers to service the mushrooming industry. In Philadelphia, the **Baldwin Locomotive Works**

*A replica of the original Stourbridge Lion, the first steam engine railroad operated in Pennsylvania.*

grew into the world's largest manufacturer, turning out hundreds of giant, powerful locomotives each year. In Altoona, the Pennsylvania Railroad built hundreds of its own locomotives. By the 1910s, Pennsylvania railroads had peaked. In another 20 years, it was the beginning of the end of the mighty railroads. The **Pennsylvania Turnpike**, partially built on land originally acquired for a railroad right-of-way, allowed easy and fast auto and truck traffic across the state. Airplanes carried passengers, mail, and some freight.

Railroads still cross Pennsylvania today. Amtrak provides passenger services to dozens of Pennsylvania communities. Freight trains move coal and other products. However, the heyday is long past. The grand days of the mighty railroads in Pennsylvania are gone.

## Reading

The City of Reading (pronounced *red-ing*) is the seat of Berks County and is located in southeastern Pennsylvania along the Schuylkill River, in a vast and rich agricultural area.

*The Pagoda in Reading, one of the city's most notable landmarks, is on Mount Penn.*

(Berks County was formed from parts of **Lancaster**, Chester, and Philadelphia Counties. It was officially chartered March 11, 1752.)

Reading was settled during the early 18th century. **William Penn** bought present-day Reading from the Indians. Penn's sons Thomas and Richard laid out the town in 1748. The city is named for Reading, England. The birthplace of the pioneer **Daniel Boone** is nearby.

An early iron making center, Reading was a military depot and a prisoner of war camp during the American Revolution. Its early iron production launched Pennsylvania as an iron producer. Industrial growth was aided by the construction of two canals in the 1820s and a railroad in 1884. Reading has railroad shops and diversified manufacturing and commercial industries. Products include electronic parts, clothing, machinery, hardware, structural steel and iron, and foodstuffs. It is the home to Albright College (1856), Alvernia College (1958), Pennsylvania State University Berks Campus (1958), and the Reading Area Community College. According to the U.S. Census Bureau, its population in 2001 was 81,207.

## Reading Railroad Massacre

Workers for the Reading Railroad had tolerated pay cuts, but the situation was getting worse. The workers in Berks County joined other railroad strikers in other cities. On July 23, 1877 in Reading, the militia fired into an unarmed crowd that blocked the trains, and ten people were killed.

## Reese, Harry Burnett

The familiar orange and gold wrapped peanut butter cups became a worldwide favorite after H. B. Reese founded his candy company. Reese started to make candy in Hershey around 1917, in the shadow of the **Hershey** Chocolate Company factory. By the mid-1920s, Reese started to make an item he called peanut butter cups. After his death, the Hershey Chocolate Company bought the H.B. Reese Candy Company and continues to sell peanut butter cups today.

## Reynolds, General John F.

Born in **Lancaster** on September 20, 1820, John F. Reynolds became one of the top Union Generals in the Civil War. He rose from commanding a brigade to commander of the Army of the Potomac I Corps. He fought at the major Battles of Second Bull Run, Fredericksburg, and Chancellorsville. President Lincoln offered him command of the Army of the Potomac, but

Reynolds turned down the appointment. During a barrage of Confederate gunfire, Reynolds died instantly when struck on the morning of the first day of the **Battle of Gettysburg**, July 1, 1863. He was the highest-ranking officer killed at Gettysburg.

## Roadside America

Somehow, it is fitting that it began as a child's dream. Roadside America is the nation's largest miniature village. In 1935, Laurence Gieringer set up a holiday display. The newspaper ran a feature story, and that was the birth of Roadside America. Today, visitors see an unforgettable and vast panorama of rural life. Over 200 years of Pennsylvania history is represented in the exquisite miniatures. The visitors to Roadside America have hands-on interaction with the trains, trolleys, lighting effects, and press-button animation. Roadside America is located at Interstate 78 and Route 22, in Shartlesville, Berks County.

## Rodale, Jerome Irving

Known by his friends as simply J.I., Jerome Irving Rodale was the founder of Rodale Press and one of the world's leading advocates of organic farming and natural food. While his ideas were first met with criticism from the scientific and medical communities, even critics

*Roadside America features over 200 years of Pennsylvania's history in this attraction located along present-day Interstate 78.*

eventually recognized him as an innovative leader. Today his Rodale Press still flourishes in **Emmaus**, publishing many magazines and books.

## Root Beer

Pennsylvania is the home of root beer. It doesn't contain any beer but it does, however, contain roots. Charles Hires, a **Philadelphia** pharmacist, while enjoying his honeymoon, discovered an herbal tea made of herbs, berries, and roots. He took his bride and the recipe home with him, and sold a packaged dry mixture. It was an instant success. He went on to develop a liquid concentrate, and introduced commercial root beer to the public in 1876 at the Philadelphia Centennial Exhibition. It became a popular drink. In 1893, the Hires family sold bottled versions of their well-known brew.

Someone made a marketing decision that it was better to call Hire's creation a "beer" rather than a "tea." Thinking it would sell better as a beer, the plan worked.

## Ross, Betsy

According to tradition, Betsy Ross modified George Washington's original design of the U.S. flag, and created the famous stars and stripes. She was a **Philadelphia** native and seamstress, whose home in Philadelphia remains preserved as the birthplace of the American symbol. Born Elizabeth Griscom in 1752, Betsy remarried several times following the deaths of her husbands during the revolution. She died in 1836.

## Ross, George

Born in New Castle, Delaware, on May 10, 1730, George Ross settled at **Lancaster** about 1751 and practiced law. Entering politics, Ross became a member of the colonial assembly 1768–1776, and served as a delegate to the State convention in 1774. Ross became a member of **America's Continental Congress** 1774–1777, and a signer of the **Declaration of Independence**. Appointed judge of the court of admiralty for Pennsylvania in April 1779, Ross served on the bench until his death near **Philadelphia**, on July 14, 1779.

## Rush, Dr. Benjamin

Born on Christmas Eve in 1745 at Byberry in northeast **Philadelphia**, Benjamin Rush became a doctor and statesman. When Rush was six, his father died. His mother made sure her son received a liberal education. He received a medical doctorate degree in 1768. While his main interest was medicine, he kept a keen interest in politics. Rush was one of the signers of the **Declaration of Independence**. In 1776 and 1777, he served as a member of **America's Continental Congress**. Rush became the surgeon general of the Continental Army during the American Revolution. Rush also

*The Betsy Ross house, in Philadelphia, where the Stars and Stripes were created.*

*George Ross, one of the signatories of the Declaration of Independence, is buried in Philadelphia at Christ Church Cemetery.*

served as the treasurer of the **United States Mint** from 1797 to 1813. In 1783, Dr. Rush founded the first free dispensary in the United States at Pennsylvania Hospital. Rush is also called the father of American psychiatry for his efforts to establish humane treatment of the mentally ill. His *Medical Inquiries and Observations upon Diseases of the Mind* (1812) was the first book on psychiatry published in the United States. He died April 19, 1813.

# S

## Salisbury

The borough of Salisbury is a town of several past names. Joseph Markley founded what is present-day Salisbury on April 15, 1795. The tract of land known as "John's Fancy" was given to Joseph by his father John Markley. The Markley's emigrated from Wurtemberg, Germany. Over the years, the town had different names. The Somerset County village located near the **Mason-Dixon Line** was called Brushtown, Salsburrich, and Elk-Lick. Dutch settlers decided on the name Salsburrich because of the salt deposits in the area. When the first post office opened, the borough officially changed its name to Salisbury.

## Salk, Jonas

In 1947, the New York born microbiologist, Dr. Jonas Salk, became the head of the Virus Research Lab at the **University of Pittsburgh**. There he worked on improving a flu vaccine and began to study the polio virus. Salk discovered a method to produce large quantities of the virus; and was able to kill it with formaldehyde so it remained intact enough to cause a response in humans. In 1952, he first inoculated volunteers, including himself, his wife, and their three sons, with a polio vaccine made from this killed virus. Refusing to patent his successful invention, Salk's vaccine wiped out the crippling Polio disease.

## Scranton

Situated in a long, narrow valley, Scranton is a transportation and manufacturing center in northeastern Pennsylvania. The area of the city was settled in 1771 and is the seat of **Lackawanna County**. It is located along the Lackawanna River and is Pennsylvania's sixth largest city.

George W. Scranton developed the city. With several associates in 1840, Scranton erected anthracite coal-fired iron furnaces in the valley. He also started a steel industry, which thrived for decades until 1902, when the production moved closer to **Lake Erie**. Scranton remained a mining hub until nearby anthracite production declined in the late 1940s. The city's manufactured produce included clothing, plastic goods, fabricated metal, electronic equipment, and printed materials. Scranton is the home of the University of Scranton (1888) and Marywood College (1915). Visitors to Scranton can see the history of steam railroading at the Steamtown National Historic Site in downtown Scranton, which includes museums, a restored railroad yard, roundhouse, and working steam locomotives. Scranton's population, according to the U.S. Census Bureau, was 76,415 in 2001.

*A commercial building in Scranton, known for its clothing, plastic, fabricated metal, and printed materials.*

## Shields, Dr. Matthew

Dr. Matthew Shields worked in the heart of Pennsylvania's anthracite coal region at Jermyn, **Lackawanna County**. In 1899, Dr.

Shields organized the First Aid Association of Jermyn, a first aid system for miners. It was from this early plan the Red Cross created industrial first aid. Dr. Shields died in Scranton on January 23, 1939.

## Sinnemahoning Path

The Sinnemahoning Indian path, now in Cameron County, ran up the valley of the Sinnemahoning Creek to Canoe Place, now Emporium Junction, and on to the Seneca villages at the Big Bend of the Allegheny. One of the earliest Indian paths through the Allegheny Mountains, it was used by the Senecas in a war against the Susquehannocks. It connected the Upper Allegheny River with the Susquehanna. The early settlers in Clinton, McKean, Cameron, and Potter Counties used this path.

## Six Nations

The Tuscarora Indians were the last to join the Iroquois Confederacy. The Iroquois had created a confederacy of five Native American peoples. The Mohawk, Oneida, Onondaga, Cayuga, and Seneca joined to create **Five Nations**. Losing their fight against the colonial settlers, the Tuscaroras fled north from North Carolina. They then joined Five Nations in 1722, and Five Nations became known as the Six Nations.

## Slaymakertown

Located on present-day Route 30 in eastern Lancaster County, Slaymakertown was previously known as Salisburyville.

The **Marquis de Lafayette** was entertained in Slaymakertown on July 28, 1825. Amos Slaymaker planned the small village before the completion of the Lancaster-Philadelphia Turnpike. Some of the village stands today. "White Chimneys," a house enlarged and developed through the years, still stands, and dates from about 1720.

## Slinkys

It still only takes about 63 feet of wire to make a Slinky®. As the story goes, Richard James was working on a tension wire experiment for the U.S. Navy in 1943. His experiment, a coiled spring, fell to the floor, and began walking. He took the spring home to his wife Betty. After showing it to her, he said, "I think I can make a toy out of this." Richard spent the next two years figuring out the best steel gauge and coil to use in making the toy. Betty James named the new toy when she found a Swedish word in the dictionary that meant traespiral—sleek or sinuous. The James had their new toy.

At first, no one wanted to sell it, because a Slinky just sitting on a shelf is not exciting until you have it in your hands or it is walking downstairs. Finally, in November, on a miserable night in 1945, **Gimbel's** Department Store in **Philadelphia** gave the couple the end of a counter. There they showed their Slinkys. That night, they had 400 Slinkys and sold them all in 90 minutes. After that, the James were besieged with orders.

*Portrait of Joseph Fayadaneega, "the Great Captain of the Six Nations."*

With $500, they started the James Spring & Wire Company. Richard James, seemingly in a midlife crisis, left his wife and six children, and went to Bolivia to join a religious order. He died there in 1974, disconnected from his family. When he left, the company that made Slinkys was nearly at its end, unable to pay its bills.

Betty James took over, and rescued the company that was nearly bankrupt. She convinced creditors to give her more time, and got a TV advertising deal. She moved the Slinky plant to her hometown of Hollidaysburg in central Pennsylvania, and slowly put the company back on solid financial footing. The TV ad brought in orders from its famous jingle. Millions of Slinkys have been made and sold over the years. College professors are known to use it in physics classes. Slinkys are still made in Hollidaysburg in a factory that employs about 100 workers.

## Smith, James

James Smith was born in Northern Ireland around 1719. He emigrated to Pennsylvania with his family when he was 12 years old. His father was a successful farmer and James received a good, simple education from a local Church Minister. He later studied law at the office of his older brother George, in **Lancaster**. Smith became a member of the Pennsylvania Bar at age 26, and then set up an office near Shippensburg in Cumberland County. Since this was a frontier area in Pennsylvania, he spent much of his time surveying, and only practiced law when work was available. After four or five years, Smith moved to a more populated **York** so he could practice law exclusively. During the 1760s Smith became a political leader. Smith attended a provincial assembly in 1774. There he presented a paper he had written, entitled "Essay on the Constitutional Power of Great Britain over the Colonies in America." In his essay, Smith proposed a boycott of British goods, and a General Congress of the Colonies, as necessary measures in defense of colonial rights. In the same year, he organized a volunteer militia company in York. He was appointed to the provincial convention in **Philadelphia** in 1775, the state constitutional convention in 1776, and was elected to **America's Continental Congress** the same year. Smith, representing Pennsylvania, was one of the signatories of the **Declaration of Independence**. He remained in Congress for only two years and, as Congress was meeting in Philadelphia in those days, provided his office for meetings of the Board of War.

James Smith retired from the Congress in 1777, and served in few public offices afterwards—one term in the State assembly, and a few months as a judge of the state High Court of Appeals. In 1782, he was appointed Brigadier General of the Pennsylvania militia. He was reelected to Congress in 1785, but declined to attend because of advancing age. A fire destroyed his office and papers shortly before he died on July 8, 1806.

## Snack Foods

Snack foods are an important part of the processed food industry and Pennsylvania ranks first in the nation in the production of potato chips, pretzels, and processed chocolate and cocoa.

Pennsylvania ranks 13th in the nation for potato production, but 70 percent of the potatoes grown are used to make chips. In 1921, two companies, Wise in Berwick, and Utz in Hanover, started production, and continue today. Herr's in Nottingham offers daily tours of its modern factory and visitors see potato chips produced and packaged. Pretzels started with **Julius Sturgis** in Lititz. Many pretzel bakeries exist throughout the state.

Hershey, the home of **Milton Hershey** and his chocolate factory, produces tons of chocolate, yet there are also other factories in the state, including Wilbur's and M&M/Mars.

## Snyder, Simon

Born on November 9, 1759 on North Queen Street in **Lancaster**, Simon Snyder served three terms as Governor of Pennsylvania from 1808 to 1817. During the War of 1812, he led the call to arms. He is also remembered for his stance of setting up and preserving a strong currency. Snyder died on November 9, 1819 at Selinsgrove. Snyder County was named for him.

## Starrucca Viaduct

Over 800 workers, paid $1 a day, built the Starrucca Viaduct for the Erie Railroad in 1848 over the Starrucca Creek. Located just north of Lanesboro in Susquehanna County, it remains the oldest stone railroad bridge still in use in Pennsylvania.

Its 18 slender arches rise 110 feet above the creek, and span 50 feet each. About 1,200 feet in length, it remains as a scenic and picturesque landmark.

## State Museum of Pennsylvania

Located at Third and North Streets in **Harrisburg**, Pennsylvania's Museum offers its visitors great exhibits that include the arts, anthropology, paleontology, geology, and Pennsylvania history. The museum, opened in 1905, includes a Planetarium.

*Left and above: The State Museum in Harrisburg offers visitors a comprehensive review of Pennsylvania's history.*

*Above: The John Stetson Factory in Philadelphia. Right: the racks where the hats were stacked in the factory.*

## Steamboats on the Mississippi

The first steamboat to sail on the Ohio and Mississippi Rivers was the *New Orleans*. Built in **Pittsburgh**, it was launched on October 20, 1811. The *New Orleans* was the fifth steamboat Pennsylvanian **Robert Fulton** built. The rapid and shallow waters of rivers like the Ohio were a greater challenge. Until Fulton's steamship, such rivers had been navigable only by canoes or keelboats. The swift currents allowed travel in only one direction. Steam power allowed riverboats to defy river currents, revolutionizing river transportation and extending the market for Pittsburgh's goods. It sank three years later, but it was the beginning of steam-powered boats on the rivers.

## Stetson, John

A simple manufacturer of hats, John Stetson grew wealthy after developing the now famous Western "Stetson" 10-Gallon Hat. He set up a factory in **Philadelphia** to produce the hats. Stetson became a philanthropist after achieving substantial financial success.

## Stevens, John

An inventor and engineer, John Stevens graduated from King's College (now Columbia University) in 1768. Admitted to the New York Bar in 1771, he served as treasurer of New Jersey during the Revolutionary War. He became interested in steam-powered navigation in 1787 and for the next fifty years was active in building and promoting steamboats and trains, securing numerous patents, and inventing. He built the first operating steam locomotive in the United States.

In 1823, Stevens secured a charter from the Legislature of Pennsylvania for the Pennsylvania Railroad, to operate from **Philadelphia** to Lancaster County. He attempted to raise financing, and made the preliminary survey of the route for his proposed

*John Stevens' Pennsylvania Railroad, Lancaster.*

railroad. It was the first exploration of a route for a railroad in the United States.

## Stevens, Thaddeus

Identified mostly as an extreme Radical Republican, Thaddeus Stevens was a champion of the equality of man—black or white, rich or poor. After moving to Pennsylvania, he went on to become one of the most powerful men in the nation, during and immediately following the Civil War.

On April 4, 1792 in Danville, Vermont, Stevens was born into a poor family. The second of four boys, his older brother Joshua was born with two club feet that made it difficult to walk. In the late 1700s, physical deformities were viewed as a sign from God that the family had committed a serious secret sin. Such a deformity was called the "Mark of the Devil" and the family was ridiculed and shunned. When Thaddeus was also born with a clubfoot, it was even worse for the Stevens family.

*The final resting place of Thaddeus Stevens. He chose this cemetery because it did not bar blacks from burial. The Stevens grave is located at Chestnut and Mulberry Streets in Lancaster.*

His father was an abusive alcoholic. The family lived on a small farm in miserable poverty. When Thaddeus was 12, his father abandoned the family and was later killed in the War of 1812.

Stevens' widowed mother worked, and ran the farm, to put him through school. Despite ridicule because of his deformity, he excelled in school. Although he was, financially, the poorest student in his class, he constantly displayed his great intelligence and a special aptitude for debating. Following his graduation from Dartmouth, he moved in 1815 to Pennsylvania. He had accepted a teaching position at a one-room school in **York**. Studying law, he passed the bar exam in a year, and set up his practice in Gettysburg. He soon became known for defending runaway slaves gratis.

In his first year, he argued nine out of ten cases successfully before the Pennsylvania Supreme Court. As word of his ability spread, he was swamped with clients. After five years, he owned a house and lot, several other properties, and was able to buy his mother a 250-acre farm and 14 cows. He moved to **Lancaster**, and invested in land and the iron business.

Stevens was elected to the Pennsylvania House of Representatives. In the 1830s, there were few free public schools. Only the wealthy families could afford to send their children to school. When a Free School Bill was introduced in the Pennsylvania House of Representatives, Stevens became a zealous supporter. He collaborated with Governor Wolfe to pass the bill. Pennsylvanians believed the new law was too expensive and some opposed the bill because they had their own religious schools. Over 32,000 individuals signed a petition to repeal the new legislation. The General Assembly was recalled and went into session to reconsider. The Senate passed a repeal bill, which then went to the House. Stevens took the floor to defend the Free School Bill. He spoke passionately, and then limped back to his seat to the cheers of the entire assembly. The Bill was passed, and Pennsylvania provided a statewide free public school system a generation before New York, New Jersey, Connecticut, Rhode Island, and the entire South.

He became actively involved in the **Underground Railroad**, aiding runaway slaves to get to Canada, as many as 16 a week. Stevens was elected to the U.S. House of Representatives and became the most powerful member of Congress in Washington. Known as "The Great Commoner," he chaired the House Ways and Means Committee and later the Appropriations Committee. Stevens often pressed President Lincoln on war and emancipation policies. He was responsible for funding the Civil War effort and later reconstruction.

Sarcastic and pompous, he was a strong and outspoken abolitionist. Before the **Battle of Gettysburg**, the Confederates punished him when they invaded Pennsylvania by destroying an iron works he owned in Caledonia.

Stevens pushed for the approval of the 13th, 14th, and 15th amendments to the U.S. Constitution, which provide the basis for all Civil Rights legislation. He wanted to punish the south for the Civil War, and wanted to treat the southern states as conquered provinces.

Stevens worked feverishly to impeach President Andrew Johnson. When the final vote fell one vote short in the Senate, Johnson was permanently weakened and reduced to a figurehead for the balance of his term. Stevens was vindictive and quick to quarrel, but personally generous. A bachelor who was devoted to his mother, he lived with his mixed-race housekeeper. He was an advocate of abstinence but was known as an avid gambler. His often zealous and frequently nasty disposition created many enemies.

Thaddeus Stevens died at midnight on August 11, 1868. The public expression of grief in Washington was second only to Lincoln's. His coffin lay in State at the Capitol Rotunda, flanked by a Black Union Honor Guard from Massachusetts. Twenty thousand people, one-half of whom were black free men, attended his funeral in Lancaster. He chose to be buried in the Schreiner-Concord Cemetery because it was the only cemetery that would accept all races. He wrote the inscription on his gravestone that reads:

> "I repose in this quiet and secluded spot, not from any natural preference for solitude, but finding other cemeteries limited as to race, by charter rules, I have chosen this that I might illustrate in my death the principles which I advocated through a long life, equality of man before his Creator."

## Stewart, James

Born May 20, 1908 on Philadelphia Street in Indiana, Pennsylvania, James Stewart was the only son of a hardware store owner. After graduating from Princeton in 1932 with a degree in architecture, Stewart joined the University Players in Massachusetts. By 1935, he landed his first movie role in *Murder Man*, starring with Spencer Tracy. Although he received an Oscar nomination for *Mr. Smith Goes to Washington*, he did not win the golden award until he appeared in *The Philadelphia Story* in 1940. Movie fans best remember Stewart for his portrayal of George Bailey in *It's a Wonderful Life*. He flew 20 combat missions in World War II; rose to Brigadier General in the Air Force Reserve; and in 1985, received the Presidential Medal of Freedom. The James Stewart Museum is located in his hometown.

## Still, William

After moving to **Philadelphia**, William Still became an operative of the **Underground Railroad**. Still kept records so relatives could later find those that passed through his station. A wealthy coal merchant, Still also helped found the first Black YMCA. He died July 14, 1902.

## Strange Names

Scattered throughout Pennsylvania are plenty of communities and towns with strange names. Some of them include:

*Paradise is among some of the towns with more unusual names.*

*Pennsylvania includes many towns with strange and unusual names.*

Apollo
Bagdad
Belfast
Berlin
**Bethlehem**
Bird-in-Hand
Birdsboro
Blue Ball
Blue Bell
Boiling Springs
**Burnt Cabins** (*see* Village of)
Bushkill
California
Denver
Dublin
Egypt
Eighty Four
Forty Fort
Houston
Indiana
Intercourse
Jersey Shore
**Jim Thorpe**
King of Prussia
Mars
Media
Moscow
Nazareth
Ohiopyle
Oil City
Paradise
Plymouth
Meeting
Roaring Spring
Sandy Lake
Shickshinny
Sinking Spring
Slippery Rock
Three Springs
Venus
Virginville
Washington
Yellow Springs

## Strank, Sergeant Michael

Born November 10, 1919 in Czechoslovakia, Strank spent his childhood in Franklin Borough, Cambria County. A United States Marine, it was "Sgt. Mike" who received the order to climb Mt. Suribachi. A flag had been raised once, but Mike explained to his men that a larger flag had to be raised so "every Marine on this cruddy island can see it." He picked his men and led them to the top. He was the oldest and highest ranking of the six men who took part in the famous raising of the U.S. flag on Iwo Jima, February 23, 1945. Photographed by Joe Rosenthal of the Associated Press, Sergeant Strank is now forever immortalized in the Marine Corps War Memorial at Arlington based on the famous photo. He never returned alive to Pennsylvania. Sgt. Mike was killed in action on March 1, 1945 soon after the famous flag raising when he jumped on an explosive to shield one of his men. He is buried in Arlington National Cemetery.

## Strasburg

A small village in southeastern Lancaster County, Strasburg attracts thousands of visitors each week. On the eastern end of this sleepy borough are the Strasburg Railroad and the

*The Strasburg Railroad chugs past the Amish farms near Strasburg. The short line railroad is now a major tourist attraction.*

222
Studebaker

Railroad Museum of Pennsylvania. Chartered by an act of the Pennsylvania legislature on June 9, 1832, the Strasburg Railroad provided both passenger and freight service. It has operated for more than 150 years, connecting its farming community with the nation's nearby rail system. The Strasburg Railroad is America's oldest short line railroad. Today, it offers visitors an excursion ride to Paradise, another small community in the heart of the **Amish** country. The Railroad Museum of Pennsylvania offers visitors a great chance to see a diverse collection of locomotive power and rolling stock dating from 1825 to the present.

## Studebaker Company

John Studebaker opened his wagon works near Heidlersburg in 1830. Six years later, he moved west. In 1852, his sons formed the Studebaker Company, the world's largest maker of horse-drawn vehicles. In 1897, the company that started in Adams County became a pioneer in the automobile industry.

## Sturgis, Julius

Legend has it that in 1850 a train-hopping hobo gave Julius Sturgis, a Lititz bread baker, a recipe to make hard pretzels. By 1861, Sturgis stopped baking bread, and instead baked pretzels, setting up the first commercial pretzel bakery. The bakery still operates and bakes pretzels today.

## Sullivan's March

In 1779, General John Sullivan and his forces marched through the northern tier of Pennsylvania. His mission was to expel the Indian menace from the **Six Nations**. The Indians fought with the British against the colonies. Washington ordered an invasion of

*Opposite: "Motor Girls" posing in and around a Studebaker auto, going to baseball game.*

*Below: Located in Lititz, the Sturgis Pretzel Bakery is the first and oldest in the country.*

Portrait of John Sullivan.

Seneca territory. Sullivan's March campaign nearly destroyed everything in its path, including about 40 Seneca villages, displacing thousands of residents who fled north to Niagara. Sullivan's group laid waste to innumerous acres of cornfields and fruit tree orchards. His expedition against the **Six Nations** continued along present-day Route 6 in Bradford and Tioga Counties.

## Sundance Kid, The

Josiah and Annie Longabaugh, who lived at 14 Church Street, Phoenixville, became the parents of five children. They named their youngest, born April 19, 1868, Harry Alonzo Longabaugh. On August 20, 1882 at the age of 15, Harry left home, and headed west. His hometown, originally an iron forge town, was filled with hardworking and patriotic citizens. There are many civil war veterans buried in the town's cemetery.

Harry became Phoenixville's most infamous native. Longabaugh took his nickname, "The Sundance Kid," from the town of Sundance, Wyoming, where he was imprisoned for stealing a horse. He was reputed to be the best shot and fastest gunslinger of the Wild Bunch, a group of robbers and rustlers who worked the Rocky Mountains region in the 1880s and 1890s. Robert Redford portrayed him in 1969 in a successful movie, *Butch Cassidy and the Sundance Kid*.

## Surrender of York, The

On June 28, 1863, the City of **York**'s officials surrendered the town to Confederate General Jubal Early. During the invasion of Pennsylvania, General Early was on his way to Columbia, and then planned to invade **Lancaster**, before heading to **Harrisburg**. But first there was York. Early demanded a heavy levy from the town. He demanded supplies worth $100,000. The town quickly worked to gather a payment. They were able to raise $28,600. General Early was not pleased, and for the next 24 hours, he would remind the York officials that he wanted more. Early had sent General Gordon further east to capture the **Columbia-Wrightsville Bridge**. The town's occupation was over in 48 hours when Early received orders from General Robert E. Lee to return to Gettysburg.

## Suspension Bridges

The first suspension bridges in America were built and used in Pennsylvania. In 1796, James Finley built the first practical suspension bridge over Jacobs Creek, near Uniontown. The world's first wire-cable suspension bridge was 408 feet long and served as a temporary footbridge. It was built in 1816 for the workers of the wire manufacturers, Josiah White and Erskine Hazard, over the Schuylkill River in Philadelphia.

## Susquehanna River

From the northeast corner of the Chesapeake Bay in Maryland, the Susquehanna River extends due north some 444 miles. It slices directly through Pennsylvania, and extends into central New York State, where it rises from its meek beginnings. The river flows south, constantly gaining in size and volume, as tributaries and creeks feed it along the way. From a system of mountain springs and brooks, streams and creeks, the river grows in strength. The water flows out of Pennsylvania a short distance into Maryland, and once there, feeds and fills the great Chesapeake Bay. In some places narrow, in other places as wide as a mile, the Susquehanna River remains a part of Pennsylvania's history. Canal traffic, the **Underground Railroad**, and the settlement of towns and villages all depended on the Susquehanna River.

## Sutter, John A.

Born in 1803, John Sutter emigrated to the United States in 1834. Sutter founded Sutter's Fort, now Sacramento, California, in 1839. Sutter helped many pioneers to settle in California. In 1848, while building a sawmill on Sutter's land, James Marshall found gold. As the news rapidly spread, gold-mad crowds poured into California during the rush of 1849. They killed Sutter's cattle and destroyed his lands in their search for gold. The gold rush ruined The California pioneer. In his last years, he moved to Lancaster County and made Lititz his home from 1871 until his death in 1880.

*The Susquehanna River provides recreation. Modern bridges span the river, allowing trains and vehicles easy crossings.*

# T

## Tanner's Alley

In the 1850s, Walnut St. near 4th St., in **Harrisburg** was known as Tanner's Alley. It was a stop on the **Underground Railroad**. Runaway slaves hid at Joseph Bustill's and William Jone's houses, both about one block apart in this area. After being fed and sheltered, they moved onto another station on the **Underground Railroad**. Both William Lloyd Garrison and Frederick Douglass spoke at the nearby Wesley Union AME Zion Church.

## Tannersville Cranberry Bog

The Tannersville Cranberry Bog is a fragile ecosystem of unique plants, animals, and of course, cranberries. Once a 715-acre glacial lake, the bog has piled up with about 40 feet of peat. Today, it stands out in contrast to the surrounding forests. Visitors see beautiful plants like calla lillies, orchids, gold thread, and the carnivorous sundew and pitcher plants. The bog is also home to bears, otters, bobcats, beavers, porcupines, minks, and snowshoe hares. Tannersville Cranberry Bog is one of The Nature Conservancy's first preserves.

## Taylor, George

*George Taylor, one of the Pennsylvania's signatories of the Declaration of Independence, lived in this house located in Easton.*

George Taylor was a working man and little concerned with politics, though he acted in service to his nation when called. He was born in Northern Ireland and emigrated to America in his early twenties. Iron production was his life's work. He was an Ironmaster at the Warwick Furnace and then at Coventry Forge, Chester County. Later Taylor and a partner leased an iron furnace in Bucks County. He moved to Durham in 1755 and served as the justice of the peace in 1757, 1761, and 1763. Taylor moved to Easton in 1763. In 1764, Taylor was elected to the provincial assembly for Pennsylvania and was reelected for five consecutive years. He was a member of the committee to draft the instructions of Pennsylvania delegates to the first Continental Congress, a member of the Committee of Correspondence, and of the Committee of Safety. In 1775, Taylor was appointed to replace a member of the Pennsylvania delegation who refused to support Independence. He arrived too late to vote, but did sign the **Declaration of Independence**. He served Congress through 1777. He was then elected to the new Supreme Council of his state, but served for only six weeks, seemingly because of illness. He died in 1781 at the age of 65 in Easton.

*Three Mile Island still functions today, generating electricity from the undamaged reactor.*

## Thanksgiving

On November 1, 1777, **America's Continental Congress**, now meeting in **York** after fleeing **Lancaster** and **Philadelphia** to avoid capture from the British, issued America's first National Thanksgiving Proclamation in York, Pennsylvania. Serving as the nation's capital, York Town hosted Congress as they adopted the **Articles of Confederation**, the nation's first form of government. Congress then proclaimed a national day of Thanksgiving to commemorate the new nation's victory at Saratoga, and the French government officially adopting treaties pledging its support to the American cause. Seldom do most Americans associate the City of York when they think of America's first Thanksgiving. It did not become an annually observed national holiday until President Lincoln proclaimed it in 1863.

## Three Mile Island

On the **Susquehanna River** southeast of **Harrisburg** and close to Middletown, Three Mile Island was the location of a major nuclear

*A historic marker now reminds visitors of the worst nuclear accident in the nation that occurred in Pennsylvania.*

accident on March 28, 1979. A partial meltdown of the overheated Unit II reactor released radioactive material and required the evacuation of thousands of nearby residents.

## TIROS

The Lavelle Aircraft Corporation manufactured the world's first experimental and operational weather satellite at State & Sterling Streets, Newtown, Bucks County in 1960. Pioneering satellite television techniques, the TIROS transmitted the first TV image from space. The success of TIROS led to enhanced satellites that provide key data to meteorologists.

## Typewriters in Pennsylvania

Today the typewriter is nearly forgotten as a machine that provided a faster and more readable substitute for handwriting. But the typewriter was an important invention. It was not invented in Pennsylvania, but one of the state's residents changed its design, making it a more useful and popular machine.

In 1881, James Denny Daugherty invented the first visible typewriter in Kittanning. As a court stenographer in Armstrong County, Daugherty became annoyed with having to constantly raise the carriage of the machine to see what he had typed. He decided to invent a typewriter where the typist could see what they were typing. His first model, made of iron, was a success and he set up a factory in Kittanning to make it. Eventually all typewriters had this design.

U

## Underground Railroad

The Underground Railroad was not underground, nor a railroad. It was a secret network of black and white antislavery Northerners and safe houses. Many of those activists and safe houses were in Pennsylvania.

One of the problems, when owning slaves, was to hold onto them. Six days of long and hard work, poor living conditions, and inadequate food versus freedom made it a simple choice. Early Pennsylvania newspapers ran ads looking for runaways such as one published on May 30, 1778 by *The Pennsylvania Gazette*:

> "Eight dollars reward. Runaway from the subscriber living at Carlisle Iron Works, a Mulattoe slave, named Anthony, about 26 years of age, 5 feet 6 or 7 inches high; had on an old blanket coat with brown stripes: buckskin breeches, white woolen stockings and old shoes. Whoever takes up the said slave, so as his master may have him again, shall have the above reward, and reasonable charges, paid by Thomas Maybury."

The Mason-Dixon Line became the point of freedom, even though Congress passed laws allowing slave holder's to hire bounty hunters to return their runaway slaves. Many followed the **Susquehanna River**. When slaves arrived in the southern counties of Pennsylvania, they disappeared as mysteriously as though "the ground had swallowed him up." Tradition says the term "Underground Railroad" started near Columbia in Lancaster County. Perplexed, the slave hunters declared, "There must be an underground railroad somewhere." The expression was adopted by many people and incorporated into the literature of the day.

The network of antislavery Northerners— many of them free black people—illegally helped fugitive slaves reach safety in the free states or Canada. They became creative in their methods of hiding

*Modernization has all but obliterated an important stop on the Underground Railroad. Runaway slaves followed the Susquehanna River to Peach Bottom. Traveling at night under the cover of darkness, they waited at the entrance where the St. Peter's Creek empties. There they would follow farm roads to safe houses in Christiana. Today, one of the roads the runaways used is still called Pilgrim's Pathway. A marina and a train bridge now mark this nearly forgotten point of the Underground Railroad.*

the runaways. Secret compartments were built in boats or **Conestoga wagons** to hide the fleeing slave. Pennsylvania Quakers and **Mennonites** often assisted the escaping runaways, even though the assistance was illegal. The male slaves dressed as women, and the women as men. Slaves with pale skin passed as whites. From the 1830s to the Civil War, the Underground Railroad grew in activity and acquired legendary fame.

Because of its proximity to the North, the upper Southern states supplied a high proportion of the runaway fugitives. The escaping slaves traveled by night to avoid detection, and sympathetic free black people often helped to conceal them. They started their flight on weekends, giving themselves a two-day head start. When possible, "conductors" met the fugitives at border points.

Pennsylvanians were opposed to slavery, and many different residents assisted the runaways. There were many safe houses in Pennsylvania. Many of the runaways only stayed a short time, moving on in fear of capture and return to an even harsher life of labor as punishment for their escape. Bounty hunting became a lucrative business for slave hunters in the 1850s, and many came to Pennsylvania in search of runaways. The conspirators talked the language of railroading. "Conductors" guided the slaves from "station" to "station." "Stockholders" financed the venture and discussed the movement of "valuable pieces of ebony" or "prime articles." Most participants probably knew little about the activities of the Underground Railroad beyond their immediate neighborhoods. They fed and hid the runaway slaves and directed them along to the next station. They asked few questions, so when slave hunters knocked at the door in search of the runaways, there was little they could tell them. Because assisting runaway slaves was an illegal activity, many accounts of assistance in Pennsylvania were never recorded. Years after the Civil War, there were only verbal accounts for historians to rely on to understand the workings of the Underground Railroad. Slavery in Pennsylvania was abolished in 1800.

*The U.S. Mint is still located in Philadelphia. It was the first public building erected by the new national government under the U.S. Constitution.*

## United States Mint

Granted the power to coin money by the U.S. Constitution, Congress made **Philadelphia** the home of the United States Mint. Secretary of the Treasury Alexander Hamilton personally prepared plans for a national Mint. On April 2, 1792, Congress passed The Coinage Act, which created the Mint and authorized construction of a Mint building in what was at that time the nation's capital, Philadelphia. The U.S. Mint was the first federal building erected under the Constitution. President **George Washington** appointed David Rittenhouse, a leading American Philadelphia scientist, as the first Director of the Mint. Under Rittenhouse, the Mint produced its first coins—11,178 copper cents, which were delivered in March 1793. Shortly afterward, the Mint issued gold and silver coins as well.

The Denver and Philadelphia Mints currently produce all the U.S. coins in circulation.

The two facilities produce 65 to 80 million coins a day. The present Philadelphia Mint opened in 1969. It is the fourth facility located in the city. The Philadelphia Mint covers five acres of land. Tours are allowed at the 5th Street facility, following strict security guidelines.

## University of Pittsburgh

The University of Pittsburgh was the first institution of higher education west of the Alleghenies and north of the Ohio River. It was first opened in 1787 as the Pittsburgh Academy. Its name changed in 1819 when it became the Western University of Pennsylvania. It became the University of Pittsburgh in 1908.

## U.S. Army War College

Home to the **U.S. Army War College** and the second oldest army post in the country, the Carlisle Barracks is open for visitors to explore America's military history. The base, founded in 1757 by England's Colonel John Stanwix, was first used for instruction on Indian fighting in 1758. The first U.S. Army educational institution, an artillery school, was also opened here in 1778. In 1863, the 21st and 22nd New York Militia Regiments withstood repeated attacks by Confederate General J.E.B. Stuart's forces. After burning down the barracks, the Confederate forces, though unbeaten, left **Carlisle** and moved on to **Gettysburg**. Over the years, ten different Army schools were located here, including the Carlisle Indian Industrial School from 1879 to 1918.

## USS *Pennsylvania*

The USS *Pennsylvania* is seldom mentioned in any reference to Pearl Harbor. During the attack, 24 men died, 14 were missing in action, and 38 men were wounded. Despite some damage while in dry dock, the battleship was one of the first to return fire at Pearl Harbor. The *USS Pennsylvania* survived to deliver incredible firepower on enemy positions for the next 4 years. She fired more rounds than any other ship in U.S. Naval history. Commissioned in 1916, the *USS Pennsylvania* (officially BB-38m originally Battleship # 38) was one of the first oil burning ships. At the end of World War II, a Japanese airplane torpedoed her. Her crew worked to save her, and she limped back to port. But her glory days were over. In 1948, the Navy decommissioned the battleship and used it for target practice.

*Cathedral of Learning, University of Pittsburgh.*

V

## Valley Forge

In colonial Pennsylvania, Valley Forge was a small village in southeast Pennsylvania, located along the Schuylkill River northwest of **Philadelphia**. It was also where General **George Washington** encamped on December 19, 1777. The Pennsylvania winter was so severe that one out of 10 of the 12,000 soldiers that marched in there never left. Many succumbed to exposure, illness, starvation, and suffering. Lack of supplies, and a harsh, punishing Pennsylvania winter forced the brave men of the Continental army to live without adequate shelter, food, or clothing. In the Valley where Washington positioned his army, he protected Congress in session in **York** from a British advance. He remained in a defensible position. Despite what had to look like a bleak future, Washington never wavered in the moral rightness of the American cause.

Washington repeatedly begged for relief. However, Congress was unable to provide it, and the American soldiers continued to suffer in the harsh, bitter winter. Women, relatives of the enlisted men, alleviated some of their suffering by providing laundry and nursing that the army desperately needed.

Valley Forge was not a battlefield. There were no military engagements or even a skirmish fought there. It was where under-supplied men somehow persevered despite ungodly hardships.

*Valley Forge, northwest of Philadelphia, is a large and beautiful park. No battle was fought there, but General George Washington and his Continental Army spent a harsh winter there. Food and supplies were sparse.*

*The soldier's huts at Valley Forge were small, cramped, and provided some protection for the rough winter weather that was unforgiving on the Continental Army.*

It was a place where men went without food, and lived in six-inch snowfalls. Men, who were dedicated to the principal of a new nation, refused to give up and made the best of their winter home. Typhus, dysentery, typhoid, and pneumonia were the killers that took as many as 2,000 men that winter. Still, giving-up was not an option. Determined, starving, and hungry, the soldiers of the American Continental army survived the horrific conditions.

In February 1778, the Prussian-American general Baron Friedrich Wilhelm von Steuben trained, disciplined, and reorganized the army at their camp in Valley Forge. He assembled a model company of 100 selected men and personally undertook its drill. The rapid progress of this company under von Steuben's skilled and masterful instruction made an immediate appeal to the imagination of the complete Continental Army. In June, Washington left the camp with a better-trained army to pursue the British in New Jersey.

## Village of Burnt Cabins

In 1750, Pennsylvania's provincial forces, who were attempting to satisfy Indian protests against the European trespassers on their lands, burnt the early settlers' cabins. This area is now known as northern Fulton County. The name of the small community remains, and is a reminder of the earlier, distressing years of the Pennsylvania frontier.

## Wade, Jenny

During the **Battle of Gettysburg**, thousands of soldiers died from their wounds. Only one Gettysburg civilian was killed during the three-day siege, Jenny Wade. As she prepared bread dough during the early morning of July 3, 1863, a bullet smashed through the kitchen door, striking her in the back and instantaneously killing her. Wade was reportedly buried with bread dough still on her hands.

*Gettysburg civilian Jennie Wade was shot in this house on July 3, 1863, as she made bread. She was the only civilian killed during the three-day Battle of Gettysburg.*

## Walking Purchase

**William Penn** became famous for his fair treatment of the Indians that inhabited Pennsylvania. Even though he was under no legal obligation to do so, he bargained with the Indians, and purchased their lands from them. Penn and his agents had made 17 such purchases from the Indians. Many of the tracts of land were narrow and overlapped each other. One of the purchases, according to a deed dated in 1686, granted lands that extended to a walk lasting a day and a half. Not an exact measurement by any means, the measurement was finally made 20 years after Penn's death.

As more settlers arrived in Pennsylvania, more land was required. Following William Penn's death in 1718, his secretary James Logan had the earlier land purchases confirmed by a single deed from Sasoonan and other Indians representing those who had made the earlier sales.

Without Penn's permission, people from New York settled along the Schuylkill River and on the Minisink Lands along the upper Delaware, where they occupied choice lands outside the area of William Penn's earlier purchases. The demand for land was strong because of heavy immigration from Europe, and the newly arriving settlers were moving north into the area from southeastern Pennsylvania and west from New Jersey. Except for the Minisink lands, the land beyond the Blue Mountains was then of little interest.

On September 19, 1737, three men—hired walkers—left Wrightstown, in Bucks County. One dropped out after 18 miles. On the second day, only Edward Marshall pressed on and, after covering about sixty-five miles in eighteen hours, eventually collapsed in exhaustion near present-day **Jim Thorpe**. The Delaware Indians had withdrawn early in the measurement in disgust, complaining bitterly that the white men did not "walk fair."

The limits of the Walking Purchase were then marked by a line, run at right angles to the direction of the walk, which extended to the Delaware River near the present-day Lackawaxen. Because of the curves of the river, this new line added to the purchase a great extent of the land north of the Blue Mountains.

Now with the new measurement, those lands no longer belonged to the Indians. Thomas Penn had reversed his father's policy of dealing fairly with the Indians, and lost their friendship. He and his brother John, as well as Provincial Secretary James Logan, were selling land to European settlers even before they had purchased it from the Indians. The Walking Purchase measurement gave them the opportunity they needed to claim ownership and deed to this land.

Outraged, the Delaware refused to leave their land. Provincial officials turned to the Iroquois to force them out, which they did in 1741. The Iroquois told the Delaware that as a subject people they had no right to sell land and insulted them by calling them "women."

Later, the Walking Purchase was used as fodder to justify Indian attacks against settlers, which led to the **French and Indian War**.

## Walsh, Loretto Perfectus

A gritty, determined woman from Olyphant, Lackawanna County is recognized as the first woman to enlist in the U.S. Navy. She enlisted on March 21, 1917, just 16 days before the United States entered World War I. Walsh served in **Philadelphia**, rising to the rank of Chief Yeomen. The Navy discharged her in 1919 and she died six years later at the young age of 29.

## Walson, John, Sr.

Recognized by both the United States Congress and the National Cable Television Association as the founder of the cable television industry, Walson created the first cable television system in the country in 1948. His company, Service Electric Cable TV, operated in the Lehigh Valley. It still provides a cable TV service today.

## Wanamaker, John

Born in **Philadelphia** in 1838, John Wanamaker created America's first department store in 1876. It was a new idea of combining many specialty stores into one large store. Wanamaker started with his men's clothing store. Another innovation Wanamaker started was a restaurant inside the store. Wanamaker pioneered the use of price tags, money-back guarantees, newspaper ads, and white sales. His landmark store in Philadelphia included the world's largest organ in the atrium, and a telegraph receiving station on the roof, which was the first to receive word that the *Titanic* had sunk. He expanded into other cities, building a chain of department stores. He also served as U.S. postmaster general (1889–1893). When John Wanamaker died in 1922, his funeral was a large public event.

## Warner Brothers' First Theater

Harry, Sam, & Albert Warner ran an early movie theater in New Castle, Lawrence County in 1906 and 1907. They were natives of nearby Youngstown, Ohio. They rented a room on the 2nd floor of the Knox building on South Mill Street, borrowed chairs from a funeral parlor, and used their hand-operated projector to show the moving pictures. Their theater seated 99 people, who could watch three movies for a nickel. Sixteen years later, the Warner Bros. Pictures Corporation was established. The Hollywood enterprise that started in Pennsylvania is still in business today.

## Washington, George

Pennsylvania's rugged and unforgiving frontier nearly took the life of a young Virginian. Had it been successful, the entire history of the United States would have been different.

George Washington, a 21-year-old major from Virginia, was returning from a meeting with the commander of a French fort north of present-day **Pittsburgh**. Christopher Gist accompanied him. Washington was on his way back to Virginia, having completed his first diplomatic mission from Governor Dinwiddie of the British Crown colony of Virginia to Legardeur de St. Pierre, the commandant of the French at **Fort Le Boeuf**. They had abandoned their Indian guides and their horses, near Venango. The animals had grown weak, snow had fallen, and the ground was frozen.

During the trip, they were fired at by Indians. After working a full day constructing a raft, they attempted to cross the swift and

*Washington's Crossing of the Delaware is depicted in this monument at the historic site in Bucks County.*

swollen current of the Allegheny River. On December 29, 1753, the stream was filled with floating ice. Both Washington and Gist tried to cross the Allegheny River near Shannopin's Town. Washington, with a setting pole that they clung onto while the ice passed by. Washington and Gist were knocked into the freezing water, which was ten feet deep, and Washington saved himself from drowning by catching hold of a raft log. The pair spent the night on an island, sleeping on the snow the entire night, hungry and half-frozen. During the night, the ice thickened over the river. In the morning, they crossed to the mainland, and toward evening, suffering from the cold and exposure, they reached the cabin of a Scotch settler. It was near this spot that a year and a half later Braddock fought the French and Indians in the Battle of the Monongahela. The island is directly opposite the United States Arsenal, at Lawrenceville, Pennsylvania, and is known as Washington's Island. It is nearly washed away.

*A marker at Washington's Crossing Park in Bucks County shows where the crossing occurred.*

## Washington's Crossing

General George Washington knew he had to strike a military blow to the British before his army melted away. On the night of December 25, 1776, Washington led a small army of 2,400 men across the Delaware River at McConkey's Ferry, in Bucks County.

Colonel John Glover's Marblehead fishermen ferried the American force across the river. They were on their way to attack a Hessian garrison of 1,500 men in Trenton. In the bleak and cold early morning hours, the Americans assembled on the New Jersey shore for the march on Trenton, about ten miles downstream. Washington's surprise attack was successful. The Hessians—mercenaries hired by the British—surrendered quickly.

The site of Washington's Crossing is a National Historic Landmark. The Pennsylvania side of the Delaware River is a state historic site and museum. Each year on Christmas day, local residents reenact the Crossing of the Delaware at Washington's Crossing.

## Watson, Henry

Henry Watson, a free black barber, and his wife Eliza, a washerwoman, lived in Chambersburg's Second Ward. There they owned a lot, worth about $200. They were the first free black people to own land in the town and two other black families lived with them. Watson assisted runaway slaves as they passed through Chambersburg. As a part of the **Underground Railroad**, he helped to keep them undetected by the slave hunters searching for them.

## Wayne, Anthony

Born on New Year's Day about five miles from Valley Forge in Chester County, 1745, Anthony Wayne excelled in mathematics as a young boy. He became a surveyor, and served **Benjamin Franklin** as an agent in Nova Scotia. Wayne studied military history, having heard stories from his father and grandfather, both having served as soldiers. When the Revolutionary

War became a reality, Wayne quickly volunteered. The 30-year-old Pennsylvanian became a colonel, and was placed in charge of a battalion. Colonel Wayne and his regiment were dispatched to Canada.

At the Battle of Three Rivers, he received a devastating wound, yet despite this serious leg injury, he ignored it and remained in charge. His service resulted in the promotion to brigadier general in February 1777.

General Wayne saw action at the **Battle of Brandywine**. When the American's retreated, Wayne's men were positioned within three miles of British troops near present-day Malvern. The British launched a brutal attack against Wayne, using swords, bayonets, and their guns as clubs. The 7th Pennsylvania Regiment, at the end of the column at camp, lost the most soldiers.

Wayne requested his own court-martial, and was cleared of any wrongdoing. He took part in the **Battle of Germantown**, and encamped at Valley Forge. In February, 1778, Washington sent him in search of food and other supplies for the starving Continental Army. Wayne's men skirmished with British forces in New Jersey as he foraged for supplies for the army.

When the British left **Philadelphia** in the summer of 1778, Wayne urged Washington to attack. Washington agreed and, after the Battle of Monmouth in New Jersey, the British left in disarray, retreating to New York.

General Wayne successfully planned a secret attack on the British fort known as Stony Point on the Hudson River. Despite suffering a severe gash on the head, Wayne successfully led the attack on the fort, capturing the strongest defended British garrison. He sent Washington a message after the capture of Stony Point:

> "The fort and garrison with Col. Johnston are ours. Our officers and men behaved like men who are determined to be free."

By now, General Anthony Wayne had earned the nickname "Mad" Anthony Wayne.

In 1781, General Wayne garrisoned in **York**, before heading south to engage in several battles that led to the eventual surrender of Cornwallis and the British army, winning independence from Britain.

President **George Washington** appointed General "Mad" Anthony Wayne as Commander in Chief of the United States to subdue the Indians in the northwest territory. Wayne reorganized the army, and deployed them into Ohio. After fighting for some time, the Indians eventually entered a treaty.

In June 1796, Wayne was back in the frontier overseeing the surrender of British forts to the United States. In November, he became ill with gout. On December 16, 1796, he died at **Fort Presque Isle**. He was buried there, only to have his son Isaac Wayne claim his body years later. The locals did not want their Revolutionary War hero's body removed, so a compromise of sorts settled the problem.

Isaac Wayne had traveled over the mountains to **Erie** in a one-horse sulky to claim his father's body. The younger Wayne enlisted the help of Dr. J.G. Wallace, who had served with Wayne at the Battle of Fallen Timbers. They opened the grave of "Mad" Anthony Wayne. When the grizzly work was done, Wayne's body was preserved remarkably well even after 13 years. There was little decay except in the lower portion of one leg. The two men decided it was impracticable to reduce the body into small packages that would fit into the back of the sulky.

With Isaac Wayne's permission, Dr. Wallace dissected the body and boiled the parts in a large iron kettle to render the General's flesh from the bones. Isaac Wayne took the cleaned skeleton back home in the sulky. The rendered

*The Conrad Weiser homestead is now a state museum. Weiser's stone house still survives on the property, located near modern day Route 422. His grave is nearby.*

flesh and the knives Dr. Wallace used in the operation were replaced in the original coffin and reinterred in the old grave.

General Wayne's skeleton was buried at St. David's Church in Radnor, Pennsylvania. In essence, he remains buried in two graves in his native Pennsylvania.

### *Weekly Advertiser, The Pennsylvania Journal and*

In 1742, **William Bradford**, grandson of William Bradford, a Quaker welcomed to Pennsylvania by **William Penn**, set up his own print shop in **Philadelphia**. From there, he published the successful anti-British *The Pennsylvania Journal and Weekly Advertiser*, which competed for many years with the *Pennsylvania Gazette*, the newspaper published by **Benjamin Franklin**.

Bradford (1722–1791) printed many books and published the *American Magazine* and *Monthly Chronicle*. Then in 1754, he opened the London Coffee House in Philadelphia, which became the seat of the merchants' exchange.

Bradford opposed the Stamp Act and took an active part in opposition to British rule, becoming a leader of the Sons of Liberty. He supported independence and became the official printer to **America's Continental Congress**. Sacrificing his business, Bradford was commissioned a major in the Continental Army and took part in the military campaign in New Jersey. During a battle at Princeton, he was badly wounded and his health was shattered. His son, Thomas Bradford (1745–1838), carried on the printing business and published the *Merchants' Daily Advertiser.*

### Weiser, Conrad

Conrad Weiser served as a diplomat, county judge, minister, community planner, soldier, and Pennsylvania's chief Indian treaty maker.

When the Weiser family settled on the New York frontier, the young German-born Conrad lived with neighboring Mohawks to learn the language of the Iroquois and serve as a go-between for the German community. By 1723, Germans in the Mohawk Valley followed the **Susquehanna River** to settle in Tulpehocken Valley, which is today's Lebanon and Berks Counties. In 1729, Weiser, his German-born wife, Anna Eve, and their children moved to the Tulpehocken region, settling on 200 acres near the present town of Womelsdorf. There he prospered as a farmer, tanner, and storekeeper, and with his wife, raised 14 children.

With his keen knowledge of the **Six Nations** language and customs, **Philadelphia** government officials learned of Weiser. Provincial Secretary James Logan hired Weiser to guide the Pennsylvania Indian policy. Over the next two decades, Weiser directed treaty negotiations, land purchases, and journeys to the Iroquois homeland. It was through Weiser that the Pennsylvania frontier remained stable and peaceful until the midcentury.

By 1755, growing competition between Britain and France had ignited. Diplomacy was set aside as the Six Nations divided over which side to join. The French set up alliances with the Indians and launched raids against eastern Pennsylvania settlements along the Blue Mountain line. Pennsylvania responded by forming provincial militia and building a line of outposts.

In 1756, Weiser received a commission of Lieutenant Colonel responsible for establishing the line between the Delaware and **Susquehanna Rivers**. He served until 1758. In that same year, General John Forbes directed an expedition to western Pennsylvania, which pushed the French out of Pennsylvania and ended the fighting.

Throughout his life, Weiser was active in local affairs. He served as a magistrate for Lancaster County, found Reading in 1748, established Berks County in 1752, and was its president judge until his death.

Though a Lutheran, Weiser joined the monastic community of **Ephrata Cloister** between 1735 and 1741. He lived intermittently as a celibate brother, withdrawing from family and political life. Weiser became disillusioned with the Cloister's leader Conrad Beissel.

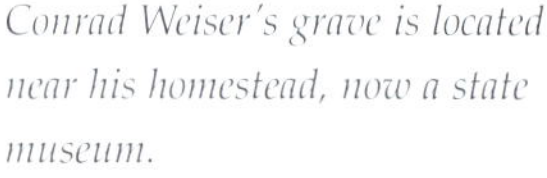

*Conrad Weiser's grave is located near his homestead, now a state museum.*

Returning to the Lutheran Church, Weiser served as a lay minister and established the Trinity Church in Reading. At this death on July 13, 1760, Weiser owned several thousand acres, as well as his farm, tannery, and the store in Reading. The Conrad Weiser Homestead in Womelsdorf is open for tours.

## Weissmuller, Johnny

Champion swimmer, gold medal Olympic winner, and motion picture hero, Johnny Weissmuller often claimed he was born in Windber, Pennsylvania. Best known as the star of a dozen *Tarzan* films, he was actually born in what is now Romania. He perpetrated the lie about his birthplace for Olympic reasons. His family arrived in Windber in 1904, shortly after his birth, where many other Austrians and Germans lived (and where his brother Peter was born in 1905). His family moved to Chicago when Weissmuller was a child.

He won fame as a swimmer for developing the "American crawl," setting 67 world records, and winning five gold medals in the 1924 and 1928 Olympics.

## Wellsboro

Tioga County's Wellsboro is built on land that the King of England granted to Connecticut and Pennsylvania. When the border was finally determined, Wellsboro became the home to settlers deep in Indian country. The town deep in the Tioga mountains woodland and close to Pennsylvania's Grand Canyon was named for Mary Wells, one of the early settler's wives. Located along Route 6, the town is noted for its gas streetlights, the only town in Pennsylvania to use gas today for illumination. The lights illuminate the entire median strip of the town.

## Westinghouse, George

George Westinghouse was an engineer, manufacturer, and the inventor of air brakes and 400 other devices. He developed the alternating current (AC) transmission of electric current. He spent his creative years in Pittsburgh and founded the Westinghouse Electric Company in 1886.

## Whiskey Rebellion, The

Being a federal tax collector in the early days of the United States was, at best, a difficult job, especially in Washington County, Pennsylvania. The fiercely independent citizens did not like the idea of paying a federal excise tax on the whiskey they produced. And any tax collector that tried to collect it was tarred and feather, then run out of town.

A series of such disturbances broke out in western Pennsylvania in 1794. Grain farmers depended on whiskey production for their income. Transporting grain was impossible in those days. It was easier to produce and transport distilled spirits of their grain to eastern markets rather than the raw grain itself.

Congress, needing money to pay off war debts, imposed the 9 cents per gallon excise tax on each gallon of whiskey. Large producers only had to pay 6 cents. The western farmers

*Gas lights still illuminate Wellsboro's streets, giving the northern Pennsylvania town a charming and unique appearance.*

felt they were unfairly burdened with the new excise tax. From Pennsylvania to Georgia, the people of the western counties engaged in harassment of the federal tax collectors, ranging from simply refusing to pay the tax or rebelling with violence.

Federal excise officers were to open an office in his county of operation, and then collect the tax. The easiest way to avoid the tax was to prevent the excise officer from setting up an office in the county. Rebels threatened anyone who offered to house the excise office. The excise officer received threats, and that was usually enough to discourage the officer from staying and collecting the tax. When an excise officer was brave enough—or foolish enough—to stay, Pennsylvanians who opposed the tax committed such humiliations as tarring, feathering, and torturing the collector. Such events set off riots. Tax rebels stole mail to discover who in their area was opposing them. Some radicals called for insurrection against the federal government.

With the encouragement of Alexander Hamilton, President **George Washington** requested the governors of Pennsylvania, New Jersey, and Virginia to mobilize contingents of militia. In October 1794, President Washington ordered the 12,950 militia to advance to western Pennsylvania, where they seized many people. Known as the Whiskey Rebellion, it is important in United States history because it provided the first real test of the federal government's choices and law enforcement power. It was the first time, under the new Constitution, that the federal government used strong military authority over the nation's citizens. It was also the first, and last time, that a sitting President personally commanded the military in the field.

Congress finally repealed the whiskey excise tax in 1802, which was seldom collected with much success.

## White Tail Deer

The official animal of Pennsylvania is the White Tail Deer. Each year, on the Monday after Thanksgiving, over one million hunters take to the woods and mountains in search of a Pennsylvania buck. A long tradition of deer hunting exists in Pennsylvania. Early settlers depended on white tail deer as an important food source.

Founded in 1895, the Pennsylvania Game Commission regulates deer hunting, monitors the yearly harvest, and protects the delicate balance between the deer population and residents of the state. Two Pennsylvania counties—Cameron and Potter—actually have a larger deer population than residents.

## Williamsport

Michael Ross laid out Williamsport in 1795 and at one time it was part of Northumberland County before it became the county seat of Lycoming County. Williamsport is recognized worldwide as the birthplace of Little League. At one time, Williamsport was the leading lumber

*Pennsylvania's white tail deer population is larger than the population of people in several northern counties. Each year, over 1 million hunters take to the woods in search of a white tail.*

center of the nation. Situated along the western branch of the **Susquehanna River**, it has long served as a trade and travel center.

## Wilson, James

James Wilson was born in Scotland in 1742. He attended a surprising number of Universities there, but for some reason never attained a degree. He emigrated to America in 1766, bringing many valuable Letters of Introduction with him. Wilson began tutoring and teaching at the Philadelphia College. He petitioned the college for a degree and was awarded an honorary Master of Arts several months later. Wilson managed to study law at the office of John Dickinson. After two years of reading the law, he attained the bar in Philadelphia, and in 1767, set up his own practice in Reading. His practice was successful and he managed to earn a substantial fortune in a few short years. Wilson bought a small farm near **Carlisle** and handled cases in eight Pennsylvania counties. He began a lifelong fascination with land speculation. In 1774, Wilson penned a pamphlet titled "Considerations on the Nature and Extent of the Legislative Authority of the British Parliament." In it, he argued the Parliament had no authority to pass laws for the colonies. It was published, and later found its way to **America's Continental Congress**, where it was widely read and debated.

In 1775, Wilson was elected to the Continental Congress, where he took a position with the most radical members that demanded a separation from Britain. Many members of the Congress favorably received James Wilson's powers of oration, the passion of his delivery, and the logic he employed during debate. But Wilson found himself in a difficult situation. Pennsylvania was divided on the issue of separation, and Wilson refused to vote against the will of his constituents. Many of his fellow Congressional members felt it was hypocritical to have argued so forcefully and so long for independence, only to vote against it. Wilson, with the support of other members who were sympathetic to his precarious position, managed to delay the final vote by three weeks, giving him time to consult with his constituents. When the vote came, Wilson voted for Pennsylvania's wish for independence. Wilson, representing Pennsylvania, was one of the signatories of the **Declaration of Independence**. Wilson resumed his activities in land speculation, including profiteering. He borrowed heavily and gambled aggressively. It all caught up with him and he was nearly arrested on several occasions. His life became miserable. His wife had died in 1786. Wilson was repeatedly accused of "engrossing," the practice of hoarding goods to drive up prices.

He petitioned President Washington to make him a Justice on the Supreme Court. In 1792, he returned to land speculation. His finances were destroyed and he spent time in a debtor's prison even while still serving on the Supreme Court. By 1798, Wilson was ruined. He complained of great mental fatigue and an inability to work any longer. His torment ended later that year when he died during a visit to friends in North Carolina.

## Woolworth, F. W.

Frank W. Woolworth failed with the first store he opened. The second try at running a store was in **Lancaster**. In April 1879, the New York native opened his nickel-and-dime store, and it became an instant success.

Woolworth pioneered the concept of buying merchandise direct from manufacturers, and setting a price, rather than having customers haggle over a price. His chain of discount stores grew to over 1,000.

## WQED TV

Pittsburgh's WQED started broadcasting in April 1954. It was the first community sponsored educational television station in America. In 1955, WQED was the first to broadcast classes to elementary schools for education. WQED was located on 5th Avenue in Oakland, **Pittsburgh**.

## Wright, John

John Wright, a Quaker, settled on the western edge of what was then Chester County, along the great **Susquehanna River** in 1726. Along with Robert Barber and Samuel Blunston, John Wright started a ferry business to provide transportation across the wide river. It offered those settlers, heading west past the Susquehanna, an easy way to cross the mile-wide river.

Wright filed a petition to create a new county, and in 1729, the provincial government set up the fourth county in Pennsylvania. The descendants of **William Penn** named the county Lancaster, taking away land from Chester County to form it. Wright had requested the name, which was in honor of his home country of England.

In the village known as Wright's Ferry, residents of the newly established Lancaster County traveled to seek provincial government assistance and to register land deeds. Indians and colonists both appeared to file claims and papers or to seek government redress of issues. Wright's Ferry was later named Columbia.

*John Wright, the man that successfully petitioned William Penn to create Lancaster County, founded the town known today as Columbia. It was originally Wright's Ferry. Wright established the community in 1726.*

## Wyoming, Battle of

Both Pennsylvania and Connecticut claimed the Wyoming Valley, a fertile, grain-producing area consisting of a 25-mile stretch along the **Susquehanna River**'s northern branch. From late 1775, the Connecticut faction had been in control of the region. There were about 400 settlers living in the disputed area. On July 3, 1778, near modern day Route 11, the massacre occurred. A force of about 1100 British, Tories, and Indians under the command of Major General John Butler defeated a company of the Continental Army under the command of Colonel Zebulon Butler. The Indians fought ferociously. They savagely killed the men as they fled, or when they stopped to surrender. They butchered and hacked the soldiers, taking more than 200 scalps. The dead remained unburied for over three months. Survivors escaped to Forty Fort.

## Wyshner, Pete Gray

Pete Gray Wyshner is the only one-armed man to play major league baseball. Born in Lackawanna County in Nanticoke's Hanover section, Wyshner lost his right arm in a truck accident when he was a child. In 1945, Wyshner played 77 games as an outfielder for the St. Louis Browns and batted .218.

His on-field exploits created an inspirational example for the disabled servicemen returning from World War II. He retired to a simple life as a recluse in Nanticoke, and died there June 30, 2002.

X

Y

Z

## Yohogania

When Virginia claimed the southwestern corner of what is present-day Pennsylvania, they called the area Yohogania County. Virginia erected a courthouse for governmental and judicial matters in present-day West Elizabeth, Allegheny County. It was active from 1777 to 1780.

## York

Located on the Codorus Creek in southeastern Pennsylvania, the City of York is also the seat of York County. Settled in 1735, York is the oldest permanent settlement west of the **Susquehanna River**. The city was named for York, England.

In September of 1777, the Continental Congress, under threat of the advancing British army, moved the location of the colonies' central government from **Philadelphia** to **Lancaster**. Since the State of Pennsylvania's Government was also located in Lancaster, officials decided that a move across the Susquehanna would separate the two sufficiently and the Continental Congress was moved to York.

On September 30, 1777, Congress convened in York. While in session there, Congress approved the **Articles of Confederation** and proclaimed the nation's first Thanksgiving. Congress remained in York until June 27, 1778. During the Civil War, there was a Confederate Invasion into York in June 1863, days before the **Battle of Gettysburg**.

Today York is a commercial, manufacturing, and distribution center for the rich agricultural Pennsylvania Dutch region.

*Left: It was in this courthouse in York where the Articles of Confederation were adopted, and the first time the new country called itself the United States of America. Below: The Haines Shoe House is built near present-day Route 30 in York County.*

Major products of the area include electrical machinery, air conditioners, metal and paper products, electronic equipment, ordnance, sporting goods, furniture, processed foods, and pottery. The U.S. Census bureau estimated York County's population at 386,299 in 2001, and the city's population at 40,862.

## York Fair

Thomas Penn, son of **William Penn**, granted the people of **York** a charter in 1765 in recognition of the "flourishing state to which the town hath arrived through their industry." America's oldest agricultural fair, the people of York held the first York Fair 11 years before the **Declaration of Independence** was signed. Stopped after 1815, the York County Agricultural Society resurrected the fair in 1853. The fair runs for two weeks each year in September. The present fairground was a former farm on 120 acres in Manchester Township, and used since 1888.

## Zippo Lighters

George G. Blaisdell founded The Zippo Manufacturing Company in 1932 at Bradford. His plan was simple. He was to create a lighter that would look good and be easy to use. He made the case rectangular, attached the lid with a welded hinge, surrounded the wick with a wind hood, and added a lifetime guarantee. Fascinated with another new invention, the zipper, Blaisdell named his new lighter after it. There have been over 300 million windproof Zippo lighters made in Pennsylvania. The factory is a tourist destination.

*Zippo Lighters are recognized worldwide, and are manufactured in Bradford. The plant has become a tourist attraction.*

# Pennsylvania Quick Facts

**Capital:** Harrisburg, since 1812. Philadelphia and Lancaster were previous capitals.

**Population:** 12,281,000 (estimated in 2002 by the U.S. Census Bureau)

**Size:** 45,333 square miles, plus 891 square miles of Lake Erie

**Rank in size to other states:** 32nd in size, 6th in population (Only California, New York, Texas, Florida, and Illinois have larger populations.)

**Length (East to West):** Longest, 310 miles, average 285 miles

**Width (North to South):** Longest, 180 miles, average 156 miles

**Highest point:** Mount Davis, located within Forbes State Forest in Somerset County, is 3213 feet above sea level.

**Lowest point:** Sea level at Delaware River

**Counties:** 67

**Bridges:** 57,000

**Roads:** 44,000

**Major rivers:** Allegheny River, Susquehanna River, Delaware River, Ohio River Monongahela River

**Named after:** "Penn" for Admiral Sir William Penn, the father of the state's founder, William Penn. "Sylvania" for woods or woodlands. Together, the two words mean Penn's Woods.

**Entered Union:** December 2, 1787 (The second state to do so.)

**Settled:** 1643

**State animal:** Whitetail Deer

**State beverage:** Milk

**State bird:** Ruffed Grouse

**State dog:** Great Dane

**State fish:** Brook trout

**State flower:** Mountain Laurel

**State fossil:** Phacops Rana

**State insect:** Firefly

**State motto:** Virtue, Liberty, and Independence

**State nickname:** The Keystone State

**State ship:** US Brig *Niagara*

**State song:** "Pennsylvania," written by Eddie Khoury and Ronnie Bonner

**State tree:** Hemlock

**Number of school districts:** 501

**Number of state parks:** 116

**Overall land use:** Forest, 55.3%; agricultural, 18.1%; pasture, 3.2%; other 23.5%

# Appendix

For more information about historical sites through out Pennsylvania, contact these organizations:

**Allegheny National Forest Vacation Bureau**
P.O. Box 371
80 East Corydon Street, Suite 114
Bradford, PA 16701
Phone: (800) 473-9370
Fax: (814) 368-9370
Web Address: www.visitANF.com
E-Mail: info@visitANF.com

**Armstrong County Tourist Bureau**
125 Market Street
Kittanning, PA 16201
Phone: (724) 543-4003 or toll free (888) 265-9954
Fax: (724) 545-3119
Web Address: www.armstrongcounty.com
E-Mail: actb@alltel.net

**Beaver County Recreation and Tourism Department**
526 Brady's Run Road
Beaver Falls, PA 15010
Phone: (724) 891-7030
Fax: (724) 891-1160
Web Address: www.visitbeavercounty.com
E-Mail: info@visitbeavercounty.com

**Bedford County Conference & Visitors Bureau**
131 South Juliana Street
Bedford, PA 15522
Phone: (800) 765-3331
Fax: (814) 623-1671
Web Address: http://www.bedfordcounty.net/
E-Mail: bccvb@bedford.net

**Bellefonte Tourism Commission**
101 West Linn Street
Bellefonte, PA 16823
Phone: (814) 353-1102
Web Address: www.bellefonte.com
E-Mail: info@bellefonte.com

**Brandywine Conference and Visitors Bureau**
One Beaver Valley Road,
Chaddsford, PA, 19317
Phone: (610) 565-3679 or (800) 343-3983
Fax: (610) 565-0833
Web Address: www.brandywinecvb.org

**Bucks County Conference & Visitors Bureau, Inc.**
3207 Street Road
Bensalem, PA 19020
Phone: (800) 836-BUCKS or (215) 639-0300
Fax: (215) 642-3277
Web Address: www.experiencebuckscounty.com
E-Mail:bccvb@bccvb.org

**Butler County Tourism & Convention Bureau**
3008 Unionville Road
Cranberry Township, PA 16066-3408
Phone: (724) 234-4619 or (866) 856-8444
Fax: (724) 234-4643
Web Address:
www.visit-butler-county-pennsylvania-pa.com
E-Mail: visitors@visitbutlercounty.com

### Centre County Convention & Visitors Bureau

800 East Park Avenue
State College PA 16803
Phone: (800) 358-5466
Fax: (814) 231-8123
Web Address: www.centralpacvb.org
E-Mail: cccvb@visitpennstate.org

### Chester County Conference and Visitors Bureau

400 Exton Square Parkway
Exton, PA 19341
Phone: (610) 280-6145 or (800) 228-9933
Fax: (610) 280-6179
Web Address: www.brandywinevalley.com

### Clinton County Economic Partnership

212 N. Jay Street
Lock Haven, PA 17745
Phone: (570) 748-5782 or (888) 388-6991
Fax: (570) 893-0433
Web Address: www.clintoncountyinfo.com

### Columbia-Montour Visitors Bureau

121 Papermill Road
Bloomsburg, PA 17815
Phone: (570) 784-8279 or (800) 847-4810
Fax: (570) 784-1166
Web Address: www.itourcolumbiamontour.com

### Crawford County Convention and Visitors Bureau

211 Chestnut Street
Meadville, PA 16335
Phone: (800) 332-2338
Fax: (814) 333-9032
Web Address: www.visitcrawford.org
E-Mail: welcome@visitcrawford.org

### Endless Mountains Visitors Bureau

712 Route 6 East
Tunkhannock, PA 18657
Phone: (800) 769-8999 or (570) 836-5431
Fax: (570) 836-3927
Web Address: www.endlessmountains.org
E-Mail: emvb@epix.net

### Erie Area Convention & Visitors Bureau

208 East Bayfront Parkway, Suite 103
Erie, PA 16507
Phone: (800) 524-3743
Fax: (814) 459-0241
Web Address: www.visiteriepa.com
E-Mail: info@visiteriepa.com

### Fulton County Chamber of Commerce & Tourism

536 East Poplar Street
P.O. Box 141
McConnellsburg, PA 17233
Phone: (717) 485-4064
Fax: (717) 485-0322
Web Address: www.fultoncountypa.com
E-Mail: fultoncountypa@earthlink.net

### Gettysburg Convention & Visitors Bureau

102 Carlisle Street
PO Box 4117
Gettysburg, PA 17325
Phone: (800) 337-5015
Fax: (717) 334-1166
Web Address: www.gettysburgcvb.org
E-Mail: info@gettysburgcvb.org

**Greater Pittsburgh Convention & Visitors Bureau**
425 Sixth Avenue, 30th Floor
Pittsburgh, PA 15219
Phone: (800) 366-0093
Fax: (412) 644-5512
Web Address: www.visitpittsburgh.com
E-Mail: info@gpcvb.org

**Greene County Tourist Promotion Agency**
417 Roy Furman Highway
Waynesburg, PA 15370
Phone: (724) 627-8687
Fax: (724) 627-8687
Web Address: www.co.greene.pa.us
E-Mail: gctour@county.greenepa.net

**Hershey-Capital Region Visitors Bureau**
4th & Chestnut Sts., Suite 208
Harrisburg, PA 17101
Phone: (717) 231-7788 or (800) 995-0969
Fax: (717) 231-2808
Web Address: www.pacapitalregions.com
E-Mail: info@hersheycapitalregion.com

**Huntingdon County Convention and Visitors Bureau**
Seven Points Road, Rural Route 1
Hesston, PA 16647
Phone: (888) RAYSTOWN or (814) 658-0060
Fax: (814) 658-0068
Web Address: www.raystown.org
E-Mail: info@raystown.org

**Indiana County Tourist Bureau, Inc.**
2334 Oakland Avenue, Suite 7
Indiana, PA 15701
Phone: (877) 746-3426
Fax: (724) 465-3819
Web Address: www.indiana-co-pa-tourism.org
E-Mail: info@indiana-co-pa-tourism.org

**Johnstown Cambria County Visitors Bureau**
416 Main Street, Suite 100
Johnstown, PA 15901
Phone: (800) 237-8590 or (814) 536-7993
Fax: (814) 539-3370
Web Address: www.visitjohnstownpa.com
E-Mail: jstcvb@visitjohnstownpa.com

**Juniata River Valley Visitors Bureau**
152 East Market Street, Suite 103
Lewistown, PA 17044
Phone: (877) 568-9739
Fax: (717) 248-6714
Web Address: www.juniatarivervalley.org
E-Mail: jrvvb@acsworld.com

**Laurel Highlands Visitors Bureau**
120 East Main Street
Ligonier, PA 15658
Phone: (724) 238-5661, ext. 14 or (800) 925-7669
Fax: (724) 238-3673
Web Address: www.laurelhighlands.org
E-Mail: aurban@laurelhighlands.org

**Lawrence County Tourist Promotion Agency**
229 South Jefferson Street, Suite 102
Cilli Central Station
New Castle, PA 16101
Phone: (888) 284-7599
Fax: (724) 654-2044
Web Address: www.lawrencecounty.com/tourism
E-Mail: tourlc@ncconnect.com

**Lehigh Valley Convention & Visitors Bureau**
2200 Avenue A
Bethlehem, PA 18017
Phone: (610) 882-9200 or (800) 747-0561
Fax: (610) 882-0343
Web Address: www.lehighvalleypa.org
E-Mail: geninfo@lehighvalleypa.org

### Luzerne County Convention & Visitors Bureau

56 Public Square
Wilkes-Barre, PA 18701
Phone: (888) 905-2872
Fax: (570) 819-1882
Web Address: www.tournepa.com
E-Mail: tournepa@tournepa.com

### Lycoming County Visitors Bureau

100 West Third Street
Williamsport, PA 17701
Phone: (800) 358-9900
Fax: (570) 321-1208
Web Address: www.vacationpa.com
E-Mail: visitorinfo@williamsport.org

### Mercer County Convention & Visitors Bureau

50 North Water Avenue
Sharon, PA 16146
Phone: (800) 637-2370 or (724) 346-3771
Fax: (724) 346-0575
Web Address: www.mercercountypa.org
E-Mail: mccvb@mercercountypa.org

### Northeast Pennsylvania Convention & Visitors Bureau

99 Glenmaura National Boulevard
Scranton, PA 18507
Phone: (800) 229-3526
Fax: (570) 963-6852
Web Address: www.visitnepa.org
E-Mail: info@visitnepa.org

### Northern Alleghenies Vacation Region

315 Second Avenue
Post Office Box 804
Warren, PA 16365
Phone: (800) 724-7802
Fax: (814) 726-7266
Web Address: www.northernalleghenies.com
E-Mail: info@northernalleghenies.com

### NW Pennsylvania's Great Outdoors Visitors Bureau

175 Main Street
Brookville, PA 15825
Phone: (800) 348-9393
Fax: (814) 849-1969
Web Address: www.pagreatoutdoors.com
E-Mail: info@pagreatoutdoors.com

### Oil Heritage Region Tourist Promotion Agency

206 Seneca Street
P.O. Box 128
Oil City, PA 16301
Phone: (800) 483-6264 or (814) 677-3152
Fax: (814) 677-5206
Web Address: www.oilregiontourist.com
E-Mail: info@oilregiontourist.com

### Pennsylvania Dutch Convention & Visitors Bureau

501 Greenfield Road
Lancaster, PA 17601
Phone: (800) 723-8824
Fax: (717) 299-0470
Web Address: www.padutchcountry.com
E-Mail: info@padutchcountry.com

### Philadelphia Convention & Visitors Bureau

1515 Market Street, Suite 2020
Philadelphia, PA, 19102
Phone: (800) 537-7676 or (215) 636-3300
Fax: (215) 636-3327
Web Address: www.pcvb.org
E-Mail: info@pcvb.org

### Pocono Mountains Vacation Bureau, Inc.

1004 Main Street
Stroudsburg, PA 18360
Phone: (800) 762-6667
Fax: (570) 476-8959
Web Address: www.800poconos.com
E-Mail: pocomts@poconos.org

### Potter County Visitors Association

519 East Second Street, Office #1
Coudersport, PA 16915
Phone: (888) 768-8372 or (814) 274-3365
E-Mail: potter@penn.com

### Raystown Country Visitors Bureau

Seven Points Road
Hesston, PA 16647
Phone: (814) 658-0060
Fax: (814) 658-0068
Web Address: www.raystown.org
E-Mail: info@raystown.org

### Reading & Berks County Visitors Bureau

352 Penn Street
Reading, PA 19602
Phone: (800) 443-6610
Fax: (610) 375-9606
Web Address: www.readingberkspa.com
E-Mail: info@readingberkspa.com

### Schuylkill County Visitors Bureau

200 East Arch Street
Pottsville, PA 17901
Phone: (800) 765-7282 or (570) 622-7700
Fax: (570) 622-8035
Web Address: www.schuylkill.org
E-Mail: tourism@schuylkill.org

### Susquehanna Valley Visitors Bureau

81 Hafer Road
Lewisburg, PA 17837
Phone: (800) 525-7320
Fax: (570) 524-7282
Web Address: www.visitcentralpa.org
E-Mail: svvb@svvb.com

### Tioga County Visitors Bureau

114 Main Street
Wellsboro, PA 16901
Phone: (888) 846-4228
Fax: (570) 723-1016
Web Address: www.visittiogapa.com
E-Mail: tiogapa@epix.net

### Valley Forge Convention & Visitors Bureau

600 West Germantown Pike, Suite 130
Plymouth Meeting, PA 19462
Phone: (888) VISIT-VF or (610) 834-1550
Fax: (610) 565-0833
Web Address: www.valleyforge.org
E-Mail: info@valleyforge.org

### Washington County Tourism Promotion Agency

273 South Main Street
Washington, PA 15301
Phone: (800) 531-4114 or (724) 228-5520
Fax: (724) 228-5514
Web Address: www.washpatourism.org
E-Mail: info@washpatourism.org

### York County Convention & Visitors Bureau

155 West Market Street
York, PA 17401
Phone: (888) 858-9675 or (717)852-9675
Fax: (717) 854-5095
Web Address: www.yorkpa.org
E-Mail: info@yorkpa.org

# Picture Credits

T = Top, B = Bottom, C = Center, R = Right, L = Left

**Allegheny National Forest Vacation Bureau:** 62T, 88, 248.

**Chrysalis Image Library:** 8, 9, 13B, 17, 21B, 29, 33, 34-35, 38-39, 44T, 49, 59, 61T, 81B, 85, 86, 90-91, 95, 98L, 100, 108T /Mark Franklin, 110-111, 114B, 119, 120-121, 123, 125T, 125B, 126, 142, 144-145, 151, 152 /Lloyd Ostendorf Collection, 160 /UK Patent Office, 167, 169T, 169BL /National Archives [B-4975], 170, 171B, 187, 193, 194TL, 194TR, 194B, 196 /Simon Clay, 197, 200L, 200-201, 202T, 202B, 205 /Simon Clay, 233 /Simon Clay, 234, 235, 239.

**Commonwealth Media Services:** 14, 57, 107 Photo by Bob Tarkowski, 180B, 243, 244.

**Corbis:** 138 © Bettmann/CORBIS

**George Sheldon:** 10B, 10T, 11, 12T, 12B, 13T, 16, 21T, 22, 24, 25, 31, 36, 37, 45, 47, 51T, 51B, 60T, 60B, 64-65, 69T, 70, 71, 72, 73, 78T, 82, 83, 89T, 89B, 92L, 92C, 93, 101, 103, 104R, 106, 112,113, 120L, 122T, 122B, 128BR, 133BR, 135T, 135B, 136L, 141T, 146T, 146B, 147TL, 147TR, 147B, 148, 154, 155, 156, 157, 171T, 172, 174, 179L, 183, 184, 195T, 195B, 198, 207, 209, 210-211, 212, 213, 217T, 217B, 219B, 221, 222, 223, 225, 227, 228BL, 228-229, 230, 231T, 231B, 232, 236, 238, 241, 242, 246, 247T, 247B.

**Gettysburg Convention & Visitors Bureau:** 136L Photo by Paul Witt.

**Greater Pittsburgh Convention & Visitors Bureau:** 43, 44B, 114T, 199B, 203T, 203B, 204.

**ibrary of Congress Geography and Map Division:** 2 [G3824.P5P3 1870.B5], 20 [G3824.G3S5 1863.D42 CW 331], 192 [G3824.P5 1796.V28 1875 TIL].

**brary of Congress Prints and Photographs Division:** 15, 18 [HAER, PA,32-LUCE.V, 1-B-2], 9T [LC-DIG-nclc-01016], 19B [LC-DIG-nclc-01103], 6-27 [LC-USZ62-133107], 40 [LC-DIG-ggbain-9764], 41T [LC-DIG-ggbain-09767], 42T [HAER, INN,38-TWOHA,1-1], 42B [LC-DIG-ggbain-543], 52 [LC-USZ62-108178], 53 [LC-USZ62-637], 54 [LC-USZ-62-45179], 61B [C-G412-T01-3-005-A-x], 62B [LC-USZ62-13758], 63 [LC-DIG-pb-01658], 66 [HAER, PA,48-EATO,6A-1], 67 ER, PA,6-BERN.V,7-15], 68 [HAER, PA,18-HA.V,4A-2], 75 [LC-DIG-nclc-01110], 76L ER, PA,32-LUCE.V,1-B-3], 76-77 [LC-USZ62-], 78B [LC-DIG-nclc-01134], 79 [LC-DIG-nclc-], 84, 96 [LC-USZ62-96106], 97 [LC-USZ62-], 98R [LC-USZ62-26777], 104L [LC-USZ62-1], 105 [HABS, PA,39-EMMA.V,2A-1], 108B SZ62-86651], 128TL [LC-USZC4-5945], 128TR SZ62-20997], 129 [LC-USZ62-110017], 130 Z62-26778], 131 [LC-USZ62-45321], 132-133 PA,51-PHILA,298-1], 158T [LC-USZ62-79335], 158B [LC-USZ62-79336], 159 [LC-USZ62-79336], 161 [LC-USZC4-3254], 162 [HAER, PA,42-MOJEW.V,1-17], 164-165 [LCPP006A-14450], 169BR, 178T [LC-USZC4-4547], 178B [LC-USZ62-3596], 179R [LC-USZ62-45328], 185 [LC-USZC4-4312], 215 [LC-USZC4-4913].

Brady Civil War Photograph Collection: 134 [LC-DIG-cwpb-00074], 137 [LC-DIG-cwpb-01640], 141B [LC-DIG-cwpb-01534].

Brady-handy Photograph Collection: 92R [LC-DIG-cwpbh-01288].

British Cartoon Collection: 115 [LC-USZ62-1509].

Farm Security Administration - Office of War Information Photograph: 175T [LC-USW3-011287-E], 175B [LC-USF34-082455-E], 190T [LC-USF34-008579-D], 190B [LC-USF34-008585-D]. Frances Benjamin Johnston Collection, 180T [LC-USZ62-63369], 69B [LC-USZ62-26788].

FSA-OWI Collection: 199T [LC-USF-34-043050-D].

George Grantham Bain Collection: 224 [LC-DIG-ggbain-04054].

Historic American Buildings Surveys: 116T [HABS, PA,51--PHILA,111-19], 116B [HABS, PA,51-PHILA,111E-2], 176 [HABS, PA,51--GERM,51-1], 214 [HABS, PA,35-SCRAN,23-1], 218T [HABS, PA,51-PHILA,458-2], 218B [HABS, PA,51-PHILA,458-17].

Historic American Engineering Record: 109T [HAER, PA,4-SHIP,1-23], 109B [HAER, PA,4-SHIP,1-26], 182 [HAER, MD,22-HAGTO.V,21], 219T [HAER, PA,36-LANC,10-1].

National Child Labor Commitee Collection: 80 [LC-DIG-nclc-01303], 81T [LC-DIG-nclc-01104].

Panoramic Photographs: 41B [PAN US GEOG – Pennsylvania no.31].

Rare Book and Special Collections Division: 226 [LC-USZ62-45270].

**Pennsylvania Historical & Museum Commission, Drake Well Museum Collection, Titusville, PA:** 99

**Pennsylvania Lottery:** 189

**Pocono Mountains Vacation Bureau, Inc:** 7, 208

**The Look In Collection:** 32

Chrysalis Books Group Plc is committed to respecting the intellectual property rights of others. We have therefore taken all reasonable efforts to ensure that the reproduction of all content on these pages is done with the full consent of copyright owners. If you are aware of any unintentional omissions please contact the company directly so that any necessary corrections may be made for future editions.

# Dedication

This one is for Matthew James Adams. He is another fine grandson.

# Acknowledgments

No book reaches the hands of its readers without the help of a lot of people behind the scenes. This one is no exception.

Special thanks to all the people on this journey that helped me with questions and provided information that I needed to write this book. I appreciate the assistance of the staffs of many libraries and museums, and tourist bureaus that directed me to sources of information.

I want to thank the staffs of the Library of Congress, the Pennsylvania State Library, and the Pennsylvania Archives. A special thank you to the nice folks at the Lancaster County Historical Society.

I would like to thank Elizabeth Stackhouse of the Pennsylvania Lottery for her special and kind assistance. Thanks to the staff of the Pennsylvania Historical and Museum Commission.

I want to thank the staff of the Allegheny Mountains Convention and Visitors Bureau, the Allegheny National Forest Vacation Bureau, Bedford County Conference & Visitors Bureau, Centre County Convention & Visitors Bureau, Endless Mountains Visitors Bureau, Erie Area Convention & Visitors Bureau, Gettysburg Convention & Visitors Bureau, Greater Pittsburgh Convention & Visitors Bureau, Pennsylvania Dutch Convention & Visitors Bureau, and the Pocono Mountains Vacation Bureau, Inc. Thanks to everyone that provided information and assistance.

I want especially to thank my wife Gloria for her countless hours of support and help, and her thoughtful edits and suggestions to improve the text. Without her, there would be no book.

I would not have written this book if it had not been for Charles W. Byrd. This is the first one I wrote without him, and I miss him. He was there in the early days, when I needed him. Thanks for everything, Charles. I will never forget you.

Special thanks to the editors and page layout folks at Chrysalis Books for doing a fine job on making this a better book, and easier to read.

Thanks to everyone else that contributed in anyway to this book. I really do appreciate it!

**George G. Sheldon**
*Lancaster, PA*